Nice Is Not Enough

Facilitating Moral Development

Larry Nucci

University of California, Berkeley

Merrill
is an imprint of

Upper Saddle River, New Jersey
Columbus, Ohio

Library of Congress Cataloging-in-Publication Data

Nucci, Larry P.
    Nice is not enough : facilitating moral development / Larry Nucci.
        p. cm.
    Includes bibliographical references and index.
    ISBN-13: 978-0-13-188651-3
    ISBN-10:   0-13-188651-7
1. Moral education.   2. Moral development.   I. Title.
    LC268.N84 2009
    370.11'4–dc22

                                        2008028400

Vice President and Executive Publisher: Jeffery W. Johnston
Publisher: Kevin Davis
Editorial Assistant: Lauren Reinkober
Senior Managing Editor: Pamela D. Bennett
Project Manager: Mary Harlan
Production Coordinator: Tanushree Kanungo
Design Coordinator: Diane C. Lorenzo
Text Design and Illustrations: Aptara
Cover Design: Jason Moore
Cover Image: SuperStock
Operations Specialist: Laura Messerly
Director of Marketing: Quinn Perkson
Marketing Manager: Erica DeLuca
Marketing Coordinator: Brian Mounts

This book was set in ITC Century Light by Aptara®, Inc. It was printed and bound by R. R. Donnelley & Sons, Inc.
The cover was printed by R. R. Donnelley & Sons, Inc.

Excerpts that appear in the book from *Charlie and the Chocolate Factory* appear by permission from Roald
Dahl. The excerpt from *Ella Sarah Gets Dressed* appears with permission from Margaret Chodos-Irvine.

Pearson Education Ltd., London
Pearson Education Singapore Pte. Ltd.
Pearson Education Canada, Inc.
Pearson Education–Japan
Pearson Education Australia PTY, Limited

Pearson Education North Asia, Ltd., Hong Kong
Pearson Educación de Mexico, S.A. de C.V.
Pearson Education Malaysia Pte. Ltd.
Pearson Education Upper Saddle River, New Jersey

Merrill
is an imprint of

10 9 8 7 6 5 4 3 2 1
ISBN-13: 978-0-13-188651-3
ISBN-10:   0-13-188651-7

To Maria, Tatiana, Michael, and Daniel

Acknowledgments

This book could not have been written without the contributions and support of many people. Many of the moral and social development lessons that appear in the book were generated in collaboration with classroom teachers and students in my courses at the University of Illinois at Chicago (UIC). I would like to especially acknowledge one of my former students, Elsa K. Weber, who worked with me in constructing several of the social studies lessons that appear in Chapters 8 and 9; and a current graduate student, Natalie Valente, who worked with me and with teachers from Park Ridge, Illinois, District 64, to develop lessons for middle school students. Other individual lessons that appear in this book were written by the following people: Roy Bounds, Eric (Rico) Gutstein, Lisa Jason, Sue Kleckner, and Emily Moravec. I thank all of them for granting me permission to use their lessons in this book.

The new basic research on moral development that appears in Chapter 3 was conducted with my colleague and longtime friend, Elliot Turiel. Our work was generously supported by a grant from the Fetzer Institute. I also wish to acknowledge the Character Education Partnership and especially Merle Schwartz for their grant in support of the integration of moral education within the UIC undergraduate program in elementary education.

Several people contributed to the book by reading earlier versions of the manuscript and offering suggestions for improvement. I want to thank my friend and colleague, Eleni Katsarou, for her comments on the book and for her invaluable support in our work with preservice teachers. Laurie LaFollett and Tatiana Nucci provided feedback on chapters for elementary and secondary schools, respectively. Tatiana offered a needed perspective from her experiences working with high school students in inner city Chicago. In this regard I want to acknowledge the input from the many undergraduate teacher education students at UIC who read through drafts of this book as part of their coursework with me over the past three years. I also want to recognize the constructive comments made on earlier drafts of the book by prepublication reviewers: Marvin W. Berkowitz, University of Missouri–St. Louis; David Diener, Indiana University;

Perry Glanzer, Baylor University; Jim Hillesheim, University of Kansas; Anthony Holter, University of Notre Dame; Joseph Lao, Columbia University; Elizabeth C. Vozzola, Saint Joseph College; Pauline Davey Zeece, University of Nebraska, Lincoln; and Ronald Zigler, Penn State–Abington.

Some passages in the book are drawn from a prior volume (Nucci, 2001) intended for educational researchers and graduate students.

Finally, I want to thank Kevin Davis and his assistant Lauren Reinkober of Pearson Education for their support in the writing of this book. Kevin never wavered in his enthusiasm for this project. Without his patience and guidance this book would have never reached fruition.

Brief Contents

Contents

Note: Every effort has been made to provide accurate and current information in this book. However, the Internet and information posted on it are constantly changing; it is inevitable that some of the Internet addresses listed in this textbook will change.

CHAPTER 1

Introduction

Anyone who has begun to think places some portion of the world in jeopardy.

—John Dewey

There is a great deal of interest in getting schools to engage in what is referred to as *character education*. Currently 80% of states have mandates for what is variously called moral/character education or social emotional learning. This flurry of activity supported by recent presidents of both political parties reflects a long-standing public desire for schools to contribute to the moral and social growth of children. Few Americans would be satisfied with schools that produced high achievers in math and science but did little or nothing to help students become good people. They would agree with Theodore Roosevelt when he said, "To educate a man [*or woman*] in mind and not in morals is to educate a menace to society."

Despite the evident interest in having schools do something to foster children's morality and character, there isn't clear public agreement about what is meant by morality and what values we want our schools to teach. The public divisions that are inevitable in a pluralist democratic society lead to concerns that moral or character education may be used as a vehicle for promoting a particular religious or political agenda within the public school system.

In addition, there is disagreement among education professionals about how to go about teaching morality. For traditional educators, moral education is about transmitting social values to children through direct teaching, role models, and systems of positive and negative consequences. The goal is to build up habits of conduct or virtues that automatically guide students' behavior toward doing the right thing (Arthur, 2008; Wynne, 1989). For other educators, the central focus is not on habits of behavior, but rather on working with the intrinsic empathic tendencies within children and adolescents to generate "habits of the

1

heart." Still others downplay the importance or centrality of moral development in favor of an emphasis on what is referred to as Social Emotional Learning in which students are taught skills for reading their own and others' emotions and how to regulate their own behavior in prosocial and acceptable ways (Elias, Parker, Kash, Weissberg, & O'Brien, 2008; Weissberg & O'Brien, 2004). Morality from this perspective becomes one aspect of a larger social skill set to allow students to become positive members of society. Finally, there are those who have tended to limit moral education to rational processes of moral reflection and moral discussion (Kohlberg & Turiel, 1971). Proponents of this perspective argue that the core of morality is moral judgment, and that moral development is less about emotion or acquiring the norms of society than it is about constructing ever more sophisticated forms of moral reasoning or problem solving.

Marvin Berkowitz (1997) has captured these disagreements by referring to the parable of the four blind men and the elephant. Each of the blind men touching a different portion of the elephant came to different albeit reasonable conclusions as to what they were touching. The blind man who touched the elephant's legs concluded that he was touching a series of columns. The blind man who touched the elephant's trunk concluded that he was touching a snake, and so forth. In similar ways, researchers and scholars focusing on different aspects of social and moral growth have drawn similarly narrow though reasonable conclusions about how to facilitate moral development.

The purpose of this book is to provide teachers and teacher education candidates with an accessible account of the process of moral development and moral education. To do this, the book will provide an integrative approach to moral education that attends to the emotional, cognitive, and behavioral sides of social and moral development. This is to say, the book will attempt to avoid the error of focusing on only one dimension of moral growth. The book will also provide concrete suggestions for how to address the affective side of social and moral development through classroom climate, relationship building, effective classroom management, and wise use of the academic curriculum.

The book is based on recent research and theory that has helped to identify the cross-cultural, universal elements of morality and to distinguish those core human values from the conventions of society. This recent work provides an analysis of when and around what sorts of values and social skills we can teach children directly, and what sorts of social values and understandings children and adolescents need to construct for themselves. Bringing these two learning processes together requires "wise teaching" that balances the role of the teacher as instructor with the teacher's role as guide and facilitator.

This distinction also allows for moral education that is more than promoting the emergence of "nice" people. Nice people are polite; they are respectful of others. They don't engage in unprovoked harm, and don't steal. They are pleasant to be around and are generally liked. Most of us would like to be thought of as nice people. However, nice is not enough. The limits of "nice" become apparent if we ask ourselves the following question, "Are people in general nicer now than they were in 1955, or were they nicer back then?" My late colleague Ed Wynne might well have answered, nicer in 1955. He once concluded, "By many measures youth conduct was at its best in 1955" (Wynne, 1987, p. 56).

If we think back to what American society was like in 1955, we would realize that a lot of "nice" people were accepting of gender roles that gave more privileges and choices to men than to women. It was also a time when racial discrimination was legal in some parts of the United States. It would be very hard to defend those social practices on moral grounds, and most Americans would agree that the changes in society that have led to greater social equality have been for the better. On that basis, one might argue that the majority of Americans are "nicer" and morally better now than people were back in the 1950s. However, few people would be willing to make that claim. It would mean that our parents and grandparents were somehow less "nice" as people than are we.

Moral education, then, is certainly about contributing to the development of caring and fair people with respect for the general conventions of society. We want to educate children who are sensitive to the needs of others and who know how to balance self-interest with justice and compassion. We want to educate children capable of regulating their emotions and handling disputes peaceably. We want them to be able to make wise choices and to avoid self-destructive behavior. As educators, then, we would want to proudly work toward the development of "nice" people.

But we would need to accomplish more than that if we are to meet our own ethical obligations as educators. Each generation inherits the social-moral system of their parents. If as educators we simply teach these inherited moral and social norms, then we contribute to the perpetuation of whatever moral contradictions are contained in those social values. People who accepted racial segregation and gender inequalities for centuries did not do so because they were less than "nice" people. These social practices continued because the majority of the population did not employ their moral understandings to evaluate the conventions of their culture.

The question, then, is not whether to engage in moral education, but how to do it effectively, meaningfully, and in a manner that contributes to the academic mission of schools. An effective and meaningful approach to moral education must do several things. First, it must be based on a philosophically and psychologically defensible definition of what we mean by morality. Second, it must be consistent with the natural processes of moral and social development. Third, it must fit within the normal flow of classroom activities rather than be an add-on or special unit. Finally, it must go beyond the socialization of conventionally "nice" children toward the development of individuals capable of lifelong moral growth and who are motivated to contribute to the morality of social institutions and the general society. This is a tall order.

This book is structured in three major sections to address aspects of what a teacher would need to know in order to be an effective moral educator. These sections presume that the reader is either in the process of developing the broader knowledge and skill base for teaching, or is a current classroom teacher. The first section addresses what we mean by morality and what we have learned about moral and social development. This first section provides the research and theory base for the sections that follow. The second section focuses on aspects of classroom and school structure, classroom rules, and forms of classroom management that are consistent with students' moral and social growth. The third section presents general principles for integrating moral education within the everyday academic curriculum and presents models of lessons employing regular academic subject matter across disciplines for moral and social growth. Because this book takes a developmental approach, the sections on classroom practices are broken down by grade level. However, the reader will benefit by reading all the chapters, because they differ in the attention they give to particular areas of academic content such as math, science, or the arts.

Moral and Social Development

What is morality? Is it the same thing as social rules? Is morality different for religious children? How do children develop morality? Does morality change with age? Is morality universal or does it change from one culture to another? What is the impact of culture on morality? Are there some things that people do that should be up to them and not controlled by social rules? How do those personal and private things relate to morality? Can morality be taught or is morality innate?

In order to provide effective moral education teachers need to have answers to these and other related questions. In this first section we introduce recent research and theory from developmental psychology that has investigated children's moral and social development. The educational principles and practices described in this book are based on this recent work. In Chapter 2 we explore research that has looked at how children and adolescents distinguish morality from the norms and conventions of society. We explore how devout Christian and Jewish children view morality and the rules of their respective religions. We also examine research on how children and adolescents define what they consider to be personal and private matters that should not be regulated by social rules.

Chapter 2 also presents research on the patterns of social interactions with peers and between children and adults that lead to the construction of concepts of morality, social convention, and personal issues. These social interaction patterns will be used in later chapters to help guide appropriate teacher responses to students' social behavior. Finally in Chapter 2 we examine how concepts of morality, convention, and the personal interact in complex social situations. We explore how cultural values influence the ways in which individuals weigh morality, convention, and personal considerations in their social lives.

In Chapter 3 we address the patterns of development within the moral, conventional, and personal domains of social reasoning. With that knowledge as a backdrop, we discuss how age-typical changes in moral and social reasoning provide a window into understanding students' social reasoning and help to account for changes we see in students' social behavior. Awareness of these developmental patterns will be essential to our discussion in Section II on the social life of classrooms, and in Section III on the construction of moral and social values lessons.

CHAPTER 2

Defining the Moral Domain

> *What is morality in any given time or place? It is what the majority then and there happen to like and immorality is what they dislike.*
>
> —Alfred North Whitehead

Before we can begin to talk about how to engage in moral education and character development, we need to know what we mean by morality. Many people would agree with Alfred North Whitehead that morality refers to the broad range of social and cultural norms that the majority accepts as defining social right and wrong. For others, morality is defined by the core set of values defined by their religion. In the United States, proponents of this view generally argue for the teaching of Judeo-Christian ethics. In a democratic and pluralist society such as the United States, however, attempts to define morality in terms of the social norms of the majority, or what the dominant religion teaches, poses problems for teachers and school systems wishing to contribute to students' moral and social growth. In some urban schools, like the ones on Chicago's north side, there can be as many as 23 different spoken languages represented among the children in a single elementary school. Children in such a school can come from Jewish, Christian, Muslim, Hindu, Buddhist, and nonreligious backgrounds. In such a context, whose moral values should we teach?

One could argue that there are moral universals and construct an educational program on that basis. But in order to do so, a teacher would need to be armed with more than personal opinion. Fortunately, we have a learned a great deal over the past 30 years about the ways that children develop morality that can help us to address these questions. It turns out that universal elements in morality become apparent when the moral domain is distinguished from norms defined by societal convention. Perhaps even more importantly, we can understand the sources of individual and cultural variation in morality by accounting for the ways in which morality interacts with religious and cultural conventions.

Morality and Social Convention

Children in any society are expected to learn to conform to a number of social rules and expectations if they are to become participants in the culture. This is a point frequently made by traditional educators (Ryan, 1989; Wynne & Ryan, 1993) and something we will return to at various points in this book. Among the rules that children in our society are expected to learn are that certain classes of adults (such as teachers and doctors) are addressed by titles, that males and females use separate restroom facilities, and that women but not men wear dresses. These are examples of social conventions. In the absence of such a shared norm, the acts are neither right nor wrong. For this reason, conventions may be said to be arbitrary. For example, we could just as easily have students address teachers by first names as have them call teachers by their last names and formal titles of Mr. or Ms.

Conventions, however, serve an important function by providing predictability and order to social life. Without social conventions it would be impossible to organize social institutions such as schools, and societies as organized systems could not exist. The arbitrariness of conventions makes their importance difficult for children to figure out. And, as we shall see in Chapter 3, it is not until some time in adolescence that children come to fully understand the function that these arbitrary conventions serve to provide predictability and order to our social interactions.

In contrast with issues of convention are matters of morality. Morality refers to issues of human welfare, justice, and rights that are a function of the inherent features of interpersonal relations (Turiel, 2002). Because of this, the right and wrong of moral actions are not simply determined by social consensus or the views of authority. For example, it is not possible to hit another person with force and not hurt the other person. Similarly, it is not possible to steal something valuable from someone else and not cause the person to experience the sense of loss. A moral judgment about unprovoked harm ("It is wrong to hit") would not be dependent on the existence of a socially agreed upon rule or standard but could be generated solely from the intrinsic effects of the act (i.e., hitting hurts). Similar analyses could be done regarding a broader range of issues that would extend beyond direct harm to concerns for what it means to be just, compassionate, and considerate of the rights of others.

These two forms of social regulation, morality and convention, are both part of the social order. Every major cultural and religious group is governed by a code that contains both conventional and moral rules. Morality and convention are not, however, reducible to each other. Instead, our concepts of morality and social convention form discrete frameworks or domains. This distinction between morality and convention is nicely illustrated by the following example. The excerpt is from an interview conducted in the U.S. Virgin Islands by one of my former students, Gloria

Encarnacion-Gawrych (Nucci, Turiel, & Encarnacion-Gawrych, 1983), with a 4-year-old girl talking about her perceptions of spontaneously occurring transgressions at her preschool.

Moral Issue

Did you see what happened?

Yes. They were playing and John hit him too hard.

Is that something you are supposed to do or not supposed to do?

Not so hard to hurt.

Is there a rule about that?

Yes.

What is the rule?

You're not to hit hard.

What if there were no rule about hitting hard, would it be all right to do then?

No.

Why not?

Because he could get hurt and start to cry.

Conventional Issue

Did you see what just happened?

Yes. They were noisy.

Is that something you are supposed to do or not supposed to do?

Not do.

Is there a rule about that?

Yes. We have to be quiet.

What if there were no rule, would it be all right to do then?

Yes.

Why?

Because there is no rule.

As this interview excerpt illustrates, very young children reason differently about moral actions that affect the welfare of others, and matters of convention in which the status of actions is a function of agreed upon social norms or the dictates of authority (Turiel, 1983). This kind of distinction has not been generally made in moral or character education until very recently (see Nucci, 2001, and Schwartz, 2007 for notable exceptions). Traditional character educators hold that moral values are established by society. They maintain that the role of character education is to inculcate children into the norms and values of the culture to produce virtuous citizens. The kind of distinction drawn here is also at odds with the accounts of moral development offered by Piaget (1932) and

Kohlberg (1984) that have had an impact on progressive moral education. For both theorists, moral development involves a differentiation of morality (fairness) out of earlier stages in which morality is defined by social norms and authority. Only at the more advanced stages of moral autonomy (Piaget, 1932) or postconventional thinking (Kohlberg, 1984) does morality supersede and operate independently of convention, according to these earlier theories. Over the past 30 years, however, more than 60 published articles have reported research demonstrating that morality and convention are differentiated at very early ages and form distinct conceptual and developmental domains (Smetana, 2006).

Research Evidence

One source of evidence in support of the moral–conventional distinction comes from interviews with children and adults indicating that people treat moral and conventional issues differently. Moral issues tend to be viewed as independent of the existence of social norms and generalizable across contexts, societies, and cultures. Social conventions, on the other hand, are rule dependent, and they hold only within the social system within which the rule was formed. Judgments that people make about moral issues are supported in terms of the harm or unfairness that actions would cause, while judgments of conventions are justified in terms of social organization, social rules, and the expectations of authority. We saw an example of this in the excerpt of the interview with the 4-year-old girl presented earlier in the chapter.

The youngest age at which children have been reported to consistently treat moral and conventional issues differently is $2\frac{1}{2}$ years (Smetana & Braeges, 1990). Other studies have demonstrated that by age 4, children have developed fairly consistent and firm differentiations between familiar moral and conventional issues encountered in home and school settings. These kinds of interview studies have not been limited to the United States or Western countries, but have been conducted across a wide range of the world's cultures. Such studies have been conducted with children and adolescents in several regions of Brazil; mainland Chinese preschool children and their mothers living in the United States and Canada; school-aged children in Colombia; preschool children in the Virgin Islands; Christian and Muslim children in Indonesia; urban children and kibbutz Jewish children and traditional village Arab children in Israel; children and adults in India; children and adults in Korea; Ijo children in Nigeria; and children in Zambia (see Turiel, 2002 for a review).

With some variations with regard to specific findings regarding convention, the distinction between morality and convention has been reported in each of the cultures examined. Children across cultural groups and social classes have been found to treat moral transgressions, such as unprovoked harm, as wrong regardless of the presence or absence of rules, and they have viewed the wrongness of such transgressions as holding universally for children in other cultural settings, and not just for their own group. Across cultures, children and adults view conventions as norms that could be altered through social agreement and as applying only to people within their own society (Turiel, 2002). However, cross-cultural studies have also shown that members of more traditional cultural settings such as Arab villages, rural northeastern Brazil, and rural Nigeria are less willing than members of postindustrial societies such as urban residents of Japan or the United States to agree that it would be acceptable to alter or remove their existing social conventions (see Nucci, 2001). This is consistent with the emphasis on cultural continuity among those more traditional groups. However, even within the most traditional cultures, children and adults differentiate between matters of morality and social convention (Smetana, 2006).

Morality and Religious Norms

If even young children differentiate between actions in the moral and conventional domains and reason differently about the two, then moral education should reflect this distinction. One obvious implication is that we may now be able to identify in a nonarbitrary way the core values that would be the focus of moral education. Perhaps the most controversial aspect of that claim is that it may help to answer whether morality can be defined independent of religious values. Responding to that issue is critical if public schools are to be able to engage in moral education without privileging the beliefs of members of a particular religious faith, or promoting values in the name of moral education that would undermine the moral beliefs of religious children. The current plea for God and prayer to be put back into the classroom derives from an old and enduring belief that morality and religion are inseparable. Even among some of those who do not seek to promote a particular faith, there is the assumption that religiously based education is somehow more grounded in morality than nonreligious schooling. Former Secretary of Education Rod Paige had the following to say in an interview in Tennessee:

> All things equal, I would prefer to have a child in a school that has a strong appreciation for the values of the Christian community, where a child is taught to have a strong faith. . . . The reason that Christian schools and Christian universities are growing is a result of a strong value system. In a religious environment the value system is set. That's not the case in a public school where there are so many different kids with different kinds of values. (Brummett, 2003)

The views of people such as Secretary Paige notwithstanding, there is now empirical evidence that will help to answer at least some of the questions and concerns regarding the role of religion in children's morality.

These findings come from a series of studies conducted with Christian and Jewish children. The Christian groups included Catholics, conservative Mennonites and Amish, and Dutch reform Calvinists. The Jewish children and adolescents came from Conservative and Orthodox communities within the United States. These studies are described in detail in Nucci (2001). In each of these studies participants were asked to make a series of judgments about the rules maintained within their religious faiths. In the study with Catholics, the issues were presented in a questionnaire format (Nucci, 1985). In the other studies children and adolescents provided detailed responses to a smaller number of issues in face-to-face interviews.

Some of the actions the participants were asked to make judgments about were moral issues having to do with actions affecting the welfare of another person. Others were rules maintained within each faith that were nonmoral issues similar to secular social conventions. Moral issues used in the studies included such things as stealing, hitting, slandering, and damaging another's property. Nonmoral (conventional) issues included working on the Sabbath, the day of worship, wearing head coverings, women leading religious services, baptism, and interfaith marriage. Adolescents over the age of 14 were also asked about consensual sex between two adults prior to marriage. Jews but not Christians were asked additional questions about dietary laws. Catholics were presented a longer list of issues in questionnaire format that included specific Church laws having to do with patterns of worship such as fasting before communion and attending church on Holy Days of Obligation.

Findings with Catholics

In each study participants were first asked if it would be wrong or all right for the authorities of their respective religions to alter or remove the rules about each given action. The majority of the Catholic high school (92%) and college students (98%) judged that it would be wrong for the pope and cardinals to alter or remove rules regulating moral actions such as hitting and hurting another person. In each case, the participants also judged that it would be wrong for a Catholic to engage in the action even after the authorities had altered or removed the rule. The reasons given for objecting to the removal of these rules and for engaging in the actions was that the acts would cause harm or unfairness to another person whether or not a rule was in place.

In contrast with these judgments about moral issues, the majority of Catholics (60%–80%) felt that it would be all right for the pope in consultation with the cardinals to alter or remove rules regulating nonmoral issues such as fasting before communion, attending church on Holy Days of Obligation, women becoming priests, premarital sex, or divorce. Thus, it was clear from the study with Catholics that they differentiated between actions that were defined as wrong as a function of being Catholic, and moral actions that were wrong because of the effects the acts had on other people.

Findings with Jews and Non-Catholics

As with the Catholics, the vast majority (93%) of the Jewish and Conservative Mennonite/Amish children and adolescents we interviewed felt that it would be wrong for the authorities of their respective religions to alter or remove rules regulating moral actions, and wrong for a person to engage in the behavior even if the authorities altered or removed the rules. Non-Catholic Christians and Jewish participants, however, did not agree to the same extent as did Catholics that their religious authorities could alter or remove the nonmoral rules of their respective religions. For example, less than 20% of the conservative Mennonite and Jewish children thought that the authorities of their religions could alter the day of worship or the rules prohibiting work on the Sabbath. These differences between the Catholics and non-Catholics with respect to nonmoral religious rules reflected the authority Catholics give to the pope as an interpreter of God's laws on earth. For the Jews and non-Catholic Christians the source of the authority for the nonmoral norms was the word of God as recorded in scripture. In order to further understand the thinking of these Jewish and Christian children we asked the following question: "Suppose God (Jesus) had said nothing about (the action), there was nothing in the Bible (Torah) about X, would it then be wrong or all right for a Jew (Christian) to engage in (the behavior)?" When asked this question less than 10% of the Jewish and Christian children and adolescents stated that it would be wrong for a person to engage in the acts we had defined as nonmoral. In fact, for the majority of issues—work on the Sabbath, not wearing head coverings, women leading religious services—*none* of the participants thought the actions would now be wrong. This finding is consistent with our definition of these actions as nonmoral. However, the finding is also consistent with the assumption that God's word determines right and wrong for these devout Christian and Jewish children. That latter interpretation does not, however, explain the findings obtained with moral issues. In contrast with their responses regarding nonmoral issues, the vast majority of Christian (87%) and Jewish (95%) children judged that it would *still be wrong* to engage in actions entailing moral transgressions (hitting, stealing, slander, damage property) even if there were nothing in scripture (God had said nothing) about the acts. These acts continued to be wrong, according to these children, because of the effects that the actions would have on other people. The distinction that our religious children made between nonmoral religious rules and matters of morality is nicely illustrated in the following excerpt from an interview with a 9-year-old Conservative Jewish girl given the pseudonym Marsha. In the excerpt Marsha talks about stealing and the Jewish norm that requires boys to wear head coverings (kippah) (Nucci, 2001, pp. 36–38). The interested reader can find several other extended excerpts from these interviews with Christian and Jewish children in Nucci (2001).

Religious Convention: Men Wearing Head Coverings

Was Jonathan right or wrong not to wear his kippah to the public school?

It was wrong because he's not showing his, uh, his, like his religion. You should always show how good your religion is, and you should always keep the mitzvah. And also, he's probably disobeying his parents.

Okay. Do you think it matters whether or not Jewish boys wear kippot?

I think it matters. For one thing, you can never tell if it's a Jewish man or not a Jewish man and you could say, "Can I, uh, can I have, can you give charity to the people, to the poor people?" And they would say, "No, I'm not Jewish." How would I know? Like you'd get really embarrassed, because you don't really know, and also like, when you are trying to do something really good and you find out he's not wearing a kippah and also it shows that he doesn't like, go in the laws of HaShem (God).

But why do Jewish boys dress differently? Why do they wear kippot?

Because it's a law of HaShem, and they're just supposed to.

Suppose that the rabbis got together and removed the rule about wearing kippot. Would that be all right?

No.

Why not?

Because it's been that way and that's a rule.

Well, if they did agree and removed the rule, then would it be all right for Jewish boys not to wear kippot?

No.

Why not?

Because the rule is there and it was meant to stay there.

The Christians don't require boys to wear kippot, is that all right?

Yeah.

Why?

Because, well, because that's not one of their rules. They don't respect God in the same way.

Is it okay that they respect God in a different way?

Yes. The religion is different. What they do is not our business, and if they want to do that they can.

Suppose that it never said in the Talmud or anywhere else in scripture any-
thing about wearing kippot, then would it be all right for Jewish boys to read
the Torah or pray without wearing a kippah?

Yeah. I mean, why would anybody need to do it if it wasn't there? How would anybody know?

Moral Issue: Stealing

Is it okay to steal?

No, because it's a law in the Torah, and it's also one of the Ten Commandments.

Does that rule have to be followed?

Yeah.

Why?

Because HaShem said so in the Torah, and, uh, you should follow all the mitzvahs of
HaShem. The Torah has 613 mitzvahs.

Suppose all the rabbis got together and decided not to have a rule about steal-
ing. Would that be okay?

No.

Why not?

Because like I said before in some of the other questions, it's a rule of HaShem. They
can't like change it 'cause like once when Moishe was walking his sons wanted, there
was a law and they wanted to change it, and they changed it and their punishment
was to die.

Suppose that people of another religion do not have a rule about stealing. Is
that all right?

Probably yes—but no. So, it's like half yes and half no.

Could you explain that to me?

Well, like if they don't have a rule they might think that it's okay to steal, and no because it still wouldn't be.

Why would it still be wrong?

Because you're taking something from another person. And the other person—let's
say it was a real gold pen or something and you really love it, like it was a present or
something from your bar mitzvah or something, or bat mitzvah, and it would be really wrong for the other people. Because it's like a treasure to them. Like on a
Peanuts show, Linus can't live without his blanket. It's like a beautiful present to
him and he really needs it. It's like a treasure. Without it he probably can't live. And
another thing is because, say there's one person and he steals from another person
who steals from the first person who stole things. Well, he would feel, both, like one
that got stolen from would get real angry and the one that already stole with the

first stealer also would get angry because his stuff was stolen. That he already stole, probably.

Suppose that there was never a law in the Torah. God never made it one of the Ten Commandments or one of the 613. He just didn't say anything about stealing. Would it be okay to steal then?

No. Still I don't think it's right because you're taking something from somebody else. But to some people probably yes, because they think it's fair because, well, they might say, "Finders keepers, losers weepers."

I see. Is it right to say that?

No, because they really took it and they didn't just find it, and the other people didn't lose it. It's not fair. And besides, it's also a lie. So there are two wrong things in that then.

What is clear from this excerpt is that the child being interviewed acknowledges that the rule about head coverings is based on the word of authority (God), that it is relative to a particular interpretation or view of that authority's norms, and that it serves the concrete social function of distinguishing girls from boys and members of her particular religious community from others. In contrast with her views about head coverings, she treated stealing as universally wrong, and wrong even if God did not have a rule about it. The wrongness of stealing, according to this child, is that it leads to hurtful and unjust consequences.

Summary of Findings on Morality and Religion

Taken as a whole, the findings from our studies with religious children indicate that children's moral understandings are independent of specific religious rules. Morality for the devoutly religious child as well as for the secular child focuses on the same set of fundamental interpersonal issues: those that deal with justice and compassion. For the public schools, this means that there can be moral education compatible with and yet independent from religious doctrine. Such moral education would focus on developing children's concepts of justice, fairness, and concern for the welfare of others.

The Personal Domain

Morality and convention are the basic forms of societal and interpersonal regulation. However, many of the social values important to us as individuals are matters of privacy and personal choice rather than moral or societal norms.

Reasoning about such issues falls within what is referred to as the personal domain (Nucci, 1996). The personal domain refers to actions that form the private aspects of one's life, such as the contents of a diary, and issues that are matters of preference and choice (e.g., friends, music, hairstyle) rather than right or wrong. A comprehensive approach to moral education would include allowance for and attention to this aspect of social life. Indeed, as will become clear in this book, many of the disputes that occur between students and their parents and teachers are over decisions that young people make within this personal zone. Moreover, the ability of children to respect the rights of others is affected by the degree to which children and adolescents have a sense of control over what is personal and private (Nucci, 1996).

Control over the personal domain emerges from the need to establish boundaries between the self and others and is critical to the formation of personal autonomy and individual identity (Nucci, 1996). Interview studies conducted in a range of cultural settings including northeastern Brazil, Colombia, Hong Kong, China, and Japan as well as the United States have shown that children and adolescents judge personal issues to be up to them (Nucci, 2001; Smetana, 2005). Research has also shown that most parents across cultures allow a certain amount of privacy and personal choice, even to children as young as three to four years of age (Smetana, 2005). Reasons that children and their parents provide for why behaviors and decisions should be treated as personal and within the child's jurisdiction focus on the role of such choices in developing the child's autonomy and personal identity, and the child or adolescent's moral right to have such discretion (Smetana, 2005).

This function of the personal is nicely illustrated in the following excerpt from an interview with a 16-year-old American boy. He is responding to a hypothetical scenario in which a boy belongs to a club in which the rules are that everyone in the club can read everyone else's mail and listen in on their phone conversations. The protagonist in the story has to decide whether or not to go along with the club rule.

> *Question:* Should Jonathan [the main character] follow the club rules and let them read his mail, or should he keep them to himself?
>
> *Answer:* Well, if that's the club rule, he might have to. But, if I were him, I wouldn't do it.
>
> *Question:* Why not?
>
> *Answer:* Well, it's carrying a group, a club, beyond the limits it needs in order to stay a group. It's just a desire to overstep and go into personal things.
>
> *Question:* Is it important to maintain the letters and phone calls private?
>
> *Answer:* Yes. It's an invasion of you, you as a person. You are losing a component of yourself. It's tearing away at that.

Question: Why would a person want to keep things private if they aren't embarrassing or incriminating?

Answer: It has its own importance. It's even one step further than being able to grow your hair the way you want. I guess your thoughts are as close to being able to describe the self that is possible. And then your physical freedoms, how long you grow your hair, just sort of build up yourself. They help to contribute on the outside to the core of your thoughts and personal ideas. (From Nucci, 1977)

The Social Experiential Origins of Children's Morality

The basic finding of a conceptual distinction between morality and nonmoral issues of convention and the personal has proven to be among the most robust phenomena uncovered by psychological research. Most recently, it has been discovered that the basic distinction between morality and convention is maintained even by children suffering from autism (James & Blair, 2005; Leslie, Mallon, & DiCorcia, 2006). The fact that morality appears to be universal and available to very young children has led some writers to conclude that morality is guided by an innate "moral sense" (Wilson, 1993). Although there is some evidence that children are primed to respond to emotional distress, there is no evidence that children are born with moral knowledge. Instead, children's concepts of morality, social convention, and the personal emerge from their efforts to make sense of everyday social experiences. Observational studies of children's everyday social interactions in the home, at school, and on the playground have demonstrated that the pattern of social interactions associated with morality is different from social interactions having to do with conventions and personal issues. As we will see in Section II of this book, understanding these natural social interaction patterns can help teachers in thinking about how to respond to misbehavior as part of classroom management.

Children's Responses to Moral and Conventional Transgressions

To explore these interaction patterns, researchers have looked at how children and adults respond to children's moral and social conventional transgressions. These patterns are illustrated in the following events observed in a study of children in free-play settings (Nucci & Nucci, 1982a). In each case, the transgression is italicized. In our studies of middle- and working-class children in free-play settings, we rarely witnessed children objecting to the use of profanity.

The use of profanity was most common in response to moral transgressions, as will be seen in the following excerpts.

Moral

1. *Two boys* (1 and 2) *are throwing sand at a smaller boy* (3). Boy (3) says, "Dammit—you got it in my eyes. It hurts like hell. Next time I'm gonna kick your heads in." Boy (1) says to boy (2), "Hey, did you hear that? Next time he's gonna kick our heads in." They both laugh and throw more sand in the face of boy (3). Boy (3) then spits at boy (1) and runs away.

2. *Two boys have forcibly taken a sled away from a younger boy and are playing with it.* A girl who was watching says to the boys, "Hey, give it back a-holes. That's really even odds, the two of you against one little kid." The girl then pulls the sled away from one of the older boys, pushes him to the ground, and hands the sled back to the younger boy. He takes the sled and the incident ends.

As can be seen in these examples, children experience moral events as victims as well as perpetrators or third person observers. The transgression (such as hitting, stealing, or damaging property) is followed by peer reactions focusing on the intrinsic effects of the act. An intrinsic effect of hitting someone, for example, is that the person will be hurt. Moral transgressions tend to be followed by statements of injury or loss and evaluations of the act as unjust or hurtful. Generally, these reactions have a high degree of emotion. With very young children, the reaction may consist solely of crying. In addition, children may avenge moral transgressions or try to avoid additional victimization through attempts at retaliation or, in the case of young children, by involving adults.

Social Convention

1. *A boy and a girl are sitting together on the grass, away from the other children, tying their shoes.* Another boy (2) sings out to them, "Bobby and Alison sittin' in a tree, K-I-S-S-I-N-G," etc.

2. A girl (1) *is sucking on a piece of grass.* Girl (2) says to girl (3), "That's what she does, she sucks on weeds and spits them out." Girl (3) says, "Gross!" Girl (2) says, "That's disgusting!" Girl (1) then places the piece of grass down and ceases placing grass in her mouth.

Peer interactions involving violations of convention tend to arouse relatively little emotion. The transgression (such as violating sex-role behavior or social decorum) is followed by peer responses focusing on social norms and social expectations. Respondents state governing rules, evaluate the acts as odd or disruptive ("gross"), and attempt to achieve conformity through ridicule (see conventional example 1 above).

Adult Responses to Moral and Social Conventional Transgressions

The pattern of adult responses to children's transgressions is also different by domain. Adult responses to moral transgressions complement those of children and often follow them in time (Smetana, 1982). Mothers of toddlers provide social messages focusing on the hurtful effects of moral transgressions and also attempt to persuade children to engage in prosocial behaviors and share or "be nice" (Gralinski & Kopp, 1993). As children grow older these adult responses become more elaborated as children are provided more explicit social messages regarding the harmful impact of their actions and are asked by teachers and parents to consider the perspective of the other person ("Mary, how do you feel when people lie to you?") and to reflect on their own motivations for acting as they did ("Why did you do that?").

Adult responses to convention also complement those of children. Mothers and teachers provide statements regarding the underlying social rules and social expectations ("Raise your hand before talking"). They also provide statements labeling the transgressions as unruly, disorderly ("It's getting too noisy in here"), or unmannerly ("Chew with your mouth closed. Where are your manners?"), inappropriate for the context ("Dan, those ripped jeans are okay for play, but not for school"), and generally inconsistent with conventional expectations ("That's not the way for a Hawthorne student to act." "Susan, act your age.") (Nucci & Nucci, 1982b).

Social Interactions and the Personal Domain

The personal represents a boundary drawn between what individuals consider to be within their area of discretion, and what is legitimately regulated by societal convention and interpersonal moral considerations. Thus, the development of children's ideas about the personal emerges from social interactions in which they stake a claim and/or negotiate for behavioral freedom. Observational studies of mother-child interactions with preschool-aged children in the United States have illustrated that children's construction of the personal is not simply a matter of accepting the default zones of control permitted by parents. This research uncovered three basic interaction patterns around personal issues (Nucci & Weber, 1995). In the first and least common pattern, mothers explicitly label certain things as up to the child. When they do give such explicit statements the mothers' instructions look like the following discussion between a mother and her daughter over the girl's hairstyle.

> MOTHER: If you want, we can get your hair cut. **It's your choice**.
>
> CHILD: I only want it that long—down to here. [Child points to where she wants her hair cut.]

More typically, the social messages mothers directed to children about personal issues were in the indirect form of offered choices such as illustrated in the following exchange:

> MOTHER: You need to decide what you want to wear to school today.
>
> CHILD: [Opens a drawer.] Pants. Pants. Pants.
>
> MOTHER: Have you decided what to wear today?
>
> CHILD: I wear these.
>
> MOTHER: Okay, that's a good choice.
>
> MOTHER: How would you like your hair today?
>
> CHILD: Down. [Child stands by the bed, and her mother carefully combs her hair.]

In the above interaction, the mother offered choices conveying the idea that dress and hairstyle are matters for the child to decide. The child might then infer that such behavior is personal. Through both the direct and indirect forms of communication, mothers show a willingness to provide children areas of personal discretion. The fact that mothers are more likely to tell children what to do in the context of moral and conventional behaviors than in the context of personal ones is in itself an indication that mothers view the former as issues in which the child needs to accommodate to specific external social demands and meanings, while the personal issues are for the child to interpret and control.

Finally, there are interactions that reflect child resistance and parental negotiation. These situations often emerged when the child attempted to exert choice around a behavior or activity that overlapped or intersected with a social convention, as illustrated in the following mother-child interaction.

> MOTHER: Evan, it's your last day of nursery school. Why don't you wear your nursery sweatshirt?
>
> CHILD: I don't want to wear that one.
>
> MOTHER: This is the last day of nursery school, that's why we wear it. You want to wear that one?
>
> CHILD: Another one.
>
> MOTHER: Are you going to get it, or should I?
>
> CHILD: I will. First I got to get a shirt.
>
> MOTHER: [Goes to the child's dresser and starts picking out shirts.] This one? This one? Do you know which one you have in mind? Here, this is a new one.
>
> CHILD: No, it's too big.

MOTHER: Oh, Evan, just wear one, and when you get home, you can pick whatever you want, and I won't even help you. [Child puts on shirt.]

This case presents a conflict between a dress convention (wearing a particular shirt on the last day of school) and the child's view that dress is a personal choice. The mother acknowledges the child's resistance and attempts to negotiate, finally offering the child a free choice once school is over. This example illustrates several things. For one, the mother provided direct information to the child about the convention in question, "This is the last day of nursery school, that's why we wear it." At the same time, she displayed an interest in fostering the child's autonomy and decision making around the issue. The child's resistance, which conveyed his personal interest, was not simply cut off, but was guided by the mother, who linked it to his autonomy: "Are you going to get it, or should I?" . . . "You can pick whatever you want, and *I won't even help you.*" In the end, there is compromise. The child got to choose, but within a more general conventional demand (enforced by the mother) that he wear a shirt.

The verbal dance engaged in by the mother and child in the above example illustrates that the mothers acted in ways that indicated an understanding that children should have areas of discretion and personal control. The excerpt also illustrates ways in which children, through their resistance, provided mothers with information about the *child's* desires and needs for personal choice. We sometimes misinterpret children's resistance as instances of disobedience or the tantrums of a "spoiled child." No doubt there are such situations and children. However, few of the interactions that we observed fit those negative patterns. Instead, most of the children we observed complied with their parents most of the time when it came to moral issues. Children asserted prerogative or choice in 98% of the cases involving a personal domain issue. In contrast, children made such statements in less than 10% of the moral situations.

Summary

In sum, children construct their notions of morality, the conventions of society, and their sense of the personal out of different aspects of their social experiences. It is the qualitatively different nature of moral and nonmoral social interactions that accounts for the fact that children think about morality, convention, and the personal in such different ways. The important point to take away from these observational studies is that children's morality is a product of their efforts to make sense of actions that affect their own well-being and that of others. Children in every culture have experiences of kindness and harm, of sharing and of injustice. It is these commonalities of social life and not an innate moral sense that accounts for the universal aspects of morality.

Moral Complexity

Domain Overlap

At this point the thoughtful reader is likely to be puzzled by what appears to be a contradiction between the research and theory on moral psychology and the reader's own knowledge of issues that seem to overlap morality and social convention. For example, most Americans have stood in line to buy movie tickets. This is clearly a social convention, and I am sure that many readers of this book have been to places where people do not line up to buy things. On the other hand, anyone who has lined up only to have someone cut in recognizes that the social convention of queuing, by establishing turn-taking, serves the moral function of distributive justice. This is an example of domain interaction, where the convention is in harmony with morality. One can also imagine domain overlap, in which conventional concerns for social organization are in conflict with moral considerations of fairness and human welfare. An example would be gender-based norms that provide opportunities to men, such as career choices and advancement, not offered to women.

These examples of domain overlap and interaction reflect the complex relations that exist between moral considerations and social structure. Our reasoning or understanding of such social issues may draw from our concepts from one or both social cognitive domains. To illustrate how we make use of more than one conceptual framework in everyday life, imagine the situation of four children trying to decide how to divide the 10 dollars they earned delivering newspapers. On the one hand, this is a mathematical problem requiring an understanding of how to divide 10 into four parts. On the other hand, this is a moral problem drawing on an understanding of equity and fair distribution. No mathematics teacher would reduce subject matter to ethics, nor would an ethicist confuse subject matter with mathematics. Yet, in this example, we see that the problem solution requires knowledge from both domains. Similar situations arise in the context of multifaceted social situations. For example, a comprehensive understanding of social norms that distribute social roles by gender requires an appreciation of the function that conventions serve for social groups such as the family to run smoothly, and a moral understanding of how such norms affect the needs of individuals to be treated fairly. To reduce the issue to a simple matter of either convention or morality is to misconstrue the situation.

There are two clear educational implications of this social complexity. The first is that a comprehensive approach to children's moral and social development needs to differentially address their concepts of morality and societal convention if children are to be aided in their ability to comprehend, evaluate, and respond to everyday social situations. The second is that any approach that reduces moral education to the social transmission of existing social norms is inherently engaged in the perpetuation of whatever immorality may be embedded within those norms. This is why moral education worthy of the name cannot follow the path of inculcation and socialization advocated by traditional character education (Ryan, 1989; Wynne & Ryan, 1993). We will return to this point in greater detail when we take up issues regarding classroom practices in subsequent chapters.

Informational Assumptions

Adding to this complexity is the role of informational assumptions on our reading of the moral implications of actions. As we have seen, young children view hitting another person as wrong because of the pain and harm it causes the victim. But what are we to make of the morality of a parent disciplining a child by spanking? Studies that have examined parental assumptions about spanking have found that parents who favor spanking do so because they consider it to be an effective educative practice that does little or no harm to the child (Wainryb, 1991). When parents were given information that spanking is no more effective than other methods of disciplining children, significant numbers of parents shifted in their views of corporal punishment and maintained that it was not right for parents to engage in the behavior because of the pain inflicted on the child. Clearly, what had changed the moral evaluation of spanking made by these parents was not the structure of their morality, but rather the assumptions they held about the effects of spanking.

Even more dramatic effects of informational assumptions on moral judgment can be seen in cultural studies of social values. In one such study University of Chicago anthropologist Richard Shweder and his colleagues (Shweder, Mahapatra, & Miller, 1987) asked adult members of a Hindu temple town in Orisa, India to rank order from most to least wrong 39 behaviors that violated social norms within their culture. The act rated most wrong was for the eldest son in a family getting a haircut and eating chicken the day after his father died. Rated thirty-fifth in seriousness was a man beating his disobedient wife black and blue. From a Western perspective these Hindu villagers would certainly appear to have a different morality from the Judeo-Christian community. As it turns out, however, the Hindu judgments of the eldest son, while morally neutral from a Western point of view, take on a different meaning within the context of Hindu beliefs about the impact of the son's actions on the father. In particular, the Hindu judgments must be seen from within the context of beliefs about the ways in which events in the natural world operate in relation to *unobserved entities*, such as souls and spirits of the deceased. In this case, the father's soul would be placed in great jeopardy by the son's actions. If we allow ourselves to role-take for a moment and imagine that we are in the son's position, we can see how the acts of getting a haircut and eating chicken become a serious matter of causing grave harm to another person. We don't need to assume a new set of *moral* understandings, but rather to apply our moral concepts of fairness and human welfare to this situation once the *facts* are understood.

Within our own culture, changes in factual assumptions have fed into shifting moral evaluations of such things as slavery and the role of women. Advances in biological sciences may alter the ways in which we view such things as reproduction, aging, and even death. How those changes may affect social morality is hard to anticipate. An educational implication of the role of factual assumptions on moral judgment is that moral education should include attention to critical thinking and academic research skills.

Summary

In this chapter we have seen that research on children's social development demonstrates that concepts of morality are distinct from matters of social convention. Morality refers to issues that affect the well-being of others. Children's morality centers around issues of caring, helping others, avoiding harm, and being fair. Moral development involves age-related changes in children's concepts of fairness and welfare and their reasoning about such issues. Moral issues are determined by the effects of actions on others such as the harm or benefit they cause, rather than by the existence or absence of social rules. Basic moral concepts emerge very early in development and appear to be universal. Morality is not determined by religious rules, and the basic moral concepts of religious and secular children are the same. Thus, public schools can engage in moral education without undermining or promoting a particular religious faith.

In contrast with morality, acts that are matters of social convention are only right or wrong if there is a governing rule. Social conventions are arbitrary in the sense that they can be changed through social consensus. Although social conventions are arbitrary and variable from one culture to another, they serve an important social function. Conventions are necessary for the coordination and smooth functioning of social groups. Conventions such as an agreed-upon dinner time, appropriate attire, and table manners provide predictability and commonality for members of a social group.

In addition to concepts about morality and convention, people maintain that certain aspects of their social life are personal matters of privacy and discretion. The personal domain is not about right and wrong, but has to do with behaviors and choices that affect the actor rather than other people. The personal includes such things as one's choice of friends, music preferences, contents of a diary or journal, and aspects of personal appearance such as one's hairstyle. Maintaining a personal domain is essential to a sense of autonomy and individuality. Development within the personal domain is structured by concepts of persons, self, and identity.

The source of children's moral knowledge is their efforts to make sense of social experiences involving harm and fairness. Every child encounters social interactions in which someone is hurt or shortchanged. As children put together their own experiences as victims, perpetrators, and observers of moral events with the views of others who have had similar experiences, children construct their basic moral concepts. These experiences of harm and kindness, fair and unfair treatment are qualitatively different from experiences concerning social conventions. Children's experiences with social conventions focus on rules and social expectations rather than on the acts themselves.

Moral complexity arises from two sources. The first is domain overlap. The second is informational or factual assumptions. Domain overlap occurs when social conventions regulating social organization are in harmony or in conflict with issues of fairness. In such cases, people may either subordinate the issue to a single domain (treat the complex issue as a matter of convention or morality only) or attempt to coordinate or integrate both moral and conventional elements.

Informational assumptions have to do with our beliefs about what is true in the natural world and may include our beliefs about unseen entities such as souls and spirits in the afterlife. Changes in our informational assumptions affect our judgments about the moral meaning of actions. For example, assumptions about the effectiveness of spanking affect whether parents view spanking as morally acceptable or wrong.

CHAPTER 3

The Development of Morality, Convention, and the Personal

The child is father of the man.

—William Wordsworth, 1882

It's a part of life to do what you want.

—A 7-year-old girl

In Chapter 2 we learned that social values are constructed within distinct conceptual frameworks or domains. The distinctions among morality, convention, and personal issues will form the framework for our approach to moral education. In order to be effective, however, our educational approach must also match up with children's development. Every teacher knows, for example, that one cannot teach a second grader what one would teach a high school senior. The same reasoning applies to moral education. In this chapter we will learn about development within each domain and what those typical developmental changes mean in terms of students' behavior and our sequencing of moral education. We will also look at how development within individual domains affects social reasoning and behavior in situations that involve the application of social knowledge from more than one domain. Many readers of this book may be familiar with Kohlberg's (1984) six stages of moral development. From the vantage point of newer research, the Kohlberg stage sequence can be best understood as an approximation of the way in which people at different ages reason about situations that require coordinating morality with other social cognitive domains. What we know now, however, is that the Kohlberg sequence oversimplifies those interactions (Smetana, 2006). A detailed comparison of the Kohlberg stage sequence with the newer work on the development within each distinct domain can be found in Nucci (2001).

Development occurs throughout the lifespan. However, we will limit our discussion to changes that take place during the school years. We will begin by looking at the broad picture of development in the personal domain, and especially its dynamic connection to social convention during adolescence. This discussion of the personal will be followed by sections describing development within the domains of social convention and morality. I have included some excerpts from interviews with children to help illustrate children's thinking at different points in development. These selections are typical of what children in research studies have had to say. Interested readers can go to the original sources for more extensive examples, or contact the author using information in the final chapter of the book.

We begin our discussion of development with the personal domain for two reasons. First, morality and convention can be seen as regulating aspects of individual behavior. There is a dynamic tension between what individual students view as personal and what is regulated by convention and moral obligation. Thus, we need to understand how development affects this dynamic if we are to appropriately navigate age-related resistance to school rules and adult authority and effectively engage in moral education.

Second, as educators, we need to recognize that it is essential for students to have a secure sense of what is personal in order for them to benefit from our efforts at moral and social development. You can only operate maturely in the interpersonal realm of convention and morality if you also have a reasonably secure sense of the personal domain (Nucci, 1996). We tend to overlook this in programs of moral education because of our focus on having children reason and act in ways that are socially appropriate and morally right. Much of the emphasis in this book will be on forms of classroom structure and curricular lessons that will build students' capacities for appreciating social norms, along with reasoning and acting in ways that are increasingly fair and compassionate. However, we will also be paying attention to the ways in which classroom structure and curricula support and foster growth in the personal domain.

Age-Related Changes in the Personal Domain

The psychological basis for children's and adolescents' claims to areas of personal choice and privacy is their centrality in the construction of a sense of identity and autonomy (Nucci, 1996). The development of students' concepts about personal issues reflects their understanding of what it means to be a person and how one establishes individual identity and autonomy. The sequence of developmental changes described here is summarized in Table 3.1. The ages and grade levels associated with each developmental period in the sections that follow reflect average trends for American children. However, individual children may enter developmental phases at earlier or later grades or ages than what is seen in the typical pattern. This caveat will hold true for development in all three domains of social reasoning.

TABLE 3.1

Development in the Personal Domain

Early Elementary

Control over the personal is tied to observable physical and behavioral aspects of self. Identity and autonomy are manifested in how one dresses and appears to others. Autonomy is literally the ownership and control over one's "own self."

Middle Elementary

The self includes a personality (as well as a physical body) described in terms of characteristic behaviors that are in comparison with the behaviors of others. Control over the personal allows for the behavioral illustration and development of the personality.

Middle School

The self is now described primarily in terms of one's ideas, beliefs, values, and thoughts. Control over the personal is necessary in order to be different from others. However, consciousness lacks depth. Being individual is defined in terms of being different; having different ideas and beliefs from others.

High School

The self is based on an interior essence of core ideas and values that are uncovered and made manifest through control over one's private and personal decisions and actions. Control over the personal allows for self-discovery and the coordination of what is "outside" with what is inside the "true" self.

DEVELOPMENTAL SHIFTS IN RELATION TO CONVENTION

Beginning in late elementary school and continuing into the second or third year of high school, children and adolescents expand what they consider to be personal and within their jurisdiction rather than under the control of parents. These shifts are in relation to family and household conventions and issues of prudence having to do with the personal safety of the child. Parents are also giving increased control of the personal domain to their children as they get older. However, the rate at which parents give over control tends to lag behind the demands of their children.

Early Elementary

Children in the early elementary grades (K–3) base their intuitions about personal control on a physical and behavioral sense of self (Nucci, 1977, 1996). Although very young children intuitively know that other people also have an interior mental life of emotions and intentions (Astington, 1993), children form their ideas about the personal domain in terms of physical and behavioral aspects of the self that are the easiest to apprehend. Susan Gelman (2003) describes young children as having the idea that the self is made up of components that are essential aspects of what that person is in actuality. We will see that these early forms of essentialism are echoed in the adolescent's concepts of a "true" inner self. Parents and teachers are quite familiar with children who insist on wearing the same pajama top to school day after day, or who cling to a particular favorite activity such as kickball or jumping rope as if their very lives depended on doing those things. For young children these clothing choices and behaviors are a part of who they are. In Chapter 4 and especially Chapter 5 we discuss how classroom rules and classroom climate should function to foster children's autonomy as well as their respect for morality and convention. Wise teachers balance the norms required for a smoothly running classroom with accommodation for children's efforts at personal expression.

The thinking of young children about the personal and its connection to a sense of identity is illustrated in the following brief excerpt of an interview with the same 7-year-old girl quoted at the beginning of the chapter. (All quotes are from Nucci, 1977.)

> *John goes to the principal and says that he wants to wear his hair the way that he wants to. What do you think about that?*
>
> I agree with him.
>
> *How come?*
>
> Because I wouldn't want to have to look like all the other boys, and I would want my hair a little different.
>
> *What would be wrong with having your hair like the other kids?*
>
> Well, he would like to be his own self, like there's all these people, they wouldn't want to look alike, then who would be who? And all their names would be alike. "Who's this? Is this you, or is this, or is this?" It would really be weird.

Middle Elementary

Children in grades 3–5 continue with the concrete foundation of the personal in observable aspects of self, but place even more emphasis than their younger peers on behaviors as the critical component that defines your personal makeup. Personality is a matter of how you do things, as one 10-year-old put it: "Well some people play volleyball, and that's their personality . . . God throws his voice; He has personality." Children at this age understand that being able to have control over aspects of your personal activities is critical to maintaining this essential component of self. As in early elementary grades students at this level require that adults provide venues within which children can carve out ways of displaying and acting out their particular, personal, physical, and behavioral modes of being who they see themselves to be. Children also, for the first time, begin to interpret themselves in terms of their relative competence within favored, personal modes of acting (Nucci, 1977). Educators are familiar with how these comparative evaluations can backfire when children are led to focus on their academic performance (Nicholls & Miller, 1984). Thus, it is crucial that children have opportunities to explore a range of activities for finding and defining themselves. The proponents of what is referred to as *developmental discipline* (Watson, 2003, 2008) include attention to children's needs for autonomy and competence as essential elements of effective classroom management and discipline with elementary school-aged children. In Chapter 5 we take up this approach to classrooms as a central feature of effective moral education.

Middle School

In late childhood and early adolescence, the elements that students use to define the self shift from the physical side of things to their inner mental life. Control over the personal now takes on a new emphasis on maintaining privacy as well as behavioral choice. Personal diaries and journals now become staples for many adolescents. However, the "interior" life of an early adolescent lacks depth, and the basis for being an autonomous individual is expressed reactively in terms of "being different from others." There is a fear of losing oneself by too closely following the crowd. This reactive notion of self is expressed in terms of the need for freedom of choice and the ability to be different from others:

> I mean everybody's got to be free you know, and growing your hair different is a way of being you know free, making a decision. I hate to be like everybody else. Because you know, I just like to look like myself, not like what somebody wanted me to look like, or you know, what my friends look like.
>
> Thirteen-year-old girl

Teachers who work with middle school students will recognize in these claims an almost Shakespearean tendency to "protest too much." The freedom expressed by the 13-year-old girl in the excerpt above hangs on a rather fragile notion of self easily threatened by moving too far away from what is acceptable to the peer group. Consider the following statement from the interview with the same 13-year-old girl cited above. In this excerpt she is talking about why she should be able to select what clothes she should wear.

> I mean your mother forces you to wear certain clothes. It makes you feel dumb, right? Dumb skirts or whatever, and then you go to school; you feel dumb, everybody's looking at you, and you can't concentrate on your work—you kind of daydream and wish you were somewhere else.

For all of her emphasis on the need for freedom and choice, this young adolescent girl is very much aware of her need for belonging and the role of peer conventions in tying her into group membership. The personal domain of an early adolescent is unstable and in flux. The surface level of her sense of self as an interior set of opinions, values, thoughts, and emotions rests on a reactive employment of discretion in her personal sphere, rather than a deeper sense of self as something other than its overt, public manifestations. In Chapters 8 and 9 we present lessons drawing from American literature that connect to adolescents' fascination with what it means to be "phony" and what it means to be genuine. One of the questions we pose is whether one can dress and act like someone else and still remain genuine. For the young adolescent this poses a near impossibility; for the typical high school sophomore and older adolescent, this question presents less of a problem. We turn now to the thinking of high school-age students.

High School

For the typical high school-aged student the connection between maintaining control over personal issues and a sense of self is thought of as a process of bringing together all parts of oneself around a core inner true self or essence. Consciousness has depth. There is a real "me" that is the core of who I am. The task is to discover that inner core and to bring the "outside self" of activities and public appearance in line with that true inner core. It is entirely possible that two people could elect to wear the same clothes and not be "phony." Because the inner selves are an essence of each person, they are not subject to change through the coincidental match of interests between two free people.

Control over a personal sphere of privacy and of thoughts is essential to discovery and maintenance of that true self, as was illustrated in the quotation from the 16-year-old boy that was included in the section on the personal domain in Chapter 2. External control over what is private and personal disrupts that process and risks damage to the construction of the true self. This notion is expressed in the following excerpt from a 17-year-old junior explaining why she thinks that a boy in a scenario should be able to determine the length of his hair.

> *You said it was important for him to display the image that he wants to. Why is that?*
>
> That's the way he thinks, and the way he acts, and the way he wants to be, and the way he wants others to see him, and the way he sees himself. It seems that you should be able to be a whole person and have your outside look like your inside looks, and people can't determine what your inside looks like, the only person who can decide is you. So it seems that those should go together and that would be why people should determine their own appearance.

In the previous excerpt you can see how she is linking the boy's decisions over his external appearance to the core interior of his self. In the following excerpt this same 17-year-old girl illustrates the self-constructive function of maintaining privacy over her personal diary:

> If I write something like that, it is really from deep down inside of me, and I feel very vulnerable . . . and to have someone just sit there and take part of that—I'd feel like it was damaged in some way.
>
> *Well, why write these things down?*
>
> Just to get your intimate thoughts on paper helps you think things out. . . . Then you have it out where you can examine yourself so to speak; your most intimate self, and you come to know how you feel and you just know more about yourself. It makes you closer to your true self I think.

Developmental Dynamics Between the Personal and Conventional Domains

The developmental patterns of thinking within the personal domain are consistent with the development of concepts of the self (Damon & Hart, 1988). High school teachers will also recognize similarities between the reasoning of adolescents about the personal domain and Erik Erikson's (1968) description of the identity crisis in youth. This is to be expected since the personal domain is generated out of children's efforts to maintain self and identity. Part of the process of becoming an autonomous self involves what psychologists refer to as individuation. This refers to the gradual separation of children from the guidance of their parents. As was mentioned in Chapter 2, we have learned that a central part of this process involves the extension by older children and adolescents of what they consider to be personal matters beyond the authority of their parents.

As children get older, and especially as they enter adolescence, they begin to push for control over a wider range of their own behaviors (Smetana, 2005). This trend holds for issues that intersect the personal with convention and their own personal health and safety (prudence). Typical issues over which American adolescents seek control include choice of movies to watch, how late they can stay out at night, where they can go for recreation, and when or whether to clean up their own bedroom. Adolescents rarely argue against parental authority over their moral conduct, adherence to basic cultural conventions, or basic safety such as drug or substance abuse. For their part, parents are also giving to their adolescent children greater authority and autonomy over personal matters. However, the time at which parents tend to view their children as ready to assume authority lags behind the time assumed by their adolescent children. As a consequence these "border" disputes over what Judith Smetana (Smetana &

Daddis, 2002) refers to as "ambiguously personal issues" account for nearly all instances of adolescent-parent conflict (Smetana, 2005). This is the case not only in the United States, but in Latin American and Asian countries where this phenomenon has been examined (Smetana, 2002). The peak ages for these disputes within the American middle class correspond to the period from middle school through the sophomore year of high school.

How parents approach their children's needs for a personal domain has an impact on adolescents' mental health. In a cross-national study of adolescents in the United States and Japan, adolescents who reported having parents who attempted to control personal issues such as the children's friendship choices, music, hairstyle, and issues of privacy such as parents reading their diary were also more likely to report experiencing internalizing symptoms of depression, anxiety, and somatization (Hasebe, Nucci, & Nucci, 2004). Essentially the same outcome was reported in a study of middle-class African American adolescents and parents (Smetana, Campion-Barr, & Daddis, 2004). The negative effects of parental control of the personal on African Americans occurred at slightly older ages than had been found for the middle class White students (Hasebe et al., 2004). For African Americans, parental control in early adolescence was associated with positive outcomes while continued control into middle adolescence (age 14 and older) was associated with negative psychological outcomes. These studies lend further support to the contention that establishing a personal domain is essential for psychological integrity.

As one would expect, there is a similar age-related trend toward greater control over the personal within the school setting. As we will see in the next section on developmental changes in concepts of social convention, these normal developmental shifts may help to account for some of the behavioral issues teachers contend with during this same early adolescent age period. According to Smetana (Smetana & Bitz, 1996), however, middle school and high school students are generally aware of the differences between the institutional setting of school and the more intimate setting of the family. Most students grant school authority over "ambiguously personal issues" such as "public displays of affection" between boyfriend and girlfriend that they would insist upon as personal matters outside the school context. Students unwilling or unable to accommodate to the regulation of such conduct in school also tend to have more general behavioral problems (Smetana & Bitz, 1996).

The Development of Concepts of Social Convention

The age-related shifts in the personal domain are taking place as broad developmental changes are also occurring in children's concepts about morality and social convention. As children sort out what areas of behavior ought to be their "own business" they are also constructing and reevaluating their concepts of moral and conventional regulation. Young children have an intuitive grasp of social conventions and by age 6 have considerable knowledge of what society expects in the way of appropriate behavior. However, the societal functions of conventions are usually quite complex, and even when children have learned what is "expected," they do not fully understand the reasons why such behaviors are considered reasonable and right. Conceptions of convention progress through seven developmental levels (Turiel, 1983) that extend into young adulthood. For our purposes we will focus on the first five levels that correspond to school-age children and adolescents.

Development follows a pattern that moves between periods affirming the importance of convention and transitional phases in which children appear to doubt or negate the reasons that they had previously given for maintaining convention. This oscillation indicates the difficulty children have in accounting for the function of arbitrary social norms and illustrates the slow process of reflection and construction that precedes the older adolescent's understanding of convention as important to maintaining the social system. We will see a similar U-shaped pattern of seeming progress and regression in the following section when we look at the development of moral concepts about helping someone in need and actions that indirectly result in harm to others. Teachers are generally familiar with what psychologists refer to as U-shaped growth patterns. Students often seem to be less competent just as they are about to make a shift to a more complex academic skill. These U-shaped patterns occur across many developmental tasks and may actually be more common than the linear patterns of steady developmental progress usually described in child development textbooks (Gershkoff & Thelen, 2004). Most teachers also understand that these "regressions" are not steps backward, but are part of the process of moving toward newer levels of competence and complexity. From an educational point of view, periods of transition are critical junctures where proper guidance can assist the developmental process. The development of concepts about convention is summarized in Table 3.2.

Early Elementary (Level I, Grades K–2): Convention as Reflecting Observed Social Regularities

Young children already understand that behaviors governed by social convention are only right or wrong if there is a social rule in place. For this reason, children need to make sense of conventions by focusing on the rules rather than the acts that rules regulate. Just as they do with rules of grammar, young children search for patterns in these social rules. For children approximately 5 to 7 years of age (roughly kindergarten to second grade), the patterns that they observe in how rules are applied, combined with the explicit information they are told (e.g., parent or teacher statements of rules or expectations) leads them to establish a

TABLE 3.2

Developmental of Social Convention

Early Elementary (Grades K–2)

Conventions are tied to observed regularities in social interactions. Conventions are connected to things as they are. Gender roles, table manners, forms of greeting, and modes of dress all conform to general patterns defined by convention. Exceptions to conventions, such as a man whom children address by his first name rather than with the title "Mr.," are viewed as errors or special cases rather than evidence that conventions do not describe "the way things are."

Middle Elementary (Grades 3–4)

Negation of convention is based on observed inconsistencies and exceptions to conventional norms. For example, knowing about a man whom children call by his first name negates the conventions for addressing elders. Conventions are applied inconsistently and therefore don't matter.

Middle Elementary (Grades 5–6)

Affirmation of convention is based on a concrete understanding that conventional rules maintain order (e.g., prevent people from running in the halls). There is a top-down conception of social authority and rules. People in charge make rules that preserve order. Rules may be changed and vary by context. There is no understanding that conventions help to structure social systems.

Middle School (Grades 6–8)

Conventions are now viewed as "nothing but" social expectations or the dictates of authority. The arbitrary nature of convention is viewed as undercutting the force of such rules. Acts are evaluated independently of rules. Students may follow conventions to avoid getting in trouble, or so as not to cause teachers problems over seemingly small matters. Students have no conceptual basis for sustaining the regulatory force of conventions.

High School (Grades 9–12)

Systematic concepts of social structure emerge. Conventions are understood as helping to maintain social systems, and also symbolically reflect the social organization and hierarchy. Referring to teachers by titles (Mr., Mrs.) symbolizes their social status and confers respect for that status. Conventions are viewed as normative and binding within a social system of fixed roles and hierarchical organization. Members of a social group are expected to adhere to conventions.

sensible but overly rigid idea about social expectations. For example, children observe that women and not men generally wear dresses. From this observed regularity, children construct a straightforward set of conclusions: Men don't wear dresses because men aren't women; therefore only women and girls should wear dresses. For a man or a boy to wear a dress would be to violate this observed regularity of the social world. Teachers of young children will recognize in this rigidity about convention similarities to what children do when they overgeneralize the rules for such things as past tense and plurals, and put "ed" endings for irregular verbs such as "drinked" for "drank," and "s" as plurals for nouns such as "sheeps" rather than sheep and "gooses" for geese. Reasoning about convention typical of young children in early elementary grades is illustrated in the following excerpt from research by Elliot Turiel (1983, p. 107) in which a 6-year-old girl is responding to a scenario depicting a boy who wants to grow up to become an infant nurse.

> *Should he become a nurse?*
>
> Well, no because he could easily be a doctor and he could take care of babies in the hospital.
>
> *Why shouldn't he be a nurse?*
>
> Well, because a nurse is a lady and the boys, the other men would just laugh at them.
>
> *Why shouldn't a man be a nurse?*
>
> Well, because it would be sort of silly because ladies wear those kind of dresses and those kind of shoes and hats.

Middle Elementary (Level II, Grades 3–4): Negation of Convention as Empirical Regularity

Children at age 5 to 7 years are aware of counterexamples to the regularities that they use to base their notions of convention. For example, they may have an adult neighbor who allows children to call him by his first name rather than by the title Mister and his last name. For the 5- to 7-year-old such a counterexample is simply chalked up to error. The neighbor is simply "wrong." As children get older, however, this instability in their assumptions about convention leads them to reconsider their position. Now such contradictions are viewed as evidence that conventions don't really matter. Children reason that if you can call an adult by his first name in your neighborhood, why can't you call a teacher by her first name at school? As one would expect, observational studies of children's violations of classroom social convention report a rise in third and fourth grade in the rate at which children break classroom rules about such things as raising your hand to speak, refraining from cross-talking, getting the teacher's permission to leave one's seat to sharpen a pencil, and lining up to enter the classroom or school (Nucci & Nucci, 1982b). Reasoning about convention at this point in development is illustrated in the following excerpt with an 8-year-old girl, again from Turiel (1983, pp. 107–108).

Right, because it doesn't matter. There are men nurses in hospitals.

What if there were not any in Joe's time, do you think he should have done it?

Yes. It doesn't matter if it is a man or a woman it is just your job taking care of little children.

Middle Elementary (Level III, Grades 5–6): Affirmation of Convention as Authority-Based Rules for Social Order; Early Concrete Conception of Social System

At approximately fifth grade (about age 10), children tend to replace the negation of the previous level with a concrete affirmation of the functional value of conventions as serving to maintain social order. Children recognize that conventions vary by context and that exceptions exist within contexts. However, they also maintain that things work "better" when there is some organization established by rules. For example, rules are needed in order to keep everyone from running in the school hallways and creating chaos. Along with this concrete conception of social order is a concrete notion of social hierarchy. People in charge make the rules, which others are expected to follow. There is, however, no understanding of societies as systems, and thus no way of justifying particular social norms beyond very obvious concrete givens. For example, children at this level do not understand the functional significance of titles (e.g., Mr., Mrs., Dr.) in forms of address as reflecting hierarchical social position. Children often state that one should use titles as a sign of respect for the person being addressed. When asked why use of the title is more respectful than use of a first name, the children are unable to answer other than to say that the authorities who have organized things favor the rule.

The following excerpt and the ones that follow were all taken from computer-generated interviews in which children typed in their responses on a laptop computer (Nucci, Becker, & Horn, 2004). The transcripts are indistinguishable in structure from what had been obtained in previous research using face-to-face interviews with a human researcher (Turiel, 1983). We have left the children's spelling and grammatical errors alone. The following excerpt is from the responses produced by an 11-year-old girl and illustrates the reasoning of a child at this point in development. The child is responding to a scenario in which a student refers to his teacher by her first name. She has already judged that it was wrong to do so and is now providing her justifications.

Why was Alec wrong to use his teachers' first names?

Because that is a sign by disrespect and the teacher asked him nicely to stop but he kept doing it.

Why is it more respectful to use titles rather than first names? What makes saying Mrs. Johnson more respectful than calling her Alicia?

Because some people like to sound older by calling them Mrs. Johnson but some people like to sound younger and calling them by their first name.

Children at this point in development also begin for the first time to respond to peer violations of adult-based conventions such as classroom rules. Prior to this, children tend to respond only to peer violations of peer norms and leave violations of school rules to teachers (Nucci & Nucci, 1982b). As one might expect, classroom observations of violations of school conventions show a decline in fifth grade relative to the levels observed in grades 3 and 4 (Nucci & Nucci, 1982b).

Middle School (Level IV, Grades 6–8): Negation of Convention as Part of a Rule System; Conventions Simply the Dictates of Authority

As children enter early adolescence (age 12 to 14) they tend to reflect on the fact that the actions regulated by conventions are arbitrary. Although they acknowledge that such norms tend to reduce chaos in some cases, such as running in the halls, many conventions, such as calling teachers by titles and surnames, seem superfluous and pointless. From the point of view of the typical middle school student or even many high school freshmen, conventions are nothing more than arbitrary rules imposed on them by authorities. At this point, young people still have no clear conception of societies as systems, and thus they have no sense of conventions as helping to form social systems.

Students who tend to be well mannered and well behaved will often follow these norms out of respect for their teachers and in order not to get into trouble. In some cases, such as norms about running in the halls, they will base their adherence on an evaluation of the behavior and go along with the rule because it seems sensible. Thus, students at this point in development will appear to selectively adhere to some conventions while disregarding others. Adding to the complexity for social reasoning at this age is the concurrent expansion of what young people consider to be personal matters. Thus, schools and teachers, especially in democratic societies, face resistance to conventions such as school dress codes that overlap with what young people view as personal matters. As can be readily imagined, observational studies have reported that the rate of violations of classroom and school conventions is higher in seventh grade than in fifth-grade classrooms (Nucci & Nucci, 1982b). In later sections of the book we will take up the implications for classroom management and the curriculum that this transitional developmental period affords.

The following excerpt provides a good illustration of how young people at this level reason about social conventions. The student was quickly responding to computer-generated questions using a laptop keyboard. Thus, there are some misspellings and grammatical errors in the student's responses. These have been left alone. The issue is the same one of teacher names as in the previous excerpt with an 11-year-old.

What do you think? Was Alec right or wrong to call his teachers by their first names?

Alec was right to call his teachers by their first names because he should be aloud to say what he wants, thats a stupid rule because just calling your teacher by whatever you want to call them should be up to you not upto a school.

Why doesn't it matter if you use first names or titles?

Because a lot of people say its a sign of respect, but just being nice is enough respect and just being kind would be respectful.

Why do you think the school would have a rule about calling teachers by titles?

For respect issues.

People sometimes respond by saying that it is more respectful to call a teacher by titles and last names rather than using first names. Do you agree with that?

No, I don't think it's more respectful to use titles because if you get a letter when you are five and its addressed to you as miss, or mr, you usually don't think of it much different as if they put your regular name.

Why do you think the kids should follow the rule?

Although I think its a stupid rule, kids should still follow it just so they don't get themselves in trouble, you could bring something up to one of your teachers, but not just start calling you by whatever name you want.

High School: Affirmation of Convention as Mediated by Social System; Conventions as Constituent Elements of Society

It is in middle adolescence that children first construct an understanding of convention as constituent elements of societies as systems (Turiel, 1983). The younger adolescent's dismissal of convention as simply the dictates of authority is replaced by an understanding that conventions have meaning within a larger social framework. Thus, conventions are viewed as normative and binding within a social system of fixed roles and hierarchical organization. This hierarchy is not the concrete differentiation of people in power from others of lower status, as was the case in middle childhood, but rather a differentiated conceptualization of the relations among differing social roles and social positions in relation to one another within a conventional system of norms. At this point in development, violations of convention are viewed as potentially disruptive of the normative system. Thus, participants within a system are expected to abide by the norms and conventions of that system.

This more sophisticated understanding of convention is illustrated in the following two excerpts. The first presents a 15-year-old's response to the issue concerning teacher names.

Level V (High School)

Why do you think the school would have a rule about calling teachers by titles?

I think they would because if the students start calling their teachers by their first names, they may get too comfortable with the teachers and consider them more as friends than people who teach them. This may cause a problem in their learning process and cause them not to learn as much as they would if they considered the teacher as a teacher instead of a friend who's on the same level as they are.

Why is it more respectful to use titles rather than first names? What makes saying Mrs. Johnson more respectful than calling her Alicia?

It's more respectful because it gives Mrs. Johnson authority, and allows her to rise above her students and not give her a strive for power, but more of a reassurance that she's "the boss," and that she teaches the students: the students don't teach her.

The 15-year-old in the above excerpt affirms the convention of students calling teachers by titles and surnames on the basis of the differential teacher-student role relationship and their respective roles within the school as a social institution. The excerpts that follow even more clearly illustrate the differences in thinking between middle school negation and high school affirmation. The responses address a series of questions based on an actual event from the period just following the American revolutionary war with England. In this incident King George of England sends a letter to George Washington to open diplomatic relations. England, however, had not as yet recognized the United States as a country. King George addressed the letter to George Washington, rather than to President George Washington. George Washington did not open the letter, but instead returned it to King George unread. First are the responses of a level IV girl.

Level IV (Middle School)

Why was Washington wrong to return the letter?

Even though he is the president, he is still Mr. Washington so it is okay to call him that.

Why shouldn't it matter how the king addressed the letter?

I don't think it mattered because like I said, that is still his name.

Why did it matter so much to him that the letter be addressed "President Washington"?

I think it mattered a lot to him because he wanted to be called the president because it made him feel good about himself and he wouldn't take anything else for an answer.

Does the way in which the letter is addressed have anything to do with having England recognize the United States as a country?

I have no idea.

The middle school student providing the above Level IV response has no real understanding of why Washington would have returned the letter. Her best guess is that the title made him feel good. She has no sense of the connection between the formal title and Washington's role within the United States as a social system. When asked about the connection to diplomatic recognition of the United States, she answers honestly, "I have no idea." In contrast, the following responses from a 15-year-old Level V girl illustrate an integration of her concepts about the social function conventions of titles as indicative of social status with their larger function as organizing elements of a social system.

Level V (High School)

Why was Washington right to return the letter?

If the problem at that time was that England wasn't giving the United States recognition, then Washington's decision paralleled the reason they were upset. Hoefully he wrote a letter back to the king telling him that he'd like to be addressed by the President, please, because if not the King would be pretty clueless.

Why does it matter how the king addressed the letter?

The whole point in their disputes was that he wasn't thinking of Washington as the leader of a real country. The king would have been pretty mad if Washington called him "Mr. George guy from that place in Europe" so I don't see why he didn't have to give Washington the same amount of respect as he expected from the rest of the world.

Why do you think Washington returned the letter?

Washington was offended with the way England constantly didn't believe the United States was a real country. If King George had referred to him as President then he would finally be saying that Washington was in charge of something real.

The Development of Concepts of Morality in Childhood and Adolescence

Whereas concepts of convention reflect an understanding of the functions of social norms, concepts of morality reflect the student's underlying conceptions of fairness and human welfare. Moral development involves shifts in the child's structures for reasoning about fairness and situations involving helping or harm to others. Moral development also involves changes in the child's ability to integrate or coordinate competing elements of moral situations. In some of our more recent work (Nucci & Turiel, 2007), we have begun to describe how the child's increased capacity for attention to moral complexity leads in early adolescence to a period of moral ambiguity or uncertainty relative to the morality of younger children and older adolescents. These changes result in a U-shaped pattern of development similar to the transitional phases we saw with social convention. The development of concepts in the moral domain is summarized in Table 3.3. We begin our discussion of moral development by looking at changes in how children evaluate or decide on the fairest way to distribute or share things between two or more people. We will then look at the recent findings that have focused on the development of moral concepts of harm and welfare.

The Development of Distributive Justice/Fairness

Early Elementary (Grades K–2): Intuitive Morality

As was described in Chapter 2, morality begins in early childhood with a focus on issues of harm to the self and others. Preschool-aged children are very concerned with their own safety and understand that it is objectively wrong to hurt others. Even 3-year-olds, for example, understand that it is wrong to hit and hurt someone even in the absence of a rule against hitting because, "When you get hit, it hurts, and you start to cry." In research on age-related changes within the moral domain, Davidson, Turiel, and Black (1983) found that up to about age 7 moral judgment is primarily regulated by concerns for maintaining welfare and avoiding harm and is limited to directly accessible acts. Young children's morality, however, is not yet structured by understandings of fairness as reciprocity. Fairness for the young child is often expressed in terms of personal needs and the sense that one isn't getting one's just deserts. "It's not fair" often means, "I didn't get what I want" or that someone's actions caused the child to experience harm.

The moral intuitions of early childhood allow children to consider the impact of actions on others. In settings where the child's own interests are not importantly at stake, young children can be touchingly generous and benevolent (Eisenberg, 1986; Staub, 1971). Preschool teachers often remark on the kindness

TABLE 3.3

Development of Morality

Early Elementary (Grades K–2)

There is recognition of primary obligations toward others (e.g., it is wrong to steal, hit, and hurt). However, the child has difficulty coordinating the needs of more than one person simultaneously. In situations with competing obligations, fairness is prioritized in terms of self-interest or arbitrary features of persons such as age or gender. Distributive justice means to share at least something. There is no clear conception that fair means equal.

Middle Elementary (Grades 2–5)

Fairness is regulated by reciprocity defined in terms of strict equality (e.g., people should receive equal rewards for equal work). There is awareness of issues of equity, but with inability to consistently integrate equity with concerns for equality.

HARM AND WELFARE

There is evaluation of actions in terms of their effects on others. Hitting is wrong because it hurts. One should help if someone is in need. There is minimal tendency to integrate contextual information. Moral situations are clear-cut. Indirect harm is viewed the same as direct harm. Actions are evaluated in terms of reciprocity. One should help because one might also need help one day. There is the beginning of paying attention to context in evaluating moral situations.

DISTRIBUTIVE JUSTICE

Middle School (Grades 6–8)

Fairness is seen as requiring more than strict equality. Concerns for equity (taking into account special needs, situations, or contributions of others) are now coordinated with reciprocity in structuring moral decisions.

High School (Grades 9/10–12)

There is consolidation of relations between equity and equality in conceptions of what is fair and an emergent tendency to apply conceptions of fairness and equity to social systems.

HARM AND WELFARE

Middle School (Grades 6–8)

Attention to context and efforts to coordinate morality with situational factors leads to recognition of "grey" areas in situations of indirect harm. There is conflation of personal choice with moral "rights" in such situations. One may have a "right" to act in ways that are morally wrong. Having choice means that one is not obligated to help someone in need.

High School (Grades 9/10–12)

Contextual factors are fully coordinated with moral considerations. "Grey" areas are acknowledged, but moral considerations are given priority. Issues of choice are clearly differentiated from "rights" in complex moral situations. Having choice does not relieve someone of moral obligations in helping situations.

exhibited by the children in their classrooms. At the same time, however, young children have difficulty balancing the needs of more than one person at a time. In the absence of some clear procedure for resolving competing moral needs, young children appear to use arbitrary standards for assigning value to persons (e.g., age, gender), and have particular difficulty in weighing the needs of others against their own desires (Damon, 1975, 1977). Thus, we witness the contradiction of the generosity and openness of young children and an arbitrariness and selfishness characteristic of the age. Resolving these contradictions involves changes in the child's conceptions of persons, in their understandings of what is required to maintain interpersonal relations, and in their general intellectual capacity to comprehend the logical implications for how what you do might affect others. This is a tall order. And these issues are revisited throughout the course of moral development.

William Damon (1975, 1977) captured the moral reasoning of young children in a series of creative studies in which he asked children to decide what would be the best way to divide candies between themselves and another child friend. In a typical situation a 5-year-old child would be asked to tell an interviewer what her favorite color of M&Ms is. She would then be shown a group of M&Ms in which the majority was of the child's favorite color. When asked the best way to divide the M&Ms between herself and her friend, the child would generally keep all the M&Ms of her favorite color and give her friend the remainder. This is considered fair by the young child because she didn't keep everything to herself, but shared some with the other child.

Middle Elementary (Grades 2–5): Morality as Strict Equality

The great accomplishment of early childhood moral development is the construction of notions of moral action tied to structures of "just" reciprocity (Damon, 1975, 1977; Turiel & Davidson, 1986). The web of reciprocal interpersonal interactions takes the child beyond the minimal moral requirements of concerns about unprovoked harm to what Piaget (1932) referred to as the social logic of justice. By approximately 6 to 8 years of age, children begin to construct a set of moral understandings that compellingly tie the actions of one person to the reactions or responses of the other. By age 10, these notions of reciprocity are generally consolidated into notions of moral "necessity" resulting from a moral logic that requires equal treatment of persons. In the case of distributing candies described above, the typical third- to fifth-grade child would distribute all the candies, including the ones of his favorite color, equally between himself and his friend. Many parents have understood this child moral logic and solve such distributive justice problems such as sharing a candy bar by having one child do the cutting and the other one getting to choose which "half" to keep.

This "strict" reading of equal treatment, however, may allow for a kind of tit-for-tat morality in which moral obligation extends only to those with whom one can expect something in return, and only to the extent that actions maintain a balanced "moral ledger." On the playground this too often translates into the tit-for-tat of getting even with name-calling or even one's fists.

Middle School (Grades 6–8): Morality of Equity and Equality

Beginning around third grade, children show signs of an awareness that differences in the capacities and needs of individuals should be met with special considerations. For example, children will generally adjust their physical play when interacting with physically handicapped peers. These intuitions are coordinated between the ages of 10 and 14 years into a notion of fairness as requiring more than strict equality. Concerns for equity (taking into account the special needs, situations, or contributions of others) are now coordinated with reciprocity in structuring moral decisions (Damon, 1975, 1977). Treating others fairly may mean treating people unequally in the sense that equity requires adjustments that bring people into more comparable statuses. In concrete terms, children begin to realize, for instance, the fairness inherent in the "unequal" treatment parents provide to siblings who are at different ages when it comes to privileges and responsibilities.

This expansion of morality frees the child from considering what is fair solely in terms of direct reciprocal exchange and allows for extensions of moral (fair) treatment to those from whom one has no expected repayment, and to those who have even been ungracious or unfair to the self. With respect to this latter point, it allows the child to go beyond a tit-for-tat morality of retribution to deal with transgressors without resorting to the same kinds of hurtful acts employed by the transgressor (Lapsley, 1996).

The Development of Concepts of Harm and Welfare
Moral Development and Its Discontents

The picture of moral development just described is one of "progress," but there is another side to the emerging capacity for moral complexity as children shift to the more abstract reasoning of adolescence. Although young adolescents have moved beyond the tit-for-tat direct reciprocity of middle childhood, their moral thinking remains in transition. This is most evident in situations where there is moral ambiguity in relation to the harm caused and the personal choice available to the actor to behave in his or her own self-interest. An ongoing study (Nucci & Turiel, 2007) is exploring the development of children's and adolescents' reasoning about situations in which they have to weigh their own self-interests against whether to help someone in need or refrain from engaging in harm to the other person. The study is investigating many variables and follows a complex design that is beyond the scope of this book. However, the basic findings can be summarized in terms of the central themes of the research.

The helping situations describe a child who falls and is injured. The protagonist must decide whether to seek help for the injured child or continue on without helping in order to be on time for an activity that the central figure in the story wants to do. The harm conditions are of two types. In one case, the harm involves directly hitting and hurting another person. In the second, an indirect harm situation, the protagonist in the scenario does not have enough money to participate in an activity with friends. The protagonist had tried to earn the money, but came up $10 short. A few days before the day of the activity, the protagonist boards an empty bus. Soon afterward a second person boards the bus and drops a $10 bill while reaching for the money to pay the bus fare. Neither the driver nor the passenger is aware of the $10 bill on the floor. The protagonist has to decide whether to tell the passenger that he or she dropped the $10 bill, or keep silent, pick up the bill, and keep it.

In addition to varying the nature of the act, the scenarios also varied the characteristics of the other child depicted in the situation. The other child was described simply as a "girl" or "boy"; as someone who had antagonized the child the previous day by teasing and making fun of him or her; or as a vulnerable child who falls or drops money because of a handicapping condition. These characteristics of the other were intended to affect the degree of empathy for the other child in the moral conflict situations. Participants in the study were in four age groups: Early Elementary (7–8 years), Middle Elementary (10–11 years), Middle School (13–14 years), and High School (16–17 years). Children were heterogeneous in terms of race and ethnicity and were drawn from urban and suburban settings in two regions of the country.

In response to the direct harm situations virtually all respondents across ages indicated that the protagonist would be wrong to engage in hitting, and that the protagonist had no right to engage in the behavior. This is not surprising, given that a 3-year-old would treat unprovoked hitting as wrong.

The indirect harm condition, however, produced a different set of outcomes. Unlike hitting, keeping the money does not result from an intentional act by the protagonist to steal from the other person. Instead, the situation presents itself entirely by chance. When the person dropping the money is described as handicapped nearly all the participants across ages judged that it would be wrong to keep the money. However, when the person dropping the money was described in generic terms or as an antagonist, the responses varied by age. Young children and 17-year-old adolescents generally viewed keeping the money to be wrong. Ten-year-olds and especially 14-year-olds were more likely to express ambivalence as to whether it might be all right to keep the money. These developmental trends became even more apparent when the children were asked to judge whether or not the protagonist would have a "right" to keep the money if that is what he or she wanted to do. Figure 3.1 presents the proportions of participants at each age who argued that one would have a "right" to keep the money. As can be seen in

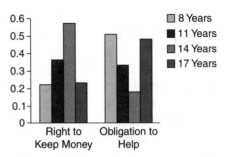

Figure 3.1
Proportions of Children at Each Age Judging That You Would Have a "Right" to Keep the Money, and That You Are "Obligated" to Help.

Figure 3.1, young children generally maintained that the protagonist does *not* have a right to keep the money because this would be a simple case of theft. More than half of the 14-year-olds, however, were of the opinion that the protagonist has a "right" to keep the money. By age 16–17, the majority of respondents again took the position that the protagonist did not have a right to keep the money. The reasoning of the typical 8-year-old is reflected in the following excerpts.

> *Suppose Judi wants to keep the money instead of giving it back to the other girl. Would she have a right to keep the $10 if that is what she wants to do?*
>
> Girl: No, because it's someone else's $10 bill, she shouldn't keep it because it's not hers.
>
> Boy: He's stealing, and you don't want to, it's not good to steal.

For an 8-year-old the situation poses little ambiguity and is responded to in the same way as if the protagonist had put his hand into the passenger's pocket and taken the money. For a 14-year-old, however, the situation is much more complex:

> *Would Jim have a right to keep the ten dollars if that is what he wants to do? How come?*
>
> Girl: Yes, because he's not doing anything wrong. He's not necessarily doing something wrong, but the right thing to do would be to give it back, but he's not necessarily, he doesn't necessarily have any wrongdoing.
>
> Boy: He's got every right to keep the ten dollars, like I said, because it's in nowhere land. And it's his, he found it. It's not in the kid's house or anything.

The ambiguity of the situation for the 14-year-old: "It's in nowhere land," "He's not necessarily doing something wrong" is coupled with confusion between what one has a right to do in a moral sense, and what legitimately comprises matters of choice that would make something a personal issue. Here, the ambiguity of the harm opens the door to the prospect that keeping the money or returning it to the passenger is a matter of free will and personal prerogative. This is nicely illustrated in the justifications the 14-year-olds provided to explain their view that the protagonist had a right to keep the money:

> Boy: I think she has a right to do what she wants to. Because it is once again, his decision to do what he wants.

> Girl: He has the right to do anything he doesn't want to, so like, if he didn't want to help he didn't have to help.

> Boy: It's his choice. It is a free country.

It is important to point out that the reasoning of these early adolescents should not be characterized as purely instrumental or operating solely from self-interest as depicted in Lawrence Kohlberg's Stage 2. The decisions to keep the money or to help someone in need were quite different when the other person in the situation was described as vulnerable. In the case of a handicapped person, the decision of nearly all participants was to help the person or to return the money.

By age 16 the majority of adolescents in the study had resolved the ambiguity of the situation as entailing a form of theft. This can be seen in the following excerpts:

> *Some girls have told us that it would be okay, because Judi didn't take the money, it just fell out of the other girl's pocket. What do you think of that? Do you agree?*

> Girl: Who are these people? I mean, it fell out of the girl's pocket!

For the typical 16-year-old the moral ambiguity posed by indirect theft is recognized as being something different from the act of intentional stealing. However, the knowledge that the money originally belonged to someone else serves as a clarification of the meaning of the situation and places moral constraints on the actor and a companion sense that the protagonist does not have the right to keep the money. This coordinated moral reasoning is illustrated in the following excerpt from a 17-year-old participant.

> *Would Judi have a right to keep the ten dollars if that is what she wants to do?*

> Like I said before, you don't have a right to steal money, and this is still stealing because you know who dropped that money. It's not like breaking into someone's house, but it's still stealing.

> *Doesn't she have a choice in this situation? Doesn't that constitute a right?*

> She doesn't have a choice! This is taking something from someone, so she does not have a choice.

The U-shaped developmental pattern for judgments about the "right" to keep the money was matched by a similar U-shaped developmental pattern with respect to judgments of an obligation to help a person in need. Figure 3.1 presents the proportions of participants by age group who argued that one would have an obligation to help. Again, it is the 8-year-olds and the 16/17-year-olds who are most likely to argue that one has such an obligation. The 14-year-olds were less than half as likely to take that position.

Summary of Findings on Moral Development

With age children and adolescents move toward increasingly equilibrated conceptions of fairness. Development moves from an early childhood set of intuitions about unprovoked harm to notions of fairness as regulated by direct reciprocity. This morality of reciprocity shifts from direct equality toward conceptions of morality in which equality is coordinated with equity.

Along with this greater understanding of fairness, however, comes an expanded capacity for incorporating facets of moral situations that render the application of morality more ambiguous and divergent. Thus, rather than presenting a straightforward picture of moral development as linear moral "progress" toward shared answers to moral situations, moral development includes periods of transition in which the expanded capacity to consider aspects of moral situations leads to variations in the application of moral criteria. In early adolescence in particular, the effort to establish the personal domain results in the overapplication of conceptions of rights in contexts that are morally ambiguous.

With development, adolescents sort out notions of free choice from conceptions of rights. They also become better able to coordinate multifaceted moral situations and to weigh the moral and nonmoral (societal, personal, prudential) aspects of particular social contexts and events (Smetana & Turiel, 2003).

Development and Cross-Domain Interactions

Chapter 2 ended with a discussion of moral complexity and domain overlap. If we apply the lessons from that chapter to the patterns of development within domains, we can begin to anticipate how students at various grade levels are likely to reason about multifaceted social situations. By way of illustration, let's consider how a cross-domain analysis affords a window into the workings of the early adolescent in middle school and the freshman year of high school. A student at this point in development is expanding the list of personal behaviors that should be matters of personal discretion and privacy rather than subject to family or school conventions (Smetana, 2005). This expansion of the personal is closely linked with the young person's efforts to establish personal autonomy and personal identity (Nucci, 1996). These developmental changes in the personal are occurring at the same time as the normative development of a phase of negation of social convention as "simply the dictates of authority" (Turiel, 1983). Thus, even those conventions the adolescent acknowledges as legitimate have little regulatory force. Finally, the young adolescent's morality is characterized by a more mature integration of notions of equality and equity in reasoning about fairness. However, moral thinking is also defined at this developmental age by an increased tendency to see the "shades of grey" in moral situations, and at times to confuse personal expression of freedom of choice in such ambiguous situations with a right to act in ways that are understood to be morally wrong (Nucci & Turiel, 2007).

Given this developmental constellation we should expect to be engaged with a young person who cares deeply about social justice and respect for personal rights and freedoms. We should also expect to interact with someone who questions existing social norms and who defines authority in terms of interpersonal qualities rather than social position (e.g., as a teacher). Personal expression in the areas of music, dress, and language will come to the forefront and may lead to conflict with parental and school rules. Our young person will also be someone who finds new complexities and ambiguities in moral situations. At a behavioral level we would expect a normative shift upward in social experimentation, challenges to authority, and engagement in petty crimes that have little or no direct impact on individuals. Shoplifting for example, tends to peak between the ages of 12 to 14 years (Wolf, 2002).

As we will see in subsequent chapters, this cross-domain developmental analysis will help to guide our grade-level-appropriate usage of the regular academic curriculum to foster social and moral growth. We can also begin to anticipate how students' social understandings will play out in terms of behavior. Teachers can use this knowledge to anticipate and respond in developmentally appropriate ways to students' misbehavior. Issues of classroom climate and developmental discipline will be the subject of the next chapter.

Summary

Maintaining a personal domain is essential to a sense of autonomy and individuality. Development within the personal domain is structured by students' concepts of persons, self, and identity. Children across cultures negotiate with parents to establish boundaries around a personal domain. Parental overcontrol of the personal areas of adolescent children has been found to be associated with psychological problems among young people in Japan as well as the United States. As children enter adolescence, they expand the numbers of behaviors they consider to be personal rather than subject to family social convention or parental jurisdiction.

Development within the conventional domain is structured by the underlying concepts about social structure and social organization. Development follows an oscillating pattern between periods affirming the functions of convention and phases negating the previous basis for justifying convention. These patterns of affirmation and negation are associated with student tendencies to adhere to or to violate classroom and school conventions. The period of early adolescence is a negation phase that coincides with the expansion of the personal domain. Middle adolescence marks the first point in which conventions are affirmed as being central elements in the structure of social systems and society.

Moral development is structured by underlying concepts of fairness and human welfare. Early childhood intuitions about morality are based on concrete evaluations of harm. In middle childhood, moral judgment becomes regulated by justice defined by direct reciprocity or equality. In later childhood and early adolescence, concerns for equity are integrated with notions of equality to produce a broader framework for fairness. Early adolescence is also marked by increased attention to competing aspects of moral situations and sensitivity to moral ambiguity. Later adolescence is characterized by an increased ability to coordinate multiple aspects of moral situations.

Social Life in Schools and Classrooms: Establishing the Foundation for Moral Development

Children's moral and social knowledge originates in their attempts to make meaning out of social experience. Thus, we must begin our discussion of moral education by examining how schools function as social and moral environments. Social life is not experienced as an abstraction, but confronts children in their everyday efforts to negotiate their desires and needs in relation to those of others, in the social rules and norms that structure social interactions, and the feelings that come along with those social experiences. Schools and classrooms are not exempt from these elemental aspects of social life. How we structure educational environments and respond to student behavior forms part of what Philip Jackson and his colleagues (1993) refer to as the moral life of schools and classrooms (David Hansen, 1996). There are three basic aspects to schools and classrooms as social environments. These are (1) the rules, norms, and procedures, (2) the emotional or affective climate, and (3) the approach to discipline and student transgressions.

In Chapter 4 we will take what has been learned from research on children's social development to explore classrooms as normative (rule-based) systems. The chapter will illustrate how classroom rules that regulate morality differ from classroom conventions. The chapter will also explore how students at different grade levels think about classroom rules that regulate morality and convention. In Chapter 5 we look at classrooms and schools in terms of emotional climate and approaches to classroom management and discipline that facilitate moral development. Although the three basic elements are discussed separately in Chapters 4 and 5, we should keep in mind that they operate in conjunction with one another in school contexts.

CHAPTER 4

Schools and Classrooms as Moral Institutions: Rules, Norms, and Procedures

> *I think there would have to be a lot of rules about hitting at school because it would hurt somebody!*
>
> —Marisha, 5 years old
>
> *If you obey all of the rules, you miss all of the fun.*
>
> —Katharine Hepburn

Marisha and Lauren are girls who live near each other, but attend different public schools in neighboring districts. At Marisha's school, children all wear uniforms. In the morning they all line up with their classmates and are led into the school by their teacher. There is no talking allowed as they walk into school in single file, being careful to space themselves two floor tiles apart as they walk through the school hallways. When they reach the classroom they each take their assigned seats. During class, students must raise their hand to speak or to get permission from the teacher to sharpen a pencil. Going to the bathroom is done as a class with everyone lining up together and led to the bathroom by the teacher at set times during the day. No one is permitted to chew gum or eat in class. There are clear rules against using swear words or fighting on the playground.

Lauren, on the other hand, can wear jeans or shorts to school, but she can't wear extra-short skirts. When the bell rings she and her classmates enter the school together, laughing and talking to each other. Once they get to the classroom they take whichever seat they wish. If they have something interesting to say during a lesson, they can speak up without raising their hands as long as they don't interrupt another speaker. If they need to sharpen a pencil, they can do so whenever they wish as long as they don't interfere with other students. Bathrooms are built into each classroom, and students may use them freely whenever they need to. As in Marisha's school, students are not allowed to eat or chew gum in class. Also as in Marisha's school, there are clear rules against fighting, and kids aren't supposed to swear, though that rule isn't strictly enforced.

Lauren and Marisha attend schools with different social norms reflecting divergent educational philosophies and ideologies. Readers familiar with variations in school structure can imagine even more divergent forms than the examples illustrated by Lauren and Marisha's elementary schools. Schools constitute mini-societies within the larger culture. They are structured by norms and conventions that frame the emotional, personal, and moral elements of the school experience. As a consequence, the sociomoral curriculum of school, unlike its academic curriculum, is not confined to periods of instruction and study, but includes the social interactions established by school and classroom rules, rituals, and practices (Jackson, Boostrom, & Hansen, 1993), and the less regimented peer interactions that take place on the playgrounds, in cafeterias and hallways.

The standard approach to this "hidden curriculum" has been to treat the entire complex of school rules and conventions as filled with moral meaning (Durkheim, 1925/61; Hansen, 1996). Although it is the case that some school rules deal with matters of morality, and also true that the manner in which even trivial rules are enforced can have moral consequences, it is a mistake to equate school norms with moral standards. This is because the differences among convention, morality, and personal discretion also hold within the micro-society of the school. As teachers and administrators wrestle with how best to establish and maintain educationally constructive school rules and discipline, they are constantly confronted with the different ways in which students at different ages react toward those different types of norms. For the most part, teachers and administrators are unaware of the systematic way in which these types of norms vary. Nor are they generally aware of the tacit ways in which their own classroom interactions are often guided by these qualitative differences. In this chapter we will examine how conventions and moral rules operate in school settings. This will include a look at what rules children expect good schools to have. We will also look at the ways in which a teacher's authority can be affected by her or his approach to these different types of social norms. One might argue that how children view such issues doesn't matter very much because teachers exert considerable power over their students. However, as Metz (1978) indicated 30 years ago, the authority-child relationship is not a one-way street. Just as teachers and schools establish rules and policies for behavior, so too do students evaluate those rules and the teachers who administer them.

Children's Concepts About School Rules

Rules and Morality

Children and adolescents expect schools to have rules governing moral transgressions such as hitting and hurting, or stealing personal property. They argue that it is wrong for schools or teachers to permit such behaviors because they result in harm to people (Laupa & Turiel, 1986; Weston & Turiel, 1980). For example, when asked whether it would be okay for a school not to have any rules about hitting, one 5-year-old said:

> I think there would have to be a lot of rules about hitting at school because it would hurt somebody! (Nucci, 2004)

In addition, researchers have found that elementary school children apply these expectations to evaluate the legitimacy of teacher authority. Laupa & Turiel (1993) found that elementary school children accepted instructions from teachers that would prevent harm to another child, but rejected the instructions of teachers to engage in such things as hitting, which if followed would result in harm to another child. This finding is entirely consistent with the basic research indicating that children do not view such things as hitting as wrong because there is a rule. Instead, they argue that the rule should be there because *hitting is wrong.*

The Laupa and Turiel (1993) study dealt with hypothetical scenarios so that children could provide responses without fear of coercion from an actual teacher. It is possible, and perhaps even likely, that a child would follow a teacher's command to hurt another out of fear of the teacher's power. Nonetheless, the study suggests that children might not view such a teacher as a legitimate authority. The one caveat that must be added to this conclusion, however, is that because teachers are presumed to have greater knowledge than children, they have great potential to alter the ways in which children read the meanings of people's intentions and actions. As was covered in Chapter 2, recent work has shown that the informational assumptions people bring to social situations can radically alter their reading of events (Wainryb, 1991). Teachers who provide children with highly biased and prejudicial accounts of the intentions of people along racial, ethnic, and gender lines have the capacity to alter the ways in which children view the actions of others. The impact of such teacher bias, particularly when enacted within the context of a shared community-wide viewpoint, has been the subject of recent research indicating that children are aware of racial and gender stereotypes by as young as 5 years of age (Bigler & Liben, 2006). As we will discuss in the following chapter, students are influenced by adult bias, but they also negatively judge teachers who display such discrimination (Brown & Bigler, 2004).

Classroom Social Conventions

If we move from the moral domain to consideration of classroom conventions, we see a very different pattern regarding children's acceptance of teacher authority. With respect to conventions, students acknowledge that school authorities may legitimately establish, alter, or eliminate school-based norms of propriety (e.g., dress codes, forms of address) and the rules and procedures for academic activity (Blumenfeld, Pintrich, & Hamilton, 1987; Dodsworth-Rugani, 1982; Nicholls & Thorkildsen, 1988 Weston & Turiel, 1980). As we saw in the examples presented at the beginning of the chapter, schools may vary widely in terms of these conventional and procedural norms, while sharing a common set of core moral rules.

The scope of the school's legitimate authority in establishing conventional norms is limited from the child's point of view by whether these norms encroach on areas of activity perceived by children as being within the personal domain. Smetana and Bitz (1996) found that children in elementary school are consistent in claiming personal jurisdiction over such issues as with whom to associate, how to spend lunch money, and choice of hairstyle. Arsenio reported that nearly 62% of all negative rule evaluations provided by fifth-grade boys involved undue teacher control of such nonacademic activities as bathroom and drinking fountain procedures and restrictions on free-time activities. In adolescence students are even less likely than fifth graders to grant legitimacy to teacher authority regarding personal or prudential areas of conduct (Smetana & Bitz, 1996).

As was noted in Chapter 2, the definition of what counts as personal is not, however, solely a matter of individual decision making. Schools are social institutions that place different sets of constraints on personal behavior than might exist in other social settings such as the family and the general outside environment. The majority of students in middle school and high school acknowledge these institutional differences and are somewhat more willing to accept conventions regulating conduct within the school setting such as public displays of affection (kissing in public) that would be considered personal in nonschool contexts (Smetana & Bitz, 1996). Students who defy these school-specific constraints on personal conduct tend to exhibit more general problems with social adjustment (Smetana & Bitz, 1996). Thus, schools represent a rather unique context within which children must learn to negotiate and accommodate their own personal freedoms in relation to the organizational conventions imposed by the varying institutions of general society.

Developmental Factors and School Conventions

There are also developmental factors that enter into students' expectations regarding school conventions. Before fourth or fifth grade children don't generally view the conventions of schools to be their business. Young children rarely if ever respond to another child's violation of a conventional school norm (e.g., talking without raising one's hand; Killen & Smetana, 1999; Nucci & Nucci, 1982b). This is not to say that young children are unaware of or disinterested in social conventions in general. Preschool-aged children do respond to violations of general social norms such as gender-inappropriate dress (Nucci, Turiel, & Encarnacion-Gawrych, 1983) and transgressions of the rules of peer-constructed games (Corsaro, 1985). Although young children have a sense of convention, they have a difficult time making a connection between themselves and the arbitrary conventional norms established by adults. In particular, they seem to maintain a distance between themselves and what they perceive to be the adult-generated rules that run schools as institutions.

One implication of these developmental trends in young children's conceptions of convention is for teachers to accept the fact that children are years away from having any real understanding of schools as social institutions, and that children view the establishment of school conventions as a task of responsible adult authority. As was mentioned above, young children view teachers as having such legitimate control over school conventions and procedures. It is reasonable, then, not only from an adult perspective, but from the point of view of the children, for teachers to establish the basic routines, conventions, and customs of the school day. As we will discuss in the following chapter, however, teachers can engage young children in helping to construct some of the conventions and classroom procedures as a way to encourage them to take personal responsibility for their actions, and also to help them construct a sense of the classroom as a community (DeVries & Zan, 1994; Watson, 2003).

As was described in Chapter 3, the development of social convention follows an oscillating pattern in which children shift between phases when they affirm the purposes of convention and subsequent periods when further reflection leads them to conclude that conventions don't really matter. First grade tends to be a period of affirmation of convention as consistent with the "natural order," for example, that girls but not boys wear dresses. Around 7 or 8 years of age (second grade), however, children start paying attention to the situational inconsistencies in the application of social conventions as evidence that conventions are not describing a "natural order." Such things as being able to call some adults by their first names rather than titles are now seen as evidence that conventions don't really matter. As you might expect, there are behavioral correlates of this period of negation, though not as pronounced as what one sees in early adolescence.

In our observations of classroom social transgressions we noted that the rates of conventional transgression are higher in grades 2 and 7 than they are in grade 5 (Nucci & Nucci, 1982b). In grade 5 children are about 10 to 11 years old, which corresponds to the modal age for Level 3 affirmation of the functional value of conventions as serving to keep social order. School rules keep things from turning into chaos. As one fifth-grade student put it: "We need rules or everybody would be running in the hallways." In contrast both grades 2 and 7 correspond to modal ages at the front end of phases of negation of convention. The main tool that teachers possess to help them in constructively dealing with the negation of convention maintained by second- and third-grade and middle school children is the general positive regard that children (especially at younger ages) have for teachers. In Chapter 5 we will discuss the establishment of a climate of *trust* between students and teachers as critical to a developmentally positive approach to student violations of classroom conventions.

One natural question that arises is whether the amount of time teachers spend on dealing with violations of classroom conventions is partially a function of having more conventional rules than necessary. In our observations of classroom interactions we have found that teachers are responding to a fairly large number of repeated violations of the same norms. The vast majority of classroom conventional transgressions committed by elementary school children fall into a few categories: cross-talking, being out of one's seat, talking without raising one's hand, and being out of line (Nucci & Nucci, 1982b). Over half of the classroom conventional violations we observed being responded to by teachers were accounted for by a single category: cross-talking (Nucci & Nucci, 1982b). Obviously second- and third-grade children in a negation of convention phase are not the best sources upon which to make such a judgment, because their lack of understanding of the purposes of convention contributes to their elevated levels of noncompliance. However, if a norm is violated at a fairly high level across grades, including fifth grade, at which point children are at their most compliant, then there may be reason to reconsider the appropriateness of the convention.

Let's consider the issue of cross-talking for purposes of illustration. Second-grade and fifth-grade children differentiate disruptive talking, which prevents others from hearing the teacher and doing their work (a moral harm), from merely chatting quietly with a neighbor. During our interviews, children expressed the view that rules against disruptive talking were good ones. In our observations, however, we witnessed teachers responding to children's cross-talking that was neither disruptive to others, nor interfering with the overall learning of the children being reprimanded. No one, including second-grade children, is in favor of a chaotic classroom. However, there is a difference between chaos and conversation. Even in the most interactive and well-organized classroom, there is bound to be "down time" in which children will want to simply talk to one another. This is particularly the case when children finish their seat work ahead of their classmates, and during periods of classroom transition from one activity to another. In addition, children (and my university education majors) often find it pleasant to occasionally chat with a neighbor while doing their work. In none of the above examples are educational goals being compromised. Reprimanding children in such situations would seem to add little to their education or their love of schooling. A far better way to make use of the children's desire to socialize is to integrate it into instruction through the uses of discourse and group activity as instructional methods. This will be taken up again in Chapter 5. A simple suggestion that DeVries and Zan (1994) make with respect to younger children, which I would echo here as a general approach, is that teachers and school administrators reduce conventional regulations to those that are actually instrumental to the operation of a school or classroom.

In deciding which conventions to maintain on a school-wide basis, elementary school teachers and administrators might consider calling on the expertise of fifth-grade children. Students at this age are both experienced with the norms and purposes of schooling and are also at a point of affirmation in their concepts of social convention. During a focus group that was part of a research project, we asked fifth-grade children to share with us some of the rules at their schools that they thought weren't especially good ones, or rules that should be modified. Their answers might serve as an illustrative example of how children at this age might be of help to teachers. One school was reported to have a "no passing" rule that forbade anyone from walking past someone else in the hallways. The children readily understood the goal of the rule as helping to reduce the likelihood that someone would run in the halls and either get hurt or knock down a younger student. However, they saw the "no passing" rule as going too far. They pointed out that the "no skipping" and "no running in the halls" rules at the school were sufficient to meet those safety goals. These same children also stated objections to the need to raise one's hand in order to say something in class. Again, they expressed an understanding of the organizational purposes of the rule, but felt that it should only apply to whole group lessons and should not be enforced in small group activities. As one girl put it, "We manage to be polite and talk at home without raising our hands, why can't we be expected to do that here?"

Many schools engage fifth- and sixth-grade children in activities such as student council and as hall monitors and assistants to school crossing guards. In these ways, schools contribute to the integration of children into the conventional structures of school society. These activities also help to develop children's sense of personal responsibility. What is being suggested here is that schools go beyond the pro forma nature of these institutions and actually engage them, particularly student council, as meaningful forums within which children can contribute to the establishment of the overall set of school conventions.

School Conventions and Adolescence

Early adolescence is a second phase of negation of convention. This is coupled with an expansion of what children at this age consider to be personal, rather than under the jurisdiction of adult authority. The developmental double whammy of the early adolescent negation of convention along with the expansion of the personal is associated with an increase in parent-child conflicts (Smetana, 1995). It also makes teacher-student relations more challenging. School norms that were annoying to fifth graders become highly objectionable to some adolescents in grades 7 through 9. Issues of appearance, manners, tardiness, talking in class may become a blur of personal choice and arbitrary adult dictate.

These adolescent behaviors often give a false impression of self-centeredness, and the resistance to authority is sometimes mistakenly responded to through harsh control. University of Michigan researchers (Eccles, et al., 1993; Eccles, Wigfield, & Schiefele, 1998) have provided evidence that despite the increased maturity of adolescents, middle schools and junior high schools emphasize greater teacher control and discipline and offer fewer opportunities for student involvement in decision making, choice, and self-management than do elementary school classrooms. Accordingly, Eccles and her colleagues (1998) have reported that the mismatch between adolescents' efforts to attain greater autonomy and the schools' increased efforts at control resulted in declines in junior high students' intrinsic motivation and interest in school.

Through it all, these students are still children in need of affection and structure. Schools are still social institutions that require compliance with certain norms in order to function. The key then in terms of positive social climate is to construct a conventional system that allows for personal expression. In many American schools this is accomplished through generous dress codes that permit oddities, such as green hair, but draw the line at obscene or immodest attire. But open dress codes needn't be the avenue that a given community or school takes. As stated above, adolescents are generally able to adjust to the idea that school is a place where behaviors (e.g., public displays of affection, such as kissing) that would be personal matters elsewhere are under legitimate conventional regulation at school (Smetana & Bitz, 1996).

As with young children, a positive approach to this age group is for the teachers to make a distinction between the norms needed to operate the school and to protect student safety and those behaviors that constitute a "minor threat" to the social order. For example, marking a student tardy for being next to his seat rather than sitting in it as the bell rings may make the adult feel powerful, but it does little to enhance the student's appreciation of the norm of promptness. Without reducing things to a cliché, this really is a phase that will pass, and some adult patience is called for. Most students who were "good kids" in fifth grade still view teachers as people worthy of fair treatment. For example, a student will call teachers by their titles in order not to needlessly offend the teacher, even though the student is clueless as to why using the teacher's first name is offensive. Firm and fair enforcement of rules with a dash of humor will work better than rigid requirements for compliance.

Eventually junior high school students and high school freshmen reach the point (14–17 years) where they construct an affirmation of convention as basic to the structuring of social systems. As one would expect, this developmental shift is associated with a marked decline in classroom misconduct (Geiger & Turiel, 1983). It is also a period in which students fully comprehend that the array of school conventions structures the high school as a societal system. Even as students move within their own particular crowds and cliques, the larger conventional culture of the high school with its norms, rituals, and traditions provides many students with a sense of belonging.

An example of how this affiliation can be leveraged within a traditional large high school is provided by the "First Class" program at Deerfield High School in Illinois. First Class originated in 1994 as a result of problems with graffiti, littering, vulgar language, and a basic lack of belonging that was perceived by some students and faculty as characterizing student life at the high school. In response, a committee was formed of students and teachers who set out to democratically establish shared norms of faculty and student conduct, and agreed-upon modes for teachers to address student misbehavior. The result of these efforts was a visible dramatic shift in the overall look of the school, in student behavior, and in a general sense of school community. The challenge faced by Deerfield High School and other schools that might wish to engage in similar sorts of activities is to keep such efforts current and alive. This cannot be done simply by addressing crises and by generating formal codes of conduct. The community discourse needs to become a much more integrative aspect of student life. For this to happen, however, schools are going to have to recognize that a portion of "instructional time" is going to have to be apportioned for these social developmental purposes.

Teacher Authority and Domain Appropriate Responses to Rule Violations

The fact that students apply their social reasoning to school rules has important implications for how they read teacher responses to moral transgressions and violations of classroom and school conventions. Researchers have explored this issue in studies looking at students' evaluations of the appropriateness of teacher responses to hypothetical transgressions of school rules. In one such study (Nucci, 1984) children in grades 3, 5, 7, and 9 were shown line drawings of children engaging in behaviors that were either moral transgressions or violations of a convention. Following the presentation of each line drawing, the children listened to a tape recording of a teacher providing five possible responses to the student behavior. Each child was asked to rate the teacher's responses on a 4-point scale as an excellent, good, fair/so-so, or poor way to respond to what the child had done. The five teacher responses were those that had been shown in observational studies (Nucci & Nucci, 1982b; Nucci & Turiel, 1978; Nucci, et al., 1982) to be the most prevalent modes of teacher response to classroom transgressions:

1. *Intrinsic features of act statement,* which indicates that the act is inherently hurtful or unjust ("John, that really hurt Mike.").
2. *Perspective-taking request* is a request that the transgressor consider how it feels to be the victim of the act ("Christine, how would you feel if somebody stole from you?")

3. *Rule statement,* which is a specification of the rule governing the action ("Jim, you are not allowed to be out of your seat during math.").

4. *Disorder deviation statement* indicates that the behavior is creating disorder or that it is out of place or odd ("Sally, it's very unladylike to sit with your legs open when you are wearing a skirt.").

5. *Command* is a statement to cease from doing the act without further rationale ("Howie, stop swearing!).

The examples presented above are all ones that would be considered domain appropriate. The reader can generate examples of domain-inappropriate responses by simply substituting the form of the responses to items 1 and 2 for the responses given to items 3 and 4 and vice versa. If the reader does this, it should be apparent that providing moral responses to violations of convention direct the student to consider a set of intrinsic interpersonal effects that simply are not there (e.g., in response to leaving one's seat during math time: "Darrell, how would you like it if other people got out of their seat during math?" or "Darrell, it upsets people when you leave your seat."). The responses that are the best fit with violations of conventions provide a rather weak basis for evaluating the effects of moral transgressions (e.g., in response to hitting: "John, it's against the rules to hit," or "John, that isn't the way a gentleman should act.").

In the study just described (Nucci, 1984) and a subsequent study with preschool-aged children (Killen, Breton, Ferguson, & Handler, 1994), it was found children prefer teachers to use domain-concordant methods of intervention (e.g., telling an instigator who doesn't share toys to give some back "because it's not fair to others who do not have any") rather than domain-inappropriate ones (e.g., telling a child who has hit another child, "You shouldn't do that; it's against the rules to hit," or simply saying "That's not the way that a student should act.").

When it comes to children's evaluations of the legitimacy of teacher authority, we found that children age 10 and older evaluate not only the teachers' responses but also the teachers themselves (Nucci, 1984). Students rated highest those teachers who responded to moral transgressions with statements focusing on the effects of the acts (e.g., "Carlos, that really hurts Mike."). Rated lower were teachers who responded with statements of school rules or normative expectations. Rated lowest were teachers who used simple commands (e.g., "Stop it!" or "Don't hit!").

As one would expect, students rated highest those teachers who responded to violations of convention with rule statements or with statements indicating that the acts were disruptive or inconsistent with social expectations, and they rated lower those teachers who responded to such transgressions in terms of their effects on others (e.g., "When you sit like that, it really upsets people.").

In studies examining how teachers spontaneously respond to actual classroom transgressions (Nucci & Nucci, 1982b; Nucci & Turiel, 1978; Nucci,

Turiel, & Encarnacion-Gawrych, 1983) we found that teacher responses were not uniform across transgressions, but instead tended to map onto transgressions as a function of domain (roughly 60% in response to moral transgressions; 47% conventional). These same studies, however, also indicated that about 8% of teacher responses were domain discordant, and another 40% domain-undifferentiated simple commands (e.g., "Stop it.").

During informal conversations, the teachers in the above studies indicated that they were unaware that they were responding in these systematically domain-differentiated ways. Their own sense of things was that, while they tried on occasion to give reasons for rules or explanations for why a given behavior was wrong, they were mostly giving commands to stop misbehavior or reminding students of how they should behave. This perception of themselves as focused on rules and social order may have been due to the fact that in proportional terms, simple commands made up a substantial proportion of their actual responses. This is interesting in light of the fact that students rated simple commands as low or lower than domain-inappropriate responses to transgression. It would appear, then, that there is room for movement in teachers' current practices toward more domain-appropriate patterns of response.

Marilyn Watson (2008) has recently identified an interesting wrinkle in how elementary school teachers may apply these lessons to classroom situations. She points out that when teachers engage students in helping to construct classroom rules, teachers would be wise to occasionally refer to that fact when addressing transgressions with students. For example, a teacher might respond to a child who blurts out answers without raising his hand, "Remember, Martin, we said we were going to raise our hand and wait to be called on to speak." In addressing the student in this way the teacher simultaneously enforces a rule and empowers the student by reminding him of the peer-based source of the rule. This approach works well as a domain-appropriate response to violations of peer-generated classroom conventions. However, it poses a potential problem as a response to moral violations. Imagine if in the example above the teacher had responded to a child who has called another child a name with the statement, "Remember, Martin, we said we weren't going to call each other names in this class." In doing so, the teacher would be making use of the peer-based source of the norm, but also would have reduced the reason that calling someone names is wrong to a matter of social consensus and convention rather than moral harm. This would be a domain-inappropriate response. Watson (2008) suggests that the teacher can avoid this problem by supplementing her reference to the peer norm with an explanation of the moral basis for the rule. For example, "Remember, Martin, we said we weren't going to call each other names in this class. People's feelings are hurt and they feel bad when we do that."

Summary

Schools and classrooms are mini-societies governed by moral rules and conventional norms. An important way in which school contributes to children's social and moral development is how rules and norms are established and enforced. Children and adolescents apply their concepts of morality, convention, and the personal to evaluate schools and teachers as legitimate authorities.

Children and adolescents expect schools to have rules governing moral transgressions such as hitting and hurting, or stealing personal property. They argue that it is wrong for schools or teachers to permit such behaviors because they result in harm to people. Children negatively evaluate schools and teachers that don't enforce rules to govern immoral (hurtful) behavior such as fighting or stealing. They also negatively evaluate schools and teachers that promote morally harmful behavior such as gender or racial discrimination.

Children and adolescents treat social conventions as something that teachers and administrators can establish or change so long as they don't overly infringe upon what students consider to be personal and private. Students' tendencies to obey school conventions fluctuates by grade level as a function of developmental changes in their understanding of the function of social convention. The middle school years are a period of transition in which students tend to negate convention as "simply the dictates of authority." Students in this developmental period are also expanding what they consider to be personal matters that should not be regulated by authority or convention. Most young adolescents, however, accept school as a special institution and go along with restrictions that they would object to in other social contexts.

Children and adolescents also apply their concepts of morality and social convention to evaluate teacher responses to transgression. Domain-appropriate responses to moral violations refer to the harmful effect of the act on another person, or direct the transgressor to take the perspective of the person who was affected by the behavior. Domain-appropriate responses to violations of convention focus on the governing rule, or the social disruption or deviation from social expectation resulting from the behavior.

CHAPTER 5

Facilitating Moral Development Through School Climate and Developmental Discipline

A morally supportive management and discipline system must foster the development of students' empathic caring, moral awareness, and moral understanding, while minimizing or avoiding the enticement of undesirable behavior through praise, rewards and punishments.

—Marilyn Watson

In Chapter 4 we looked at how classroom rules help to structure schools as cultural and moral institutions. We also considered how students' concepts of morality and social convention enter into their willingness to comply with school and classroom rules, as well as their evaluations of teachers as legitimate social authorities. In this chapter we will continue to explore how the social life of the classroom can contribute to students' social, emotional, and moral development. Our approach will be guided by attention to the developmental needs of children and adolescents. There are two related issues that we will address in the chapter. The first is the overall social, emotional, and moral climate of the classroom. The second is how teachers and schools address behavioral issues through classroom management and discipline.

Establishing a Moral Atmosphere

Moral Development and Emotion

Children's concepts of morality are about fairness and the welfare of others. These moral understandings include feelings and emotions associated with experiences of harm, unfairness, selfishness, and loss, as well as kindness, generosity, and fair treatment. William Arsenio and his colleagues (Arsenio & Lover, 1995) have carefully studied how emotion is included in children's construction of morality and social convention. Experiences of moral transgression are associated with "hot" emotions such as sadness, fear, anger, or outrage. Engaging in morally positive action is associated with happiness and a sense of satisfaction. These feelings are incorporated into the schemes that form the child's moral understanding. One outcome of this developmental process is that variations in the emotional experiences of children can influence their moral orientations. For example, variations in the child's temperament (Kochanska, 1993), the amount of anger displayed by adults in reactions to children's transgressions, or the warmth in reaction to children's prosocial behavior (Cumberland-Li, Eisenberg, Champion, Gershoff, & Fabes, 2003; Emde, Birigen, Clyman, & Openheim, 1991) appear to affect the way in which children construct their basic concepts of the social world and how to react to social situations.

The development of morality in children is supported by environments in which the child experiences emotional warmth and fairness. Growing up in such an environment increases the chance that a child will construct a view of the social world based on "goodwill" (Arsenio & Lover, 1995). This goodwill goes along with the positive feelings and happiness that children experience when they engage in acts of kindness and helping (Eisenberg, 1986). In contrast, children with long-term patterns of victimization and peer rejection tend to establish a pattern of "ill will" distorting the construction of moral reciprocity in support of aggressive actions toward others (Arsenio & Lover, 1995). In summary, a climate of predictability, trust, emotional warmth, and reciprocity are the key elements to establishing a pattern of goodwill (Arsenio & Lover, 1995) conducive to the emergence of the moral self (Noam, 1993).

From the perspective of the classroom teacher, this effect of early emotional experience helps to explain the variations they observe in children's tendencies to respond to peers in fair and caring, or aggressive ways. It also means that an important element of a teacher's approach to children's moral and social growth is the establishment of a classroom climate that maximizes the likelihood that students will experience goodwill during their time at school.

The importance of an emotionally supportive environment has not been lost on proponents of moral education. For some educators the establishment of a caring environment and an overall "ethic of care" is the most essential component of moral education (Noddings, 2002). A child who develops a caring orientation is able to *care for others*, and is also able to *accept care from others*. This requires a school and classroom climate in which students can afford to be emotionally vulnerable, and in which that vulnerability extends to the student's willingness to risk engagement in acts of kindness and concern for others (Noddings, 2002).

An ethic of care is related to a more general approach to the school and classroom environment around the establishment of relationships based on trust (Watson, 2003). Trust carries with it the emotional connections of care integrated with moral reciprocity and continuity. Thus trust corresponds essentially to what Arsenio and Lover describe as an "orientation of goodwill." Trust is basic to the construction of an overall sense of school or classroom community that in turn is one of the primary predictors of prosocial conduct in schools (Battistich, Solomon, Watson, & Schaps, 1997).

The Basic Elements of a Moral Classroom Climate

The development of trust and self-discipline in schools and classrooms builds on four basic needs of children. These are: autonomy, belonging, competence, and fairness (Nucci & Katsarou, 2004 Watson, 2003).

Autonomy. The need for autonomy is expressed in two ways. The first is through the construction of the personal domain of prerogative and privacy. A child's sense of him- or herself as an individual with a unique social identity is gained through control over activities, friendship choices, personal expression, and privacy (Nucci, 1996). In the classroom and school setting this translates into providing children some space for decision making both in the social arena and, where appropriate, over academic issues.

The second component of autonomy is the child's exertion of self-control and self-determination. Moral autonomy refers to a commitment to what is right based on moral judgment rather than social pressure or social convention. It also means doing what is right for one's own reasons. There are two basic ways in which individuals are motivated to do something. One is to respond to external incentives in the form of punishments and rewards. The second is to engage in actions because of their perceived value to the individual (Deci, 1995). It is obviously much easier for teachers and schools to manipulate external rewards and punishments than it is to somehow connect up with or influence students' intrinsic reasons for doing something. Yet it is the connection with intrinsic, non-pragmatic motivation (Subbotsky, 1995) that is the most effective and enduring way in which to link moral reasoning with action. Unfortunately, the most common way that children's moral autonomy is diminished is through teacher efforts at controlling them with rewards and punishments (Deci, 1995). We will return to this issue again in a discussion of consequences for students' classroom behavior.

Belonging. The need for belonging is built into human beings from the time we are born. Our first expression of this need for belonging is in the attachment we establish as infants with our caregiver, usually our mother. Attachment theory argues that the quality of the mother-infant relationship plays a critical role in a child's capacity to love and trust (Ainsworth, 1973; Bolby, 1958; Sroufe, 1983). The need for belonging does not end in early childhood, but extends throughout the lifespan. Classroom teachers cannot be expected to replace parents and family as basic sources of love and belonging. However, the classroom and school can go a long way toward supporting children's sense of connection and their beliefs about their own self-worth and the trustworthiness of others.

Competence.   The need for competence is expressed in children's curiosity and efforts to solve puzzles, master skills, and get along with others. Competence is enhanced when students succeed at academic tasks and when they are successful in making friends and sustaining relationships. Moral education does not occur in a vacuum. It is connected to the entirety of the academic and social life of the classroom.

Fairness.   Fairness is what links autonomy, belonging, and competence to morality. Children construct their sense of fairness in early childhood and employ their understanding of fairness to evaluate teachers and schools as valid institutions. Fairness emerges in relationships based on reciprocity. Children expect and seek fairness from adult authority (Laupa & Turiel, 1986). Teachers who treat students with respect receive respect in return. Students are quite sensitive to teacher displays of unfairness. For example, children are aware of discrimination based on gender and race at early ages and by third grade are able to form expectations that a teacher who was discriminatory in one context is likely to show preferential treatment toward members of a particular gender or race in other situations (Brown & Bigler, 2004). Finally, as we saw in Chapter 4, children and adolescents expect schools and teachers to protect them from harm and exploitation by other students. This protector role of teachers extends from basic safety on the playground to the fair treatment of students through classroom procedures and grading of students' work (Hansen, 1996).

Moral Development and the Social-Emotional Climate

Early Childhood (Preschool Through Grade 2)

A climate of acceptance and warmth toward students is an essential element of moral education at any grade level. However, these elements are expressed differently toward students at different ages. Because young children are in the early phase of integrating feelings within their moral and personal schemas, classrooms need to be characterized by positive emotion. Young children are particularly open to warmth from adults and particularly susceptible to the negative effects of adult displays of anger (Cumberland-Li, et al., 2003; Katz & Gottman, 1991). In early childhood classrooms, it is important that teachers be even tempered and refrain from emotional outbursts or shouting at children. The desire that young children have for emotionally calm environments accounts for the immense popularity of television characters such as Barney and Mr. Rogers whose soporific manners bore most adults and older children.

In a broader sense, it is essential that school be perceived as a benign environment in which children are safe from harm and exploitation by others. We want to do whatever possible to enable young children to construct a view of the world as benevolent and fair so that they might construct an orientation of goodwill toward others. This would be particularly important for young children whose experiences outside of school may be less than benign, and which may contribute to an experience of ill will and a consequent tendency to act in terms of self-interest rather than fairness.

Middle Childhood and Early Adolescence (Grades 3–8)

The climate of acceptance and warmth that characterized the good preschool is also essential at the elementary and middle school levels. Children at this age range are less dependent on adults, but still look to them for emotional support and social stability. Because the formal academic curriculum now assumes greater importance, one critical arena in which teachers determine the emotional climate is through their approach to academic instruction. A positive climate for social and moral growth is enhanced by academic experiences that foster peer interaction and discussion within a setting that allows for people to make mistakes without the risk of being made to look "dumb." This means that children should be encouraged to ask questions and to risk making mistakes in the process of learning. The key element for the teacher is to convey to students that mistakes are necessary to learning, and that children need to make mistakes if they are to grow. In doing so, the teacher establishes a social context in which differences among people in ability and interest are not used as criteria for inclusion or exclusion from academic activity. In a subtle, experiential way, students are being exposed to a social world in which issues of equity and equal treatment are being integrated. Although this is an important feature of teaching at all ages, it is especially important for children in middle childhood and early adolescence.

A central issue of middle childhood and early adolescence is how the self appears relative to the competencies of others (Nicholls, 1984, 1989). In a focus group that we conducted with fifth-grade children, we learned that the primary source of conflicts at school was peer exclusion. The instigators of the conflicts were said by both boys and girls to be children who were not well liked because of their lack of social skills (shy, nerdy), their inability to perform well in team sports (kickball), or their tendency to pick fights (bullies). An interesting sidelight of these discussions was the spontaneous tendency of the children to recognize that it was the act of exclusion that was the primary problem, and not just the characteristics of the children who instigated the fights or arguments that followed.

Being made to look dumb in class or being made the outsider on the playground is not simply a problem of peer culture, but of the school and its values.

Schools can enhance the sense of inclusion through the judicious use of cooperative modes of teaching (Aronson & Patnoe, 1997). They can reduce the harmful effects of peer competition and comparison through recreational forms of team sports (e.g., American Youth Soccer Organization–style soccer) that focus on participation, skill enhancement, and camaraderie rather than loss or victory (Shields & Bredemeier, 2008). Finally, they can refrain from engaging in practices that magnify peer comparisons, such as posting lists of children who have displayed "good character" (Character Counts Coalition, 1993). Such practices do not serve to enhance the values schools wish to promote, but on the contrary exacerbate tendencies toward invidious social comparison—one of the truly negative features of this developmental period.

Adolescence (High School)

The social climate of the high school should continue to underscore the basic elements of safety and of academic and social participation discussed in regard to earlier grade levels. Integrated participation of students is particularly important at the high school level in order to offset the tendencies toward segregation into cliques and crowds that characterize peer relations at this age. While this self-selection serves the purposes of identity formation, it also works toward exacerbating the problems of social exclusion that emerge during earlier developmental periods (Horn, 2003). Although it should not be the goal of schools to interfere with students' friendship networks or associations (elements of the personal domain), school should promote a broader sense of community in which students of diverse interests and abilities interact with one another.

This is of particular relevance for students who may be gay, lesbian, bisexual, or transgendered (GLBT). In many schools the climate for gay and lesbian youth is negative. Students who are thought to be gay or lesbian frequently report hearing negative comments from other students and school staff, and a high number of students report that they are harassed on a daily basis by other students because of their sexual orientation (Bochenek & Brown, 2001; Rivers & D'Augelli, 2001; Russell, Franz, & Driscoll, 2001). This type of victimization can lead to multiple negative developmental outcomes for youth including such things as depression, substance abuse, and suicide (D'Augelli, 1998). Recent work by Stacey Horn (2006) has shown that there are some positive factors in adolescents' views about homosexual peers that could be used as the basis to offset this negative situation. What she has discovered is that a large majority of those high school students who have objections to homosexuality also believe that it is wrong to tease or harass fellow students simply because they are gay or lesbian. This rather positive finding, which she has replicated in several settings, indicates that adolescents, including those who hold negative views of homosexuality, are open to moral arguments that would deter peer harassment and teasing of GLBT classmates. Schools can build on this latent tolerance by doing such things as allowing students to construct Gay-Straight alliances in which hetero-sexual and homosexual students collaboratively work to improve school climate (Horn & Nucci, 2006). Efforts by schools to support students' moral inclinations against harming fellow students do not require teachers to alter their basic views of homosexuality. However, such efforts do call on teachers to act as moral exemplars of fairness and compassion.

One obstacle to constructing community in American high schools (and in some middle schools) is their sheer size. The advantage of these larger schools with populations in excess of 800 students is that they can offer a much richer curriculum and broader array of extracurricular activities. The disadvantage of larger schools is that on a percentage basis, there is actually less student partic-ipation in a given activity and less student participation in such things as sports, school newspaper, and theater, overall.

A number of strategies have been devised to offset the social costs of the large comprehensive high school. What these approaches share in common is the goal of breaking down the total population of the school into smaller, socially diverse units within which students can generate a sense of community. In gen-eral these strategies use a common set of courses (e.g., English, history) or a class period (e.g., home room) as a way of identifying "houses" or communities within the school. Teachers and students in a given house remain together for at least one academic year and may use specified times throughout the year to col-lectively address or discuss social issues. The most well-researched of these school within a school programs are the "Just Community Schools" developed by Lawrence Kohlberg and his colleagues (Power, Higgins, & Kohlberg, 1989). Published reports indicate that this approach is quite effective in reducing stu-dent misconduct and contributes to students' moral development.

A more eclectic recent revival of the school within a school is being at-tempted on a reasonably large scale within the Chicago Public School system through the Small Schools Workshop originally operated by the University of Illi-nois at Chicago and now a national organization located at the College of Educa-tion of the University of South Florida (Klonsky, 2007). A small school in this approach has a population of 250–400 students. This project and others, such as the Just Community Schools, are pointing the way toward practical approaches for reducing the population of the comprehensive high school into human-scale, diverse social communities. Unlike the Just Community Schools these more eclectic attempts to break down the size of the comprehensive high school are not based on a specific theoretical orientation toward moral development. Nonetheless, research done on the effectiveness of *small* high schools indicates that they contribute to improvements in attendance and graduation rates, sense of community and belongingness, reduction in violence and disruptive behavior, higher academic achievement, and increased teacher satisfaction (Small Schools Workshop Web site: http://www.smallschoolsworkshop.org/info3.html).

Facilitating Moral and Social Development Through Discipline

Establishing an overall school and classroom moral climate extends beyond the emotional tone of the school to include methods of classroom management and discipline. All approaches to classroom management have two goals in common: control and efficiency. With variations in underlying theory and recommended practices their primary intent is to make academic instruction run smoothly (Evertson & Weinstein, 2006). Over the past twenty years, however, developmentally oriented educational researchers have generated approaches to classroom management that have the additional goal of fostering students' social and moral competence (DeVries & Zan, 1994; Nucci, 2006; Watson, 2003). There are some differences in the underlying theories that support the work of these newer developmental approaches. However, they share enough in common that I will borrow from Marilyn Watson (2003) and refer to them collectively as *developmental discipline.*

Developmental discipline is aimed at having the student do what is right for his or her own reasons rather than to receive external rewards or to avoid punishment. The particulars of developmental discipline adjust according to students' age and grade level. There are, however, four central strategies that characterize developmental discipline across grade levels.

1. Focus on building the classroom and school community by:
   a. Establishing caring, trusting, respectful relationships with each student
   b. Building respectful, caring relationships among students
2. Teach students the social knowledge and skills they need in order to act in ways that are kind, fair, and responsible.
3. Attend to the antecedents of misbehavior by
   a. Examining teacher-generated procedures and policies that make student misbehavior likely
   b. Examining school policies and procedures that make student misbehavior likely
   c. Examining student needs and motives that are contributing to misbehavior
4. When external control is needed, keep it "light." When possible, choose ways that are noncoercive or punitive. Respond to misbehavior in ways that effectively control or stop the behavior, but that also
   a. Help the student learn from her or his mistake.
   b. Minimize the pain or shame that the student will experience.
   c. Minimize the harm to the student's relationship with the teacher or peers.
   d. Minimize the student's loss of autonomy or sense of competence.

In this chapter we have already addressed many of the elements of establishing a moral classroom community. What we will take up now are some suggestions for how to respond to misbehavior in ways that foster students' moral and social development. We will begin with a discussion of how to handle moral conduct through social problem solving. We will then explore how to appropriately employ positive feedback and consequences for misbehavior.

Facilitating Moral Development Through Social Problem Solving

Early Childhood (Preschool Through Grade 2)

The great moral achievement accomplished by young children is the construction of an understanding of fair reciprocity. Because young children generate their initial understandings of morality out of their direct experiences in social interactions, the primary contribution that schools make toward young children's moral development is through the framing of these direct moral experiences. Teachers do this by helping children focus on the effects of actions and their reciprocal implications. For example, a teacher might respond to moral transgressions in the following way:

> "Mike, Matthew needs some clay. Please give him some."

> "Veronica, Dawn hasn't had a turn on the swings. Please let her have one."

In both cases, the teacher statements focus on the needs of the other child, and not simply on the power of the adult. But even these domain-appropriate moral statements lack the element of reciprocity. Although they do connect with the young child's concepts of morality, they do not explicitly direct the child's attention to the reciprocal nature of turn-taking or distribution of goods.

There are two ways for a teacher to do this. One is for the teacher to do all the thinking and lay out the reciprocal implications in statements to the children:

> "Mike—how would you like it if Matthew had all the clay, and you didn't have any? He needs some too. So please share with him."

This is a reasonably efficient way for a teacher to handle the situation, and it makes sense in contexts where the teacher's time is at a premium. The teacher's response is domain appropriate, and it lays out the reciprocal nature of morality and moral justification. However, it does not engage the students in active problem solving and is therefore not an optimal way for a teacher to make use of this situation. A better use of this teachable moment is for the teacher to assist the children in conflict resolution.

The value of engaging children in conflict resolution is that it engages the child in recognizing the contradictions that exist between his own initial way of looking at things, and what is necessary for his own needs and those of another person to be met. This is a slow process that is helped along by the child's inevitable experience of being on more than one side of these prototypical childhood disputes. One day's owner of the clay or the swing is the next day's child on the sidelines. In Piaget's terms, what takes place is the gradual disequilibration of the child's current way of thinking, and its gradual replacement by a more adequate reequilibrated form that resolves the contradictions arising from the initial way of looking at things.

From this viewpoint, there is an argument that can be made for allowing the children to solve such problems on their own (Killen, 1991; Piaget, 1932). Allowing children to solve their own problems has the advantage that the solutions generated are "owned" by the children, and the process contributes to the child's autonomy and social efficacy. In point of fact, teachers cannot enter into every conflict situation that arises among children, and observational studies have indicated that teachers allow a fair number of social conflicts among preschool and early elementary children to be resolved without adult intervention (Killen, 1991; Nucci & Nucci, 1982b). In many cases young children handle these disputes quite well. Approximately 70% of preschool children's disputes during free play are resolved by the children themselves either through reconciliation by the instigator, or through compromising and bargaining (Killen, 1991).

Although these findings are impressive, the value of allowing children to solve their problems on their own can be overstated. Adults have the developmental advantage of being able to see both sides of a moral dispute in ways that young children cannot. Moreover, children look to adults to provide protection from exploitation and harm, and to help them work through social problems (Killen, 1991; Nucci & Nucci, 1982b; Youniss, 1980). As was stated before, adults impede moral growth when they reduce moral situations to ones of convention and adult power. Adults contribute to moral growth when they engage children in moral reflection. With respect to conflict resolution, adults contribute to young children's moral growth by assisting them in identifying the sources of the conflict, by helping them to consider the perspective of the other, and by helping them to arrive at mutual solutions. This approach also provides children with experiences that counter the tendency to conclude that the use of sheer power and intimidation are the only methods by which one can achieve personal goals.

In the swing set example above, the teacher might begin by first asking the children to describe what the problem is, to hear each other's viewpoint and feelings, and then help them work toward a solution. We can imagine the following interchange described in Nucci (2001, p. 154):

T: Okay what's the problem?

D: Veronica has been on the swings for a long time, and I haven't had a turn.

T: Veronica, what do you have to say to that?

V: I got on the swing first, and I didn't even get to swing yesterday.

T: Dawn, how do you feel about what Veronica just said?

D: Well, this isn't yesterday, and she is making me really mad.

T: Why is that?

D: It isn't fair. She only gets a turn, and I don't!

T: Well, what do you think we should do?

D: We could share. Veronica could let me swing for a little and then I would let her swing some more.

T: Veronica, Dawn is suggesting that you guys share. Is that something that you can do?

V: Maybe . . . but I should get to have more time than her because I got here first!

T: Well, Dawn—how do you feel about that?

D: Okay, but not all day. I need turns too!

T: Okay, why don't you guys give it a try. I bet you can work something out. Call me if you need any help.

This scenario was loosely based on events commonly observed in our classroom observations, and the discourse format of teacher-child conversations in DeVries and Zan (1994). It illustrates how a teacher can provide a scaffold for children to build their own approach to moral problem solving. The key elements are that the children hear each other's point of view, attend to the harm or fairness issues involved, and offer a mutually satisfying resolution. The key roles for the teacher are to act as an honest broker, to assist in thinking about possible solutions, and to offer support for follow through. This provides a context in which the work is done by the children in an atmosphere of safety and mutual regard.

Naturally, real children do not always engage in cooperative resolutions of conflicts. In such cases, the teacher will need to make a judgment as to whether sufficient harm or injustice is being perpetrated as to warrant a direct intervention by the teacher, or if the issue is one of relatively minor consequence where the children will simply need to deal with the fact that not all situations turn out nicely. For example, if Veronica simply is not interested in sharing, but hasn't really been dominating the swingset, the teacher may simply decide to let things stand as they are. She might say to Dawn, "Well, I am sorry to say that Veronica isn't going to share right now. Perhaps you can come back and use the swings later." One might argue that in doing so, the teacher has rewarded Veronica's "selfishness." This is where a teacher's judgment has to come in. If Veronica does not generally behave in a selfish manner, there is little likelihood that an occasional act of self-interest marks a major shift in "character." It may well be that Veronica has a special desire to swing that day, or that she doesn't particularly like Dawn and is momentarily acting on that dislike. Unless the teacher is clairvoyant, she will have no way of knowing why Veronica has chosen this moment to act as she has. In this scenario, Veronica's failure to be "nice" may be irrelevant to her level of morality. As for Dawn, she will live to swing another day. In this case, disappointment would not entail moral tragedy, but a practical lesson in human psychology and interpersonal relations. The children's attempt at moral discourse would not have resulted in a solution, but it would raise the underlying issues to a level of consciousness from which both children would stand to benefit.

If, on the other hand, Veronica has dominated the swingset and is simply unreasonable, the teacher would have a moral obligation to protect the rights of the other children and would step in to ensure that Dawn was given a turn. The teacher might also take disciplinary action toward Veronica. We will take up the issue of consequences later in the chapter.

Middle Childhood (Grades 3–6)

The morality of children by the third or fourth grade of elementary school has the element of reciprocity lacking in the preschool child. However, it is a very literal reciprocity in which fairness requires simply that one not come out on the short end of things. On the plus side, children are now much better able to take into account the needs of the other as well as the self in making moral decisions. On the down side, this tit-for-tat morality has a basic limitation that elementary school teachers will recognize being expressed in the kinds of trouble that elementary school children sometimes get themselves into, and in the instances of insensitivity that children of this age sometimes exhibit.

The social exclusion that our focus group children so readily identified as the primary source of social problems at school is sustained by a morality that views fairness in terms of providing rewards in direct proportion to the quality or amount of one's deeds (Damon, 1977). From this moral orientation, a child who is not a good kickball player is simply not as entitled to play as someone who is a good player. A child who is shy or not socially skilled is less worthy of invitation to a party than someone who is more socially adept. Excluding these children is therefore, not unfair. In addition, there is an element of personal choice involved in that children may view the selection of whom to involve in play or social activity as an aspect of social relations that is a matter of personal prerogative.

Generally, teachers are not involved in helping to resolve these social problems. Unlike the failure to engage in turn-taking, which is an overt act of excluding others from common playground equipment, the decision by children not to include a particular child in their games or activities is often viewed by the teachers as well as the children as a peer matter of choice. On the other hand, children do recognize teachers as having legitimate authority to ensure that school resources (in this case opportunities to play) are distributed in a fair manner. In addition, children expect teachers to protect not simply their physical safety, but their feelings as well. For a teacher to become involved requires a judgment that a child's exclusion is becoming systematic and, therefore, potentially harmful to the child.

Name calling and fighting are other common examples of moral problems that are compatible with the direct reciprocity morality of middle childhood. One consequence of a morality based on direct reciprocity is that it can lead to the view that any harm requires a commensurate harmful response. This eye-for-an-eye morality leads to a vicious cycle in which, as Martin Luther King put it, all parties end up blind. Virtually every parent and teacher has heard the phrase, "He started it!" as an explanation for name calling or fighting. And, as every parent and teacher knows, the tit-for-tat mentality of children makes efforts to determine "who started it" usually futile.

Domain-appropriate responses to social exclusion and fighting are somewhat different, though in both cases the goal is to direct children to consider the intrinsic moral consequences of their actions. Teachers may do this by engaging in the sorts of domain-concordant feedback described with reference to younger children. In applying this to older children, however, the goal is not simply to get each child to consider the other's perspective, but to help them recognize the limitations that result from strict reciprocity moral reasoning.

Another strategy is to extend the effort at social problem solving described with reference to preschool children by bringing in a peer mediator (Deutsch, 1993). The advantages of engaging a peer mediator to help with conflicts among elementary and middle school children are several. First and foremost, it reduces the tendency for children to see objections to immoral conduct as simply a matter of adult authority. Second, it causes the disputants to see their situation from a third, disinterested vantage point. This third-person perspective moves the issue out of one of direct reciprocity and offers a window into a new way of looking at moral issues. Finally, the act of peer mediation is of benefit to the mediator, who is necessarily engaged in moral discourse and reflection. For example, a study examining the impact of peer mediation on second- through fifth-grade students found that students who had served as peer mediators more often resolved their *own* interpersonal conflicts in ways that took into account the needs of both parties, and were also less likely to ask for adult intervention than children who had not had this mediator experience (Johnson, Johnson, Dudley, Ward, & Magnuson, 1995).

Adolescence (Grades 7–12)

The rate at which teachers respond to children's moral transgressions begins to decline by the time children enter the fifth grade. By seventh grade, teachers and other school personnel are rarely respondents to children's moral transgressions (Nucci & Nucci, 1982b). The lack of adult response observed at the seventh-grade level was in part a function of the reduction in rates of moral transgressions that involved overt acts of aggression and squabbles over such things as playground equipment. Most of the moral transgressions observed at the seventh-grade level were in the form of name calling or other forms of psychological harm (Nucci & Nucci, 1982b). Teachers provide relatively low response rates to such transgressions at all age levels including preschool (Killen, 1991), leaving such issues up to processes of peer interaction. Commensurate with the observed decline in adult response rate, older children and adolescents tend to seek out adult intervention for moral interactions at much lower rates than do young children (Nucci & Nucci, 1982b).

At both the junior and senior high school levels, school authorities appear to respond only to severe breaches of moral conduct such as fighting and theft. In most schools, this means that teachers and other school personnel have little direct input into the moral interactions of the vast majority of their students. The contributions that traditional junior and senior high schools make to students' moral growth are through the degree to which conventional norms are fairly applied, the degree of respect and mutuality that exists between teachers and students, and the degree of openness and interaction that exists in the discourse over academic subject matter. In other words, the contribution of junior and senior high school faculty and administrators to students' moral growth (beyond moral elements of the academic curriculum) is through these general structural features of the school and classroom rather than any form of direct teacher involvement in student moral interactions.

Objections to this traditional perspective have been raised by those who argue that it is only through direct social experience that students can develop as moral beings, and that academic discourse is insufficient without a direct linkage to students' actual lives (Power, Higgins, & Kohlberg, 1989). The primary proponents of this point of view are the advocates of democratic education (Lind, 1996; Oser & Veugelers, 2003) and the Just Community school (Power, et al., 1989). What these approaches share in common are mechanisms by which students come together as a community to openly discuss the moral issues they are confronting within the school context (e.g., thefts, student exclusion or isolation, sexual conduct, racism), in order to arrive at a rational moral consensus (cf. Habermas, 1991; Oser & Veugelers, 2003) for how such issues should be resolved. Often these resolutions involve the construction of shared moral norms, which are then used to guide the conduct of members of the Just Community (Power et al., 1989).

In order for these "just communities" to work, schools must give instructional time on a regular (weekly) basis for students to hold these town hall–style meetings. They must also give to the students and their community advisors the authority to alter, add to, or abolish existing school rules that affect these "quality of life" issues for students. Students are not empowered to change the basic academic framework of the school, but rather those norms that pertain to problematic areas of their moral interactions. Despite evidence that such just communities result in behavioral and cognitive moral growth, few schools in the United States have adopted this holistic approach.

The value of working with high school students to help solve moral problems is being highlighted in a recent controversial effort to reduce gang-related violence in the Chicago public schools. Many inner city high schools are plagued with violent fights instigated by gang affiliations. In the past, the typical response of Chicago Public School authorities has been to call in police and attempt to quell violence through force and punishment. In 2003 there were 8,900 arrests of students for participation in fights. In 2006 the rate of such arrests dropped by nearly 20% (*Chicago Tribune*, Nov. 19, 2006). This drop in the arrest rate is directly attributable to a policy adopted by some high schools in which fights are quickly quelled by school staff, and gang leaders are brought in by the school principal to gain an understanding of the causes of the fight. Rather than arrest or expel the students involved in the fight, the principal engages in discussion with the students along with a parent or guardian. Generally, there are consequences, but not incarceration. Discussions with gang leaders often lead to information that permits the administrator to alert neighborhood police to head off any escalation outside the school.

This is an extreme situation at the end point of experiences in which some students have long since lost their sense of trust. A school principal involved in this new approach acknowledges the difficulty of the task brought on by his commitment to negotiation over suppression. However, he is convinced that his school is safer than when he resorted to simply handing the problem over to police. In his words, "You never give up your building . . . and you don't let it fester. This is my reality, and I can't make it go away by hiding from it. We owe it to these children to do everything we can to help them" (*Chicago Tribune*, 2006).

Facilitating Social Development Through the Judicious Use of Consequences

As was evident in the example of gang-related fighting, there are some situations in which consequences for misconduct are clearly called for. The goal of all effective classroom management is to anticipate problems and to avoid the need for consequences. In Chapter 4 we discussed the wisdom of eliminating unneeded classroom conventions that are guaranteed to generate high levels of noncompliance. Managing the antecedents to misbehavior would also include attention to the academic demands of the classroom that might tax the ability of a student to stay on task. This can be as simple as making sure that all students have access to materials at their reading level to providing synopses of longer readings that would exceed the ability of attention deficit disordered students to complete. However, even when a teacher attends to students' needs for attention and power, and does all that is reasonable to address academics and school norms, children will still misbehave. This should come as no great surprise to teachers who, having brilliantly taught an academic lesson, will nevertheless see mistakes on tests. Social development is no exception to the simple fact that making mistakes is part of the process of growth and development.

Supporting Positive Behavior

One way to avoid discipline problems in the classroom is to provide feedback that supports children's positive behavior. This feedback can come in the form of tangible rewards, but most often comes in the form of adult praise. Although the use of positive feedback and rewards can help sustain and guide a child's developing morality, an overreliance on rewards and positive adult feedback can backfire and actually undermine the child's moral motivation (Deci, 1995). The limitations of external reinforcement are most readily apparent with the case of offering children tangible rewards for their good behavior. There is a substantial research literature indicating that providing external rewards to children, such as gold stars or stickers, reduces their tendency to spontaneously engage in the rewarded behavior. In other words, children shift from engaging in the behaviors for their own intrinsic reasons, toward doing things simply for the "money."

Marilyn Watson (2003) strenuously argues that any use of rewards is antithetical to her conception of developmental discipline. I would argue in contrast that one can distinguish between the use of rewards that serve to *validate* what the student is already motivated to do, and the use of rewards as a means of "shaping" the student's behavior to conform to the wishes of adults (Deci, 1995). For example, a student who has consistently treated classmates with kindness and generosity might well respond to a "citizenship" award as reflecting social validation for her actions, rather than as an effort to shape her behavior. On the other hand, the routine awarding of pins or other emblems and the weekly public listing of the names of students who have displayed "virtue" or "character," as advocated by some neo-traditionalist programs (cf., Character Counts), exemplify how *not* to support children's positive behavior (Kohn, 1997). In such cases, the rewards become overt sources of competition, and commodities in and of themselves. They may temporarily serve to mold and shape students' conduct, but they also undermine the very motives such programs seek to instill.

Similarly, in providing praise to a student, we need to differentiate positive statements that validate children and encourage their efforts at moral action from "controlling praise" that serves the adult's desire to "mold and shape" the student. Controlling praise focuses attention on the child rather than the child's actions, is nonspecific in content, and often employs terms that are superlative in nature. Examples of such praise are: "Allison, you are such a good girl"; "Jack, you are the nicest child I have had in class in years." The effect of controlling praise is to give the child a momentary boost in self-esteem, but at the cost of setting the bar at an unrealistically high level. Is it realistic to assume that Allison and Jack are always going to be so superlatively well behaved? Second, the feedback to the child says little about what it is that warranted being labeled "such a good girl" or "the nicest child in years." Any reasons that the children might have had for doing the behaviors that won them their accolades are lost in the focus on the evaluations of the children themselves. Thus, one risk associated with controlling praise is that it moves the desire to engage in a behavior from intrinsic valuing of the action to an ego-oriented focus on one's own perceived social status (Nicholls, 1989). The moral self that is constructed on this basis may be superficially oriented toward behaving morally, but not for moral reasons. The child who needs to always be "such a good boy" in order to fit social expectations is not operating out of moral motivation, but in order to sustain external approval.

In contrast, praise that takes the form of encouragement uses moderate language and focuses on the specifics of the action. Such praise lets the student know that his actions are appreciated, and also indicates that it is the actions that are being evaluated, and not the child himself. Examples of validating praise would be: "Tatiana, that was a kind thing that you just did. I am sure that Marcy appreciated the time you spent with her when she wasn't feeling well." "Mike, thanks for helping clean up the room. It makes everything better for everyone. I really appreciate it." Encouraging praise is especially effective as a response to what we might refer to as "everyday acts of character." In the previous example, Mike might have been one of the children who never helped with cleanup time. For him to have done so might well have taken considerable personal effort. Acknowledgment from the teacher in the form of thanks would let him know that his efforts were recognized and his contribution validated. The teacher might even add a word of encouragement to "keep up the good work." Of course, a behaviorist might justifiably argue that such positive feedback is serving to shape Mike's positive social behavior. There is no reason to quibble over this point. The key elements are whether the teacher acts out of a genuine sense of appreciation, and whether Mike interprets the statement as validating his own efforts. In any case, praise should be used *sparingly* and directed at specific acts rather than at the characteristics of children.

Responding to Misbehavior

An essential aspect of all learning is making mistakes. It would be nice to believe that moral education is a matter of guiding children down the "right" path, but the fiction of "error-free" learning has even less to do with morality than other aspects of education. Although children are rarely, if ever, motivated to purposefully make mistakes in academic areas, the very nature of moral misconduct is that it often involves actions that are counter to what the child knows to be the "right" thing to do. Correcting errors in the moral area is not simply a matter of pointing out mistakes, but also helping the child to choose to act in ways that are not always concordant with his or her immediate desires. What Piaget (1962) referred to as a "conflict of will" is what is at stake, and not simply a question of the "objectively" right thing to do.

Helping the child to choose to want to do the right thing is in part a function of teachers' disciplinary responses to children's misbehavior. Consequences provided to students in response to their misbehavior should not take the form of expiatory punishments designed solely to inflict discomfort or cost to the student (DeVries & Zan, 1994). A classic example of an expiatory punishment is spanking. A classic example from school would be detention. Expiatory punishments are to be avoided because they do not provide the student with any reason beyond the pragmatic goals of punishment avoidance as a motivation for action. Because students associate expiatory punishments with the person meting them out, rather than with their own misconduct, such punishments invite revenge and provide students with a sense that they have the right to retaliate. In other words, the morality of the situation becomes turned on its head as the student, guilty of misconduct, now becomes in his or her own mind the aggrieved party. An example that some readers might relate to would be getting "grounded" by your parents for some misbehavior. My university students can invariably recall examples from adolescence when this happened to them. To a person, they have difficulty even remembering the specifics of their misbehavior. However, they have no problem whatsoever in conjuring up the sense of outrage they felt toward their parents at the time. Frequent use of expiatory punishment by a teacher transforms the emotional climate of the classroom into an environment of "ill will" that supports students' self-protective and "selfish" motivations.

Instead, sanctions should take the form of logical consequences connected in a meaningful way with the nature of the transgression (DeVries & Zan, 1994). Logical consequences include such things as restitution, depriving the transgressor of the thing misused, and exclusion. Because of the nonarbitrary, reciprocal nature of morality, it is somewhat easier to envision logical consequences for moral transgressions than for violations of social conventions. For example, if a child takes something away from another child, a logical consequence would be for the child to have to replace it. However, even conventions, once in place, have a logic associated with their function. A student who talks disruptively during story time might be asked by the teacher to leave the story area until he or she is able to rejoin the group and sit quietly. If this sanction is coupled with a domain-appropriate statement of the rule or social organizational function of the norm, the student is likely to see the connection between the sanction and the misbehavior. An indefinite or extended expulsion from the story area, however, would shift the consequence away from the behavior, and become an arbitrary, expiative punishment rather than a logical consequence (DeVries & Zan, 1994).

Teachers can increase the likelihood that students will accept the logical consequences of misbehavior by engaging them in group discussions about patterns of misbehavior occurring in the classroom, and seeking their advice on how to avoid or reduce such problems in the future (Battistich et al., 1997; DeVries & Zan, 1994). In Chapter 4 we discussed the use of group discussions as a way of engaging children in the consideration of what rules should be in place to regulate or help guide students' conduct. In this case, the discussion concerns what to do about behaviors that the children agree are problematic. Through group discussion, the teacher can guide students, especially in elementary and middle school, to generate ideas about what would constitute appropriate logical consequences. Part of the teacher's role is to help the children focus on prevention of misbehavior. By engaging children in such discourse, the consequences of misconduct are moved from a top-down, adult-imposed act of power, to autonomously constructed, logical outcomes reflecting values shared by the children.

Finally, an ethical response to students' misconduct must allow for student reentry and acceptance into the social group. Once the logical consequence has been met, the child must have the opportunity to move forward as a class member. Otherwise, the logical consequence is transformed into expiatory punishment with all the negative ramifications already discussed. This is a fairly easy requirement to meet when it comes to typical transgressions of social convention. It is not always so easy when the transgression involves moral consequences to other classmates. Although the teacher may be willing to move forward, the students may be unwilling to risk interactions with someone who had caused them pain or injustice. In such cases, as with an aggressive child, the teacher needs to help the transgressor understand the connections between aggressive conduct and the responses of his or her classmates. The teacher must also help the other students to recognize that they would not want to be permanently excluded either. This requires patience and persistence on the teacher's part and is helped or hindered by the overall moral and emotional climate of the school and classroom.

Summary

Schools and classrooms contribute to students' moral development through the nature of the overall social and emotional climate. This includes the way in which teachers and schools address behavioral issues through classroom management and discipline.

Paying attention to the emotional climate of classrooms is important because children incorporate emotional experiences within their social cognitive schemes.

Variations in the emotional experiences of children can affect their moral orientations. The development of morality in children is supported by experiences of emotional warmth and fairness. Children who grow up in such environments tend to construct a view of the world based on goodwill. A child who maintains an orientation of goodwill feels emotionally secure and expects the world to operate according to basic moral standards of fairness. Children who maintain this orientation are more likely to engage in prosocial behavior. A moral classroom climate is one that fosters this tendency toward goodwill. The elements of a moral classroom climate address the following four needs: autonomy, belonging, competence, and fairness.

In early childhood it is especially important to construct a classroom climate characterized by positive emotion. In middle childhood students are less dependent on adults. However, they become more susceptible to social comparison and peer exclusion. A positive moral climate reduces competition and increases opportunities for peer collaborative learning and social problem solving. In adolescence the challenge is to offset the negative impact of student cliques and tendencies toward alienation. Large high schools pose special challenges for the creation of moral community. The Just Community School and the Small Schools movement are efforts to address this challenge through "schools within schools."

A positive moral atmosphere is complemented by behavioral management in the form of *developmental discipline*. In addition to the goals of control and efficiency common to all approaches to behavioral management, developmental discipline includes the additional goal of fostering students' social and moral competence. Developmental discipline engages students' intrinsic motivation to do what is right for their own reasons. Developmental discipline deemphasizes the use of external rewards and punishments to shape behavior. Conflicts and misbehavior are addressed primarily through social problem solving. Teacher discourse provides suggestions and scaffolding to support students' efforts to resolve disputes and arrive at fair solutions.

Teacher feedback in support of positive behavior avoids the use of external rewards such as gold stars or certificates of recognition for good conduct or character because such external rewards reduce intrinsic moral motivation. Moral action and compliance with school conventions is aided by teachers' judicious use of positive feedback in the form of validations that use moderate language referring to specific behavior and not the characteristics of the student. Responses to misbehavior should minimize the use of consequences when alternative problem-solving methods are available. When consequences are to be employed they should be "light" and in the form of logical consequences that are connected in a meaningful way to the nature of the transgression.

Facilitating Moral Development Through the Academic Curriculum

In Section II we explored how to use the social climate and social interactions of everyday life in classrooms to build the foundation for moral development. That foundation emerges from the natural tendencies of children to seek love and social connection along with autonomy. Those affective tendencies feed into children's efforts to try to make sense of their encounters with other people and with social norms. Through the appropriate structuring of school experience teachers and administrators can help students to generate basic moral understandings and an orientation of goodwill. A healthy classroom and school moral atmosphere will also contribute to students' ability to balance their own personal needs for autonomy and privacy with the needs of all social groups to operate with shared norms and conventions. These basics of moral and social development provide the foundation for a conventionally good, moral person.

Our ability to develop this foundation solely through the direct experiences of social life at school, however, is limited. The range of conventional and moral issues that students encounter through direct experience at school is confined to the particular features of schools as social institutions. In addition, observational studies of naturally occurring interactions indicate that teacher responses to students' moral or conventional violations tend to decrease as students leave elementary school (Nucci & Nucci, 1982). Finally, naturally occurring social interactions in traditional school settings do not afford much in the way of time for reflection or discussion. We have discussed ways in which schools can improve their effectiveness through developmental discipline and related strategies for classroom management. But even the most developmentally appropriate school environment is not designed to allow for extensive discussion and reflection around social issues.

The educative role of schools, however, is not limited to direct social experience. Schools are specialized institutions designed to bring students beyond their own direct encounters with the world to acquire information and to construct understandings that are valued by their culture. This is accomplished through the formal academic curriculum. The curriculum is rife with moral and conventional content as well as issues of personal choice and identity. Schools, then, have an opportunity to engage in meaningful moral and social education through an integration of values education with the teaching of regular academic subject matter. This becomes increasingly important from the third grade of elementary school on through high school as students become increasingly capable of reflection, and as the involvement of teachers in the moral lives of students lessens. Employing domain-appropriate practice to integrate values education within the academic curriculum is the subject of Section III.

As we will see in the next section, the academic curriculum can be used to supplement and extend students' direct social experience to help them build the basic social knowledge and skills to become a conventionally good, moral person. As we will also see, the academic curriculum can do more than this. It can form the context in which students can learn to take a critical moral perspective toward their own conduct and values, as well as the social norms, beliefs, and institutions of society. It is through the academic curriculum that students encounter great literature, history, and the treasure trove of factual information that comes from the natural sciences. It is through the academic curriculum that students can learn how to question existing beliefs, develop the skills to create new knowledge, and the capacity to express themselves in writing, speaking, and the arts. Integrating moral education within the academic curriculum can help to foster the development of students' concepts of morality, convention, and the personal. It can also enable them to apply that knowledge to critically evaluate the social world around them. As any teacher can tell us, this capacity will be dependent on the students' level of development. However, the basic skill of applying moral knowledge to critical thinking is something that can begin in elementary school. Developing students who approach themselves and the social world from a critical moral perspective is how we engage in moral education that goes beyond fostering conventionally moral, nice people.

Chapter 6 in Section III will present the basics for how a teacher would go about integrating domain-appropriate practice for moral and social development within the regular academic curriculum. This will include how to identify moral, conventional, and personal domain issues within regular classroom materials and academic assignments. The chapter will provide basic guidelines for constructing lessons and leading discussions. Finally, this chapter will describe how to prepare students for effective discussion and follow-up academic work.

Chapters 7, 8, and 9 will present examples of lessons that employ the regular academic curriculum for moral and social development. Chapter 7 will focus on the elementary school setting; Chapter 8 will focus on middle school; and Chapter 9 will focus on high school. All three chapters will include examples from literacy and social studies. The uses of math, natural sciences, and the arts are distributed across chapters. In using these chapters, teachers should keep in mind that development is not tied to specific ages or grade levels. For this reason teachers should read all three chapters, because some activities designed for students in grades above or below the classes they teach may actually be appropriate for some students in their classrooms. Finally, in order to reduce duplication, the chapters vary in terms of lesson formats and strategies. Reading all three chapters provides the best picture of how teachers may effectively integrate moral education within the regular curriculum.

CHAPTER 6

Using the Academic Curriculum for Moral Development: The Basics

> *The overall goal of any program must be to help children reason autonomously about moral problems. No amount of rote learning or indoctrination will prepare children for the many diverse situations that they will face in life.*
>
> —William Damon (1988)

In this chapter we will go over the basic process for using the academic curriculum to facilitate moral and social development. A central premise of this approach is that each lesson will generate a "2 for 1" set of benefits. A successful lesson or unit should serve *both* academic achievement and social and moral development. Adopting this 2 for 1 approach allows teachers and schools to contribute to students' moral development without sacrificing instructional time. More importantly, evaluation research has demonstrated that programs for emotional or moral development that are implemented in isolation have little long-term effect on children and tend to be short-lived (Greenberg et al., 2003). Thus, the 2 for 1 approach is not only the most efficient way to go; it is also the most effective.

The use of the curriculum should go hand in hand in with the establishment of a socio-moral atmosphere and practices of classroom management and discipline as described in Section II. This will result in a holistic approach to academic teaching and social development that benefits academic achievement as well as emotional and moral development. Developing social knowledge within domains has been shown to contribute to students' academic achievement in specific content areas such as social studies and language arts (Nucci & Charlier, 1983). In a meta-analysis of existing research, Roger Weissberg (2006) concluded, "There is an inextricable link between students' social-emotional adjustment and their academic achievement. They are not just relevant to academic achievement, they are central to it."

This holistic and integrated approach to teaching is consistent with the intuitions and practices of many successful teachers. Thus, the practices that will be described in this chapter and the ones that follow should be seen as extensions of good teaching, rather than a radical departure from what good teachers have been doing in their classrooms. In our work with classroom teachers, we have found that there is an initial adjustment period as teachers work through their existing materials to identify moral, conventional, and personal issues within their academic lessons. It also takes some time to help students develop the listening and discussion skills needed for effective moral lessons. However, once things are in place, the application of domain-appropriate social and moral education becomes a natural part of academic instruction. We recently integrated domain-appropriate social and moral education in our undergraduate elementary teacher education program at the University of Illinois at Chicago. The evaluation of that initiative demonstrated that when our students had completed student teaching their knowledge of children's social and moral development and their own sense of efficacy in contributing to children's moral education was significantly higher than graduates of our program from prior years (Nucci, Drill, Larson, & Browne, 2006). This project along with our work with experienced teachers provides a basis for confidence that the practices that will be presented are ones that most teachers can readily adopt. This is not to say that the skill to integrate moral education within the curriculum will come simply as a result of reading this book. Developing that skill will take time and practice just as in any other aspect of classroom teaching. A novice using this approach needs to be patient and willing to stick with it through early phases of implementation. It is also a good idea to collaborate with a colleague. The concluding chapter of the book contains contact information and other resources to provide support to teachers implementing this approach.

Goals

In addition to having the 2 for 1 goal that social and moral development lessons contribute to academic learning, there are seven other basic goals for use of the regular curriculum for domain-appropriate moral and social developmental education. Some of these goals need to be further specified by grade level in relationship to normative patterns of social development. In Chapters 7–9 goals will be defined in relation to examples of lessons for students at different grade levels. What follows is a description of the general goals for use of the curriculum for social and moral education that cut across grade levels.

- **Goal 1.** *Moral domain.* Students will develop their concepts of fairness and understanding of their obligations with respect to the welfare and rights of others. This goal means extending students' prevailing concepts of fairness to begin to question their assumptions about what it means to be treated fairly and to reevaluate their moral obligations toward others.

- **Goal 2.** *Conventional domain.* Students will develop their understandings of the functions of societal convention in everyday life. In middle school and high school students will coordinate their concepts of convention with an understanding of societies as rule-governed systems. Although Goal 1 is included in all developmentally based programs of moral education, Goal 2, the fostering of concepts about convention, is not generally included as an aspect of social developmental education. This is because traditional moral education programs based on the work of Kohlberg and Piaget have regarded social convention as an inferior basis for structuring morality. Research demonstrating that convention and morality are different conceptual frameworks contradicts those older assumptions. Goal 2 stands as recognition that mature and competent members of society must have an understanding and appreciation of the functions served by convention if they are to function within society, and if they are to be able to stand outside of their own social and cultural framework. The latter is an essential component for membership in a pluralist democracy in which respect for the culture and traditions of others is needed. Finally, it is only by first understanding the functions of convention that students can apply morality to evaluate society as a system of norms and rules from a moral perspective.
- **Goal 3.** *Personal domain.* Students will develop an understanding of the role of a zone of personal choice and privacy for maintaining a sense of autonomy, individuality, and the capacity to create a self consistent with one's own sense of identity. Development within the personal domain is tied to the student's developing understandings of self and personhood. This is an essential aspect of establishing the ability to function as a competent person. It is also critical to the person's ability to appreciate the rights and needs of others.
- **Goal 4.** *Coordination across domains.* Students will develop their capacity to employ knowledge from more than one domain to reason about and evaluate their own social behavior and the conduct of others. Students will also develop in their capacity to apply knowledge from more than one domain in evaluating the norms of social groups, social institutions, and the general society.
- **Goal 5.** *Factual assumptions.* Students will develop the skills and attitudes consistent with an inquisitive and critical orientation toward the factual assumptions associated with social and moral value judgments.
- **Goal 6.** *Critical moral perspective.* Students will develop a critical moral perspective. Goals 4 and 5 should combine to result in students who approach their own personal moral positions with humility and willingness to change in the face of new information or a more compelling moral argument. Goal 6 also means that students will apply their moral under-

standings to evaluate the morality of existing social norms, institutions, and practices. This goal moves moral education beyond the task of fostering conventionally moral, nice people toward encouraging the development of citizens who can contribute to the moral growth of society.

- **Goal 7.** *Moral self.* Students will connect moral and social knowledge to their sense of themselves as moral agents. This goal might be considered similar to the goals of character education. The aim would be to connect the processes of reflection, discussion, meaning making, and reasoning to the student's core personal values and sense of self. The assumption is that genuine moral development will result in more than a surface change in moral language, but a deeper shift in the student's moral perspective and worldview. Unlike traditional character education, however, there are no particular virtues that would be presumed to attach to all students as they construct themselves as moral beings. Nor would the goal of connecting to the moral self be aimed at attaining a decontextualized "good person" whose conduct would always be guided solely by moral considerations.

Basic Principles

There are four basic educational principles for constructing domain-appropriate lessons to attain the moral and social development goals listed above. In addition to these social development aims, however, a successful lesson should also be evaluated in terms of its connection to the academic standards and goals of the subject matter. Thus, each lesson should be consistent with principles of sound academic instruction as well as social development in order to meet the 2 for 1 objectives of academic and social and emotional learning.

1. *Generate reflection and construction of knowledge.* Lessons that facilitate moral development engage students in actively figuring out increasingly more adequate ways of understanding and reasoning about the social world. This principle draws from the basic premise of all constructivist teaching. Genuine understanding and the ability to reason can only result from the active efforts of students to recognize and resolve contradictions, build from the hints and suggestions of others, and generate novel insights through personal reflection. These processes map onto Piaget's notions of cognitive equilibration, Vygotsky's ideas about co-construction and the zone of proximal development, and Bruner's concept of scaffolding. Teachers will recognize that this principle means that simply memorizing rules, maxims, and definitions has little effect on students' development. Successful lessons are those that generate controversy, pose problems to solve, and require the students to come up with ideas and solutions rather than simply model the views and behaviors of others.

2. *Employ age/development–appropriate activities, terms, and discourse.*
   This principle acknowledges that students at different ages and points of
   development will process information differently and provide different
   resolutions to social and moral issues as a function of their level of understanding of the social and moral world. Teachers must select issues
   that match the developmental levels of their students and frame questions and activities that will generate student reflection within the developmental frame (zone of proximal development) appropriate to their
   level of social and moral understanding. This principle fits the intuitions
   of most teachers and has been supported by a generation of research. We
   will provide general guidelines for selecting materials and constructing
   lessons to fit developmental level in the following chapters.

3. *Employ domain-concordant issues, terms, and discourse.* This principle states that the tasks assigned to students in a social and moral development lesson need to be in sync with the domain of the focal issues.
   We will provide examples of how to identify and select curricular issues
   by domain in a later section of this chapter.

   Several years ago, we set out to address whether attention to the domain of social values in teaching social and moral lessons makes a difference in the development of children's moral and social conventional
   concepts (Nucci & Weber, 1991). The setting for our study was an
   eighth-grade American history course and a companion course in English
   composition. Together with the history teacher, we identified a series of
   issues from American history that were primarily either moral or social
   conventional in character as well as events and issues that involved domain overlap. Examples of the moral issues were slavery and the forced
   removal of Indians from their lands. Conventional issues included such
   things as the adjustments in modes of dress, work conventions (such as
   time schedules), and dating patterns that resulted from the influx of im-
   migrants and the shift from an agrarian to an industrial society. Changes
   in laws permitting women to vote is an example of a mixed domain issue
   used in the study.

   Students participated in small-group discussions of these issues once
   each week for a period of 7 weeks. In addition, students were given essay
   homework assignments based on the issues that they had discussed.
   These homework assignments were graded by the classroom teacher as a
   part of his assessment of their learning of history. Finally, students wrote
   essays on related moral, conventional, or mixed issues in their English
   composition class. Students were assigned to one of three forms of instruction. In one condition (Convention), students were directed in their
   small group discussions and in their essays to treat all issues as if they
   were matters of convention. Discussions centered around the norms in-

volved, and the function of norms in structuring society, and the impact that altering or violating the norms would have on the social order. In the second condition (Moral), students were directed to treat these same issues as if they were matters of morality. Discussions and essay instructions directed students to consider the justice and welfare implications of the issues under consideration. The third instructional mode fit our definition of Domain-Appropriate values education. The focus of discussions and essays was matched with the domain of the particular issue under consideration. In the case of mixed domain issues, students were asked first to consider normative, conventional aspects and then to consider the justice or welfare features of the issue. Finally, students were asked to integrate or coordinate the moral and conventional features of the event. This latter exercise was one that we hoped would increase the capacity of students to spontaneously respond in a critical way to contradictions between morality and conventions, and to seek moral resolutions of those contradictions in ways that also respected the need for social organization. Examples of how these discussions were structured will be presented in some detail later in Chapters 7 through 9 when we look more closely at examples of domain-appropriate lessons.

Several findings from the study are important for this discussion. First are the outcomes regarding development of morality and convention. What we found was that students in the Moral condition and students in the Domain-Appropriate condition had moral reasoning scores that were very similar to and significantly higher than the scores of students who had been in the Convention condition. With regard to the development of reasoning about convention, the outcome was the inverse. Students in the Convention and Domain-Appropriate conditions had similar levels of conventional reasoning, and both were on average nearly half a stage higher than the conventional levels of students in the Moral condition. These results indicate that attention to domain does matter in terms of efforts to affect students' social conceptual development. Students who received instruction focusing in one domain developed in that domain, and not the other. Only the students in the Domain-Appropriate instructional condition developed in both domains.

A second noteworthy finding of the study had to do with how students dealt with overlapping issues. At the end of the 7-week instructional period all students were asked to write an essay discussing their views of the social values issues raised by an event in which morality and convention were in conflict. The matter concerned an actual event in which the king of the Gypsies of the Chicago metropolitan area refused federal money for scholarships to attend a local public university because it would require him to permit Gypsy women to attend as well as Gypsy men. This event pitted the gender-based conventions of Gypsy society against the unfair provision of educational opportunities for one gender and not another. The student essays were scored in terms of whether or not they subordinated the issue to either morality or convention, vacillated between the two domains without coordination, or integrated the moral and conventional elements of the event through domain coordination. Findings were that students who had domain-appropriate teaching were the only ones to spontaneously coordinate elements from both domains. In contrast, two thirds of the students in the Moral instructional condition subordinated the issue entirely to its moral elements. Conversely, and as we had expected, a majority of students (including females) in the Convention instructional condition subordinated the issue to its conventional elements.

This last set of findings has particular relevance for our aim to develop students' capacity for critical moral reflection. Obviously, the students in the Convention instructional condition were hampered in their ability to attend to the moral implications of the gender-based conventions of Chicago's Gypsy community. Their prioritization of concerns for social organization was fostered by their recent educational experiences, which heightened the salience of those conventional elements. The social conservatism of their curriculum appeared to foster a similar conservatism in their reading of this real-life social issue. Conversely, the students in the Moral instructional condition prioritized the moral elements of the situation and guided the social arguments made in their essays. The prioritization of morality is recognized in philosophy as a requirement for ethical judgment and behavior (Baumrind, 2004). However, the "idealist" social critics in the Moral condition of our study did not spontaneously consider the social organizational ramifications of their single-minded attention to morality. In real life, however, there are always organizational costs to any change in the conventional social structure. For example, a single-minded attention to needs for gender equality in careers leaves unanswered any number of practical questions in terms of how one should restructure the conventions of the family. When all is said and done, somebody has to do the dishes, raise the children, and so forth.

The students in the domain-appropriate instructional condition did prioritize the moral elements of the situation and argued in their essays against the Gypsy king's decision. However, their arguments also acknowledged the ramifications this decision might have for the conventional organization of Gypsy society and offered constructive suggestions for how those changes might be resolved. When we argue for a critical moral perspective as a goal of domain-appropriate moral education, we are not simply advocating the development of single-minded moral criticism of social conventional systems, but rather this more integrative form of social critique.

In sum, attention to domain in the selection of issues that are the focus of lessons and the wording of questions and assignments is critical to maximizing the effectiveness of lessons for social and moral development. Attention to domain is also critical to the goal of developing students' critical moral perspective.

4. *Make connections to students' own feelings, beliefs, and sense of self and not just to abstract principles or norms.* This principle is consistent with the accepted educational practice of making connections to students' prior knowledge and interests in order to maximize student learning and motivation. It also refers to the goal of engaging students in connecting their social concepts and moral judgment to their construction of a moral self.

Putting This Into Practice

There are some general strategies and practices for attaining the goals and implementing the basic principles listed above. These strategies fall into three basic categories: selection of lesson formats, identification and domain categorization of social development issues, and structuring effective developmental discussions.

Lesson Formats

There are several formats that lessons can take and still be effective for moral and social development. In some cases, lessons, and especially units, will use a combination of formats. However, the one constant across formats is that the lessons include some time for reflective discussion. In most cases it is advisable that the lesson include a written reflection or interpretation either as homework or as an in-class assignment. This encourages additional reflection and further identifies the lesson as an academic activity to be taken seriously by the students. It also provides the teacher with an academic product that can be graded using regular academic standards. We will take up the issue of grading and assessment at the end of the chapter.

Exceptions would be lessons for young children below third or fourth grade where writing is still in the early phase of development. Other exceptions regarding writing could be made for lessons involving artistic expression or mathematics. In these cases the provision of a verbal explanation along with the performance or artistic product would serve as the product to be assessed or graded by the teacher.

Curricular Issue Discussion

The most common format and the one that is most readily used with language arts and social studies content is *issue discussion*. In this format, the teacher identifies moral, conventional, or personal issues ahead of time that are contained within the material that the students are covering. The teacher constructs questions in advance that will be used to guide students' reflective discussion. The lesson can be based directly from the reading the students have done at home or in class, or from a summary provided by the teacher. Some of the teachers we have worked with have created brief fictional scenarios based on the curricular unit to bring the values dimensions of issues to light.

Role Play

In a role play social values issues are embedded in a dialogue created by the teacher, or in collaboration with the students. The dialogue is then acted out and serves as the basis for a related discussion and possible homework assignment. The content of the role play should be connected to the academic content being covered in the class. Teachers we have worked with have created social development role plays based on issues raised in history, language arts, and biological sciences.

Representation Through the Arts

The arts can be employed for social and moral education in two ways. With students in secondary school, the arts can be used as the basis for an issue discussion. In this case, students are asked to respond to the social and moral themes represented in artwork, music, or drama. Examples of such lessons are presented in Chapter 9. The other primary use for the arts is to allow students to represent social or moral issues or concepts through visual media, music, theater, or dance. This is an especially effective mode for students who have difficulty expressing themselves in writing. Representation through the arts can be employed across grade levels.

Representation Through Mathematics

There are several ways in which social and moral issues can be integrated within mathematics lessons. Educators who connect issues of mathematics to social justice have created lessons that ask students to reflect on social issues, such as the relationship between poverty and the likelihood of incarceration, and then use mathematics to investigate available data on those relationships. Mathematics can also be used to represent distributive justice issues in everyday life, such as how four kids would most fairly distribute the money they make working together on a paper route. Such lessons typically involve using statistics, graphing, and constructing equations. Graphic representations are also a good way for students to sort out what they would consider to be moral, conventional, and personal matters. Students can construct Venn diagrams to represent areas of domain overlap to guide their reflections on complex, multifaceted social and moral issues.

Empirical and Library Investigation

Finally, lessons can include the investigation of underlying factual assumptions associated with moral issues. Students might use the library and Internet resources to gather information that would inform their discussions, and/or to find artistic and mathematical representations of social and moral issues. They can also use the tools of empirical sciences, thus combining the learning of scientific methodology with social development. For example, students can construct surveys to sample student opinion about complex issues, such as teasing or bullying. They might also construct simple social psychological experiments with peers to investigate their assumptions about how young people react to moral and social conventional situations.

Identifying and Categorizing Issues by Domain

In order to construct effective moral and social values lessons, the teacher needs to be able to identify the domains of the issues that are to be the focal point of the lessons. The primary reason for doing this is to ensure that the discussions and activities of the students are concordant with the type of issue being considered. The other reason is to ensure that students confront issues from several domains rather than focusing predominantly on either morality or convention, or only considering complex multifaceted issues without the opportunity to hone their concepts and reasoning within each particular domain.

One factor that enters into domain classification of issues is that most real-life events occur in contexts that include some elements from more than one domain. For example, using titles and surnames to address teachers is a matter of social convention. However, respect for other people that can be conveyed through convention does have an element of morality. Constructing lessons that would focus on a single domain, such as convention in the case of teacher titles, means selecting events or issues that are predominantly characterized by features consistent with one domain. What follows are criteria that a teacher can use to identify issues by domain.

Morality

- Does the act affect the welfare of others? If yes, then the act is likely to be moral.
- Would a transgression still be wrong if there were no rule or norm about the act? If yes—because it affects others' welfare—the act is an issue of morality.

Social Convention

- If there were no rule or norm about the act, would the act still be considered a transgression? If no—then the act is a matter of convention.
- Could things be set up differently so that the purposes of the norm could be achieved through a different arrangement? For example, boys could have long hair and girls short hair to differentiate between sexes. If yes—the norm is a convention.
- Is the primary purpose of the norm to coordinate the interactions of people or to organize the system in some way? For example, we walk on the right-hand side to allow efficient movement through the school hallway. If yes—the norm is a convention.

Personal

- Do the effects of the act fall primarily on the actor? Are the effects on the actor benign? If yes to both, then the issue is personal. If yes to the first question and no to the second, then the act is a matter of prudence. Children and younger adolescents generally view prudential issues such as whether to eat healthy foods as matters that parents and teachers can influence or control. Older adolescents and adults generally treat even these latter issues as personal.
- Is the act a matter of privacy? If yes to this question and to the first question above, then the act is personal.
- Is the act an aspect of constructing autonomy and a unique sense of identity? If yes to this question and to the first question above, then the act is personal.

Overlapping or Multifaceted Issues

The above criteria can be used to identify complex social issues that have elements from more than one domain. For example, rules and laws that define who is allowed to vote help to structure how people contribute to governance of a particular social group. Thus, these rules have to do with social organization. These rules can also be changed through social consensus. Thus, voting laws are a matter of convention. On the other hand, voting rules also differentially treat people in ways that give one group of people, voters, more power than other people, nonvoters. Thus, the rules that govern voting have a considerable element of morality to them. A lesson that focused on voting rights and suffrage would, therefore, be one that would address both morality and convention, and how these elements of social life interact with each other. We could do a similar analysis for issues that involve considerable overlap between social convention and the personal domain.

Structuring Effective Developmental Discussions

The key element for moral and social cognitive development is engaging students in meaningful reflection. This can be accomplished in a number of ways including providing students with provocative problems to solve, or assigning readings and written work that provokes reflection. Some examples of provocative writing assignments will be provided in the following chapters. However, the primary tool for engaging students to think in new ways about moral and social issues is developmental discussion. It is through open discussion that students hear differing perspectives and points of view, and experience challenges to their own positions coming from peers as well as the teacher. We see this at an early level in the arguments and negotiations among young children. Without such argumentation, there would be no reason for children to assume that others do not hold the same position as they do, and certainly no reason to assume that the other person might be in the right (Piaget, 1932). At an advanced level, discussion can take place through interactive writing, and we are beginning to see a revolution in that form of communication through the Internet.

There are three general forms that discussions can take. These differing forms map onto conceptual tasks that are associated with the characteristics of domains.

- *Dilemma discussion.* This entails pitting two moral principles against each other, such as stealing versus human welfare. Should you steal bread from a store in order to feed a hungry person?
- *Conflict discussion.* This pits social norms against either moral or personal domain considerations. An example would be whether a boy should follow a school dress code or wear a T-shirt with a rock band logo if he feels it is important to his personal identity.
- *Conceptual discussion.* This form of discussion would be a group effort to try to generate an understanding of the purpose or meaning of a social norm or social or moral construct. An example would be a discussion of the social functions served by differing forms of clothing for formal and informal occasions. Generally, conceptual discussions center on social conventions. However, they can also focus on discussions of moral concepts such as what is meant by fairness, or personal concepts such as why it would matter to maintain some things as matters of personal choice.

In whatever form discourse takes, it must result in changes in the ways that students think about social and moral issues if it is to have an impact on development.

Communicative Discourse: Nine Rules for Having a Good Discussion

In early efforts at moral education, it was assumed that discussions had to take place between people who were within one developmental stage of each other in terms of their moral reasoning (Blatt & Kohlberg, 1975). This was based on experimental research indicating that students do not benefit from exposure to arguments that are either too primitive or too advanced for the student to understand. For this reason, teachers were instructed when leading moral discussions to provide statements one stage above the modal level of the class. This is different from the general educational principle of employing developmentally appropriate issues and posing questions or assignments that are within the developmental range of students. The notion contained in the "plus one" assumption was that teachers should adjust their statements within a free-flowing classroom discussion to match the modal level of the arguments being used by the students.

Research on this "plus one" assumption proved it to have little use in actual classroom discourse (Berkowitz & Gibbs, 1983; Berkowitz, Gibbs, & Broughton, 1980). What this research uncovered is that it is very difficult for teachers to generate plus-one statements in the flow of actual classroom conversation, and they were in fact rare in occurrence. More importantly, even when such plus-one statements were provided by experts, their input into the discussion had less of an impact on students' moral reasoning than did the statements of their classmates. Given that most classrooms have students who vary in level of development within one level or stage of one another, the concern for plus-one discussion is essentially met through the normal range in student diversity of typical classrooms.

Transactive Discussion

When the researchers looked at the factors that made for effective discussion, they discovered that the most important variable was whether or not the statements made by students were efforts to actively transform the arguments that they had heard others make. The researchers labeled such statements *transacts*. Transacts are responses that attempt to extend the logic of the speaker's argument, refute the assumptions of the speaker's argument, or provide a point of commonality between the two conflicting positions. Passive listening and simple efforts to restate or give back the speaker's argument were not associated with conceptual change. This last finding is a rather revealing indictment of simple direct instruction and regurgitation as an educational method.

Communicative Discourse

Encouraging students to engage in transactive discussion has clear developmental and educational benefits. However, there are two important caveats to this statement. First, transactive discussion is not something that can generally be accomplished by children before second or third grade since generating this type of discussion requires linguistic skills and perspective taking that is beyond the developmental levels of young children. Young children are, however, very capable of listening to another child's statements when directed at their own conduct. They can also listen to others and add ideas of their own. As we will see in a moment, young children can be encouraged to engage in what we will refer to as communicative discourse.

A second limitation of a reliance on transactive discourse as the sole element of classroom discussion is that such transacts can be used in two fundamentally different ways. Here we are going to loosely borrow from the distinction the philosopher Jurgen Habermas (1991) makes between strategic action and communicative discourse. When we are engaged in strategic action, our goal is to somehow get the other person to agree with and go along with our own point of view and our own goals. A great deal of our conversations are of this strategic kind. The prototype of strategic discourse is debate. In a debate, the goal is to win the argument. It doesn't matter whether or not the position we take is the most defensible, but whether or not we are able to convince the other, or convince the judges, that we have been able to outdo our opponent in presenting our case. When we are engaged in communicative discourse, however, the goal is to arrive at the best, most compelling position regarding the issue. It is the shared recognition of the force of the reasoning and not the power or skill of the debater that is the winner. In a strategic discourse, the outcome is unilateral; someone wins. In a communicative discourse, the outcome is mutual; the argument wins.

The goal of a developmental discussion is to have the argument win and not an individual student or elite group of students. In our approach to social and moral education, we attempt to engage students in activities that move toward communicative discourse. The approach we have taken makes use of the work on moral dilemma discussion (Lind, 2006; Oser, 1986; Power, Higgins, & Kohlberg, 1989) along with the suggestions and guidance of experienced teachers we have worked with. We are especially indebted to Georg Lind for his guidelines on the pace and timing of dilemma discussions in classrooms. In the recommendations that follow we are assuming that the overall moral atmosphere of the classroom is compatible with this form of instruction. In effect, the use of communicative discourse contributes to an overall moral climate of mutual respect and cooperation that not only serves social growth, but academic achievement as well. As part of a project we did with Elementary District #64 in

Park Ridge, Illinois, we worked with teachers and fifth- and sixth-grade students to come up with the following guidelines for how to structure a good classroom discussion. These guidelines incorporate elements of transacts and translate the basic notions of communicative discourse into language readily accepted by students and teachers. Although these guidelines are the handiwork of elementary school students, they have also been embraced by undergraduates to frame their discussions in my university-level courses.

Nine Rules for a Good Discussion

- *General principle:* The purpose of a good discussion is to work with others to come up with the best set of ideas or ways to deal with a situation. In an argument or a debate, only one side wins. In a good discussion, everybody wins!
    1. Think before you speak.
    2. Listen carefully to what others have to say.
    3. Do not interrupt when some one else is speaking.
    4. Make use of what others have to say when it is your turn to speak.
    5. Only say what you truly believe.
    6. Do not remain silent. Make sure to contribute to the discussion.
    7. Let other people speak. Do not hog the discussion. Once you are done speaking, let at least two other people talk before you speak again.
    8. Support good ideas that other people have, even if they are different from your own.
    9. Search for the best solution even if it is different from the way that you thought at first.

Preparing Students to Engage in Productive Discussion

In working with teachers, we have found that implementing the above nine rules works best when students have an opportunity to discuss what these rules mean, and then to consider which ones they would find difficult to put into practice. We have found that elementary school students from grade 4 through middle school take this discussion very seriously. High school teachers may or may not feel the need to have this list of rules, though as I have mentioned, my own undergraduates have found them useful. This list of rules should also be viewed as a starting point, as students may wish to alter, delete, or add new ones to reflect their own approach toward communicative discourse. The purpose, of course, is to reach consensus on the process of discussion that will lead to genuine efforts to find the best argument rather than to win a debate.

Implementing a communicative discourse of the sort described by the above nine rules requires skills that not all students have developed as part of their linguistic repertoire. What follows are some suggestions for how to prepare students to effectively engage in moral discussion. Students and teachers find these exercises fun. They should be used early in the term to prepare students for later work. They may be used sporadically thereafter, as a way to develop discussion skills, but shouldn't be overdone. These exercises were constructed with the help of Marvin Berkowitz. They make use of the discoveries from his research on transactive discourse, and borrow from practices that teachers have long used to help students engage in productive discussions. The initial listening exercise may be used at all grade levels. The transactive discourse exercises are intended for use with students in grades 4 and above.

Warm-Ups: Learning to Listen

In order for students to discuss one another's ideas and points of view, they need to be able to listen to what each person has to say. There are many exercises that teachers have developed over the years as ways to help students learn to listen. This first one is taken from Aronson and Patnoe's (1997) book, *The Jigsaw Classroom: Building Cooperation in the Classroom*. It is intended to help students realize the importance of turn-taking in a group discussion. Place students in groups of 5 seated in a circle facing one another, and ask them on the count of three to say their names out loud all at once. A brief follow-up discussion with students will quickly reveal that it was very difficult to make out anyone else's name under those conditions.

The second activity is intended simply to address the tendencies among some students to listen to others only in the sense of hearing their voices in order to tell when they have stopped talking so that the listener may begin. This sort of parallel conversation is common among very young children, but it is an affliction that many older students and adults share as well. The purpose of the game is to get each player to accurately paraphrase the statement of another speaker. It is similar to the game "Telephone" except in this case, the goal is accuracy.

> Place students in threes. Player (1) tells something brief about himself to player (2). Player (2) restates it as accurately as possible to player (3). Player (1) then evaluates whether or not the paraphrase was accurate. Player (2) then tells something brief to player (3) with player (2) as the "checker" until all players have had a turn at each role.

Transactive Discourse: Elaboration Game

One of the simpler transacts is to extend the arguments made by a previous speaker. This game may be used directly after the listening game because it extends the use of paraphrase. In this game the student must take into account what the previous person said and elaborate on it. Prior to play, the teacher models a simple elaboration of a previous statement. The teacher then gives the class an interesting issue to discuss. Over the past three years we have used the following issues: Should the Chicago Cubs rehire Sammy Sosa? Should Congress permit stem cell research? Should the mom have a say in whether or not a person your age cleans up his or her room?

> Place students in circles of up to 6 players. Player (1) begins by expressing a point of view. Player (2) paraphrases the statement made by player (1) and elaborates or extends it. Player (3) does the same with the statement made by player (2). This continues until all students have had a turn at extending the argument. With elementary-aged children, the teacher should circulate from group to group to hear whether or not children are accurate in providing elaborations, and help out when this doesn't occur. With junior and senior high school students, the teacher can assign one member of each group to serve as "checker."

Transactive Discourse: Rebuttal Game

The rebuttal game is an extension of the elaboration game and uses the same procedure except that each student must paraphrase and offer a refutation of the argument advanced by the previous speaker.

Transactive Discourse: Integrative Resolution

This final version is intended for use with high school sophomores and above, or very advanced younger students. It requires the students to listen to both an initial argument and its refutation, and then, taking both arguments into account, offer an integrative resolution of the two positions. Prior to this exercise, the teacher should model an integrative resolution.

> Students are placed in groups of six. Player (1) states a position, which player (2) then paraphrases and refutes. Player (3) then paraphrases the positions taken by both players (1) and (2) and offers an argument that resolves the differences between the two positions. Player (2) then offers a new position, which Player (3) refutes and Player (4) integrates. This continues until each player has had a turn at offering an integrative resolution.

Common Questions for Setting Up Discussions

We will close this section by reviewing and providing answers to some common questions teachers raise about how to use discussions for social and moral lessons. These answers are based on our own experiences and those of others who have worked with dilemma discussion (Lind, 2006).

- How do I structure groups? For students in grades 4 and above, groups should have 5 or 6 children. In younger grades children can work in pairs or triads. Groups should be heterogeneous with respect to gender, ethnicity, and academic ability. For dilemma and conflict discussion groups should include children who hold opposing views with at least two members on each side of the issue (in grades 4 and above).

- How do I introduce and sequence the lesson? The following chapters will provide examples of lessons with model questions that the teacher should have prepared in advance to structure discussions.

    1. *Clarify the issues.* To begin the lesson, make sure that everyone understands the issue. Does everyone agree on the facts? It can help to have a brief prepared summary of the particular issue that you want students to focus on. After the initial phase of some moral issue discussions it may be important to help students identify situations where their disagreements are about factual assumptions. For example, discussions about controversial issues such as the death penalty often center around assumptions about whether the death penalty acts as a deterrent, whether it costs less than life imprisonment, if it is applied unevenly by race, if innocent people are put to death, and so on. When such factual assumptions lead to disagreement it is best to have the students research the facts and then return to the moral discussion.

    2. *Clarify feelings and engage in person perception.* This applies to moral, personal, and overlapping issues. This is an especially important element of social emotional learning in elementary and middle school.

    3. *Connect the academic issue to students' personal experience.* There is some disagreement as to whether to begin an issue discussion with the moral or social issues raised in the academic content, or to begin with questions that connect the underlying theme to students' personal experience. Generally, teachers in elementary grades find it more engaging to start with everyday experience and then move toward the more distal academic lesson. However, this is not always the case, especially when dealing with literature or stories. In most cases the lesson should make a connection to personal experience, whether at the beginning or end of the lesson.

    4. *Connect to an academic assignment.* Lessons should generally end with an academic assignment either for in-class work or homework.

- Do I also use whole class discussion, or only small groups? A pattern employed by many teachers is to have a small group discussion followed by a whole class discussion. This allows everyone the benefit of hearing a range of solutions or positions. Generally students participate at a greater level in small group rather than large group discussions.

- Can I use this type of discussion with young children? The short answer is yes, especially with regard to moral dilemmas or moral conflicts. However, these discussions should be integrated into reflective "pairs" reading or other academic activity. Teachers can effectively lead small group and whole class discussions with young children similar to what older children can accomplish in groups on their own. Generally, young children do not have much to say about social conventions. Discussions about conventions are more fruitful in relation to classroom rules or in the context of understanding a story plot than in trying to get young children below grade 3 or 4 to try to figure out the social functions of conventional norms through academic content.

- Can I take a moral position as the teacher? The short answer is yes, but with this caveat. Every time that a teacher provides an answer, it robs the students of the opportunity to construct their own understanding and to come to hold a moral position firmly on their own. The better role for the teacher is to ask the provocative questions, and to prod students into looking for solutions beyond pat answers that will cause them to grow in their moral and social understanding.

- Should I connect the discussion to some other academic assignment? Yes, have homework or other assignments connected to the discussion. This will increase the likelihood of on-task behavior and will help students to deepen their understanding and knowledge.

- How long should this take? For simple issues, about 20 minutes. For complex issues in middle school and high school, it can last up to 35 minutes across two sessions. For children below grade 4, a discussion should last no longer than 10 minutes.

- How often should this be done? No more than twice per week, and no less than once every two weeks.

- Should I plan for particular days each week for moral lessons and discussions? This should be a function of the connection between the academic work of the class and the issues that emerge within the academic content. Social and moral lessons should not occur on an "if this is Friday, it must be honesty day" formula. As in other good teaching always be prepared to raise moral issues during a "teachable moment."

Summary

This chapter provided an overview of the basic elements for constructing a moral and social values lesson using the regular academic curriculum. A guiding principle for constructing such lessons is that they provide a 2 for 1 benefit of increasing moral and social development and contributing to academic learning within the same lesson. The purpose of using the academic content for social and moral lessons is to contribute to the development of students' social and moral knowledge and understanding. A particular advantage of integrating social and moral development with academic content is that it affords an opportunity for reflection on issues that go beyond personal experience. It also allows students to apply their moral knowledge to existing social norms and social structures, particularly as students enter upper elementary grades and secondary school. This gives students the chance to become morally reflective and develop a critical moral perspective, which they can apply to themselves and society.

The basic principle that guides lesson construction is that lessons generate reflection and construction of new social and moral understandings. In order to do this effectively, lessons must be appropriate for the students' age and the activities of the lesson must match the moral, conventional, or personal domain issues contained in the lesson. Finally, lessons should connect to the students' own feelings and sense of self.

Lessons can take several formats including discussion around issues raised in the regular curriculum, role plays, representation through the arts, representation through mathematics, and empirical (scientific) or library investigation. In most cases, lessons will make use of developmental discussion.

Discussions should take the form of communicative discourse in which the goal is to have the best argument or idea emerge, rather than for the most skilled debater to dominate and "win" the discussion. Effective discussions involve having students think about and reflect upon what they are hearing and offer suggestions that make use of what others have to say. This process is referred to as transactive discussion. Teachers can develop students' listening and discussion skills. The chapter offers nine rules that can be helpful for classroom discussion. The chapter ends with answers to common questions teachers raise about how to implement values lessons.

CHAPTER 7

Using the Academic Curriculum for Moral and Social Development in the Elementary Grades (K–5)

Maybe because the other ones were so small and he was the biggest one, and maybe they were all small and friends with each other. He probably thought they were making fun of him because of his height and that's why he started to bully.

—A second-grade girl, the tallest and biggest child in her class,
responding to a student's question as to why Bimbo the pilot whale began ramming
dolphins with his nose.

In this chapter we will look at examples of moral and social development lessons for the elementary grades. It is important to keep in mind that the lessons presented in this chapter and in the subsequent chapters represent a sampling of possibilities. The primary goal is to illustrate lessons that address moral, conventional, personal, and overlapping issues in relation to students' likely developmental levels. A second goal is to provide sample lessons from varying subject matters and formats. We will not provide an example of every format and issue type with every age group or grade level. However, by reading these chapters one should get a very clear picture of how a teacher working at any grade level can construct moral and social development lessons that achieve the 2 for 1 goal of contributing to academic growth along with moral and social development.

Nearly all of the lessons come from work that we have done with classroom teachers and lessons that have been created and implemented by our preservice teacher education majors. In a few cases we have drawn from Internet resources to stimulate lesson structure. With each lesson we will spell out the moral and social development goals of the lesson and describe the academic goals in more general terms. In the work we have done with our students, we have required them to indicate which specific learning standards each lesson addresses. However, because learning standards vary by state, that information will not be included here.

Morality

The Primary Grades (Kindergarten–Grade 2)

The great achievement in the moral development of the young child is the construction of the concept of fairness as just reciprocity (Damon, 1977; Piaget, 1932). The goal of curricular lessons for moral development in the primary grades is to help children to read the emotions and intentions of the protagonists in stories or historical events, and to take them into account when judging what would be the moral or fair outcome of a situation. Lessons should direct children to try to work out solutions that take both sides of a dispute into account. The first step in a moral lesson with young children would fall under the rubric of Social and Emotional Learning (SEL). This initial step involves getting the children to identify the feelings and motivations of the protagonists.

Language Arts

The following example is from the second-grade reading selections of the Chicago Public Schools. It is based on the story of "Bimbo the Big Bully" from the book *Nine True Dolphin Stories* by Margaret Davidson (1974). This story can also be read aloud to younger children who are not yet able to read on their own. The central issue is the fairness of different ways to respond to a bully. It also raises the consciousness of "bullies" to let them see what happens when they act as they do, and also allows the other children to have empathy for what may motivate the bully. The goal is to engage children in seeing the perspectives from both sides and bringing those perspectives together. The tendency for children at this age is to view a tit-for-tat response as a fair way to deal with an aggressor. The dolphins in the story, however, respond differently. This opens up space for children to consider other ways to handle similar situations from a moral perspective.

BIMBO THE BIG BULLY

This story presents an actual incident in which the directors of an oceanarium in San Diego introduced a pilot whale into a tank with several dolphins. At first things went well. But then Bimbo, the pilot whale, began ramming the dolphins with his nose. The director decided to intervene by draining much of the water from the tank so that the dolphins could still swim, but Bimbo could not. When that happened Bimbo became very scared and made sounds that showed how scared he was. The dolphins, hearing his cries, came to comfort him. After that the director raised the water level and Bimbo no longer rammed the dolphins.

LESSON GOALS

1. Identify feelings and motives of characters in the story.
2. Consider what is fair in dealing with someone who harms you by taking into account the perspective of both the character who is harmed and the character doing the harm.

PROCEDURE

Have students read the story in pairs, or for nonreaders, the teacher would read the story out loud. Following the reading, work with students in small groups of up to 7 children for discussion.

Questions to Guide Discussion

1. Do you think Bimbo was trying to hurt the dolphins? Why do you think he would do that?
2. How do you think the dolphins felt when Bimbo kept trying to ram them with his nose?
3. Do you think it was wrong or all right for Bimbo to do that? How come?
4. The director of the oceanarium drains the tank so there isn't enough water for Bimbo to swim around. That scares Bimbo. Why did the director do that?
5. Do you think it was fair for the director to do that to Bimbo?
6. Bimbo was hurting the dolphins. Suppose the dolphins got together and hurt Bimbo back. Do you think that would have been okay? Do you think Bimbo deserved that?
7. When Bimbo was scared the dolphins came to help. What do you think of that? Do you think that the dolphins should have helped Bimbo? After all, Bimbo had hurt them.
8. This story tells us that Bimbo was scared because he was the only whale in the aquarium and was without any whale friends. Have you ever been somewhere without friends? How does that feel?
9. How did what the dolphins did help Bimbo not to feel afraid?
10. Do you think if Bimbo is less afraid he won't act like a bully?

SEL SUPPLEMENTS

This lesson provides several opportunities for children to offer emotions or feelings terms to account for the behaviors of the characters. The creators of the PATHS social-emotional learning curriculum at Penn State advocate having children construct an emotions dictionary. One way to supplement this and other moral lessons is to add these feelings terms to an emotions dictionary that the children can generate as part of their language arts curriculum. The majority of English-speaking children at this age can read and define global terms such as *happy, sad, angry, mad, lonely, scared,* and *worried* (Dale & O'Rourke, 1976).

Beyond using the curriculum to help young children construct their knowledge about feelings and their concepts of fairness, language arts can also be a good context within which to work on children's fears and help them to generate a sense of trust (Watson, 2003) and to construct a worldview based on fairness (Arsenio & Lover, 1995). These early emotional patterns are important for the construction of morality. Teachers we work with in the Chicago Public Schools have supplemented their classroom practices with stories read with their students that deal with some of the sources of their fears and concerns. For example, teachers have used the book *Stars in the Darkness* by Barbara Joosse (2002) to explore and confront children's fears about gangs and street violence. The book tells the story of a kindergarten-aged boy whose fears of the gangs and violence of his neighborhood are elevated when it appears that his older brother may become a gang member. The story is resolved when the mother firmly but lovingly confronts the older brother, and then works with other parents to establish a neighborhood gang watch. The story generally evokes strong and heartfelt responses from children whose own lives touch upon some of these uncomfortable social realities. The messages in the story mirror the messages of trust and support the teachers try to convey through their classroom climate. This social and emotional aspect of the curriculum is not always recognized. However, there are now considerable resources online for teachers interested in making use of what is referred to as "bibliotherapy," the use of children's literature to help children address social and emotional issues.

The Middle Elementary Grades (Grade 3–Grade 5)

Children between grade 3 and grade 5 consolidate their ability to coordinate the perspectives of both sides in a moral situation. However, their notion of fairness still tends to be dominated by a tit-for-tat mentality. Two aspects of development mitigate against this raw form of justice as direct reciprocity. The first is the gradual emergence of concerns for equity in children's moral thinking (Damon, 1977). The other is the tendency of children typically by age 8 to 10 years to begin to attribute mixed feelings to the perpetrators of moral harm. At these ages the child who victimizes another is not viewed simply as experiencing "happiness" at having gotten his way, but is also thought to experience negative emotions such as sadness or sorrow at having caused harm to another (Arsenio, Gold, & Adams, 2004). The goals for curricular lessons focusing on moral development in these middle grades are to engage children in seeing the limitations of a morality based on strict reciprocity, and to move them toward moral positions that are based on "justice as fairness." With respect to related issues of Social and Emotional Learning, moral lessons broaden the horizon of children's knowledge about emotions and engage children in thinking about others in terms of their personalities and personal characteristics.

Language Arts

The first issues we will use to illustrate moral lessons are drawn from Roald Dahl's book, *Charlie and the Chocolate Factory* (1973/2005). The basic plot of this well-known story revolves around a contest run by Willy Wonka in which five child winners and their families will receive a guided tour of his famous chocolate factory. To win a tour a child must find a golden ticket inside the wrappings of a chocolate bar. The hero of the story is Charlie Bucket, a young boy who comes from a poor but loving family. Charlie finds the last golden ticket and goes on the tour with his grandpa Joe. The other four winners are children with notable character flaws. Each of these children ends up being transformed into a confection consistent with his or her character. The story raises moral issues of sharing limited resources and fair responses to offensive behavior. The story also affords excellent opportunities to discuss issues of personality, and allows students to get some perspective on why certain behaviors are unfair, while others are simply socially unappealing. Finally, the story presents several situations that highlight social convention. Those issues will be discussed when we look at lessons focusing on social convention. The lessons that follow are a sample of the moral lessons that could be generated around the events in this book.

CHARLIE AND THE CHOCOLATE FACTORY (GRADE 3)

Lesson 1 (Characteristics of main characters)

GOALS

This first exercise engages children in an evaluation of the personal characteristics of the main child characters in the story. The goal is to engage children in a discussion about aspects of personality (an SEL goal), and also to begin to connect moral and social values knowledge to evaluations of personal behavior.

PROCEDURE

There are two phases to this exercise. In phase one students work either in pairs or small groups. The teacher asks the students to list the five children who won golden tickets and describe the personal characteristics of each child. The teacher should expect the students at this age to describe each child in terms of overt behaviors rather than personality traits. The use of internal personality descriptors does not generally appear in children's language until about age 12. The teacher may provide the students with a worksheet that list the names of the five characters with space for them to write in descriptors.

   a. *Augustus Gloop*—very fat and eats so much candy that he locates a ticket.
   b. *Veruca Salt*—who is so rich she gets what she wants by screaming and demanding things from her parents.
   c. *Violet Beauregard*—a girl who chews gum all the time and puts it behind her ear when she eats.
   d. *Mike Teevea*—watches television all the time.
   e. *Charlie Bucket*—a poor but loving and generous child.

Once children have listed descriptors ask them to rank order the characters from one to five, from least to most likeable, and tell why.

In phase two, the teacher leads a class discussion of the descriptors and rankings the children arrived at in their work in pairs. The teacher should be careful to withhold judgments and let the students sort this out. The teacher can help clarify terms and descriptors. Terms and descriptors can be added to the class vocabulary list.

Lesson 2 (Sharing versus personal property)

GOALS

The goal of this lesson is to engage children in reflection on the morality of sharing versus one's right to maintain control over one's own possessions. The issue of sharing is a complex one that has both developmental and cultural elements. The question is when and under what conditions you are obligated to share as opposed to when sharing is a matter of personal discretion. Children in third grade have generally just entered the phase of moral thinking in which they can take the perspectives of two people into account when arriving at a decision of what is fair. However, sharing is complicated in that the person who is in possession of goods generally has a legitimate personal claim to those goods. So, sharing is not a simple moral issue, but one that also touches on the personal domain of choice and discretion. Our adult social messages to share, along with messages that one should defend one's entitlements, and that one should not expect things from others, make this very confusing for children.

PROCEDURE

Phase 1

The teacher begins by asking children to summarize the main events of Chapter 7. Following this, the teacher provides the following summary and discussion questions to children to work on in pairs.

"Charlie's family is quite poor. For his birthday they buy him a WONKA'S WHIP-PLE-SCRUMPTIOUS FUDGEMALLOW DELIGHT candy bar. When Charlie opens the wrapper, he finds that there is no golden ticket inside. He shrugs his shoulders and then says, 'Here, mother, have a bit. We'll share it. I want every-body to taste it."

1. Why do you think Charlie started to share his candy bar?
2. Should Charlie have to share his candy bar if he doesn't want to?

Phase 2

Following the pairs discussion, the teacher leads a whole class discussion em-ploying the following questions as a guideline.

Questions to Guide Discussion

1. What do you think of what Charlie did?
2. Why do you think Charlie started to share his candy bar?
3. Should Charlie have to share his candy bar if he doesn't want to?
4. It is his birthday present. Should he share his birthday present?
5. None of his family would accept any of his candy. Why do you think that is?
6. Charlie's family is very poor. Do you think that is why Charlie shared? How come?
7. When do we have to share? How can you tell when you have to share and when you don't?

Homework or In-Class Writing

Students are asked to write two to three sentences answering the following questions.

1. Do you think Charlie should have shared his candy bar? How come?
2. Should Charlie have to share his candy bar if he doesn't want to? How come?

Lesson 3 (Justice versus vengeance)

GOALS

Children at this age have a moral perspective that defines justice in tit-for-tat terms. This is why teachers should be careful not to simply allow children to de-termine punishments. The book *Charlie and the Chocolate Factory* comes very close to simply feeding into those atavistic impulses of young children who like to see the moral ledger balanced in a very direct way. The goal here is to get children to begin to consider that vengeful justice may not be fair.

PROCEDURE

Once students have completed their reading of the book, place students in pairs with a handout listing the names of the four child characters (other than Charlie).

1. Ask students to list what happens to each of the four children while they are in the chocolate factory.

2. For each character have the students consider whether the punishment was fair, or not.

Following the pairs work bring the class together for a discussion about each character employing the following format. First read lines from the book that describe what occurs to each character. Then follow each description with discussion questions. For example, for Augustus Gloop ask the children to consider the following lines from the "Oompa Loompa" song:

This boy, who only just before

Was loathed by men from shore to shore,

This greedy brute, this louse's ear,

Is loved by people everywhere!

For who could hate or bear a grudge

Against a luscious bit of fudge?

Questions to Guide Discussion

1. Do you think it would be right to turn Augustus into fudge? Would that be fair?
2. How come Charlie asked if they were joking?
3. Why did his grandpa say, "At least I hope they're joking, don't you?" (p. 86).

Do a similar sort of analysis with the children of the other characters. Veruca and her parents end up covered in garbage; Violet ends up permanently purple; Mike Teevea ends up stretched out to 10 feet.

Homework or In-Class Writing

Select one of the four characters and write a three- to five-sentence paragraph describing what you think would have been a fair way to help your character change his or her behavior.

Role Play Justice versus Vengeance (Grade 5)

The issue of justice versus vengeance is one that emerges in language arts and in social studies. It is also an issue that recurs throughout the curriculum across grade levels. We will end the presentation of lessons focusing on moral issues with a role play that was developed for use with students in grade 5 by teachers in Park Ridge, Illinois, District #64. The title of the role play is "The Movie." However, the teachers gave it the subtitle "Sweet Revenge." This particular role play was very highly rated by students who evaluated it as part of a more general program evaluation. The story makes use of issues of peer pressure and peer inclusion and exclusion. These were issues that our focus group found were central concerns of the students.

PROCEDURE

The teacher prepares copies of the role play narrative for all students in the class. The narrative presented here is the teacher's version. It contains the script to be given out to students along with the script to guide the teacher in running the class discussion.

The teacher selects six students (3 boys, 3 girls) to enact the role play. Two of the boys are assigned roles as narrators (Narrator 1, 2). One of the girls is assigned the role of Caitlin, Popular Girl 1; a second girl is Ginny, Popular Girl 2; the third girl is Jennifer, an Unpopular Girl. The third boy is assigned the role of Jennifer's brother Jack.

The teacher allows time for the six students to absorb their roles. The teacher then introduces the role play and leads an ongoing class discussion following the script.

Script

Teacher Okay, let's shift gears a bit. We've been talking today about different things that have to do with fairness and how we treat other people. Sometimes it happens that we are the ones who end up on the short end of things.

How do you guys feel when someone does something mean or unfair to you? What do you feel like doing to the person who was mean or unfair to you? Okay, that's what this next situation is about. [The teacher signals the students to begin.]

Narrator 1 In this scene we see two popular girls, Ginny and Caitlin, discussing whom to get together to go to see the movie "(name of current movie title)."

Ginny Boy, I would really like to invite Jack—he is sooo cute. But if we invite him, we have to invite his creepy sister too.

Caitlin Ugh, she is the worst. I, like, have to hold my nose to be near her, she's so fat and gross. I mean, is she adopted?

Ginny I know! We can tell her that we are all going to see the movie in the next theater. We can get Jack to get her into the theater and then once it starts he can say he has to get popcorn and ditch her and then join us.

Caitlin Oh—you are so evil. I love it. But we have to get Jack to go along.

Ginny Don't worry, he'll do it. Besides, his mother always makes him drag her along. He doesn't like her any more than we do.

Narrator 1 At the movies: Jack and his sister are sitting together.

Jennifer Jack, where is everybody else?

Jack Don't worry, they'll be here soon. Hey, listen, I have to go get some popcorn. [Jack leaves]

Narrator Half an hour passes.

[The girl portraying Jennifer acts this out as the narrator reads.] Jennifer is really anxious. She looks in the lobby. Then she pokes her head into the next theater and sees Jack with the other kids. Jennifer is devastated, and goes back to her seat in the other theater.

When the movie ends, Jack and the other kids leave without Jennifer, who is left alone at the theater.

Teacher Okay folks, let's just take a second here. How does Jennifer feel right now?

How do you think she feels toward her brother and his friends? Okay. Try to get that feeling for yourself for a minute and let's follow the rest of the story.

Narrator 2 It's a week later and Jennifer is still upset at what happened to her. And then it happened! The school arranges for everyone to go to Great America as long as they have their money and parent permission forms in on time. The day before the Great America trip, Jennifer goes to the school office to do her service hours helping the school secretary. When she arrives, the secretary asks her to take care of things in the office while the secretary goes to the bathroom. Jennifer is all alone in the office when she notices something amazing. All the Great America parent permission slips are sitting on the secretary's desk. Then Jennifer gets an idea for what she calls "sweet revenge." All she has to do is go through the pile quickly and get her brother's and the popular girls' permission forms from the pile. No one will know until it's too late—and the kids who treated her so mean at the movie won't get to go to Great America.

Teacher

1. What do you think Jennifer should do? Why? (There is no chance that she will get caught or get in trouble.)
2. Well, let's say that Jennifer does destroy the permission forms and the kids who treated her badly don't get to go to Great America. Wouldn't that be justice? Why?/Why not?
3. Have you ever gotten "sweet revenge" on somebody? How does it feel?
4. Is there any difference between justice and revenge? What would the difference be?
5. If you were Jennifer's friend, and you knew how hurt she was by what her brother and the girls did, what advice would you give her? How come? Why is that good advice?

Those were some great ideas. Let's take a moment and write down some suggestions for what a person should do when someone else has done something unfair or mean to them. How should you react? What are some good ideas about what to do in that kind of situation?

[After the students have had some time to write down their ideas, the teacher would then ask:]

Okay, let's share some of these ideas. [The teacher asks students to share their suggestions.]

Homework

As a homework assignment the class is asked to write a two-paragraph essay responding to the following questions:

What do you think Jennifer should have done? Why?
Is there any difference between justice and revenge? What would the difference be?

Social Convention

The Primary Grades (Kindergarten–Grade 2)

As we learned in Chapter 3 children at this age tend to have a fairly fixed notion of conventions as describing this aspect of social reality as the way it is supposed to be. For example, boys don't wear dresses because that is what girls are supposed to do. Most of the growth in young children's concepts about convention is going to emerge from their everyday lived experiences of witnessing contradictions to these assumptions of consistency. An example would be interacting with a neighbor man whom children call by his first name rather than Mr. Initially these inconsistencies are simply chalked up as error by children. Eventually (generally grade 3) children use these counter examples as evidence that conventions do not matter. This later period of transition opens up the shift to the construction of a concrete understanding of convention as structuring social order that emerges in the middle grades (generally grade 5). Given these developmental constraints, the most constructive way to integrate the curriculum with young children's concepts of convention is to help them to attend to the contextual nature of these norms.

Typically, primary grade social studies includes units on community. In some cases these units provide young children with introductions to modes of dress and everyday customs of different cultures. These units can often afford the teacher a chance to ask children to make note of the differences in the ways in which people dress in one culture versus another. At a more concrete level children can discuss everyday contexts such as school and play where people dress and speak to one another differently.

The Middle Elementary Grades (Grade 3–Grade 5)

Children in grades 3 and 4 tend to view conventions as unimportant because there are exceptions to their application, such as the neighbor man whom children can call by his first name instead of Mr. In fourth grade children are shifting to an understanding of conventions as reflecting a concrete social hierarchy that serves to provide order and reduce chaos. At this point norms are not yet integrated within a conception of societies as systems. However, by fifth grade most children affirm conventions as important to uphold because they reduce "running in the halls" and other forms of social disorder. Lessons designed for third and fourth grade should direct children to try to figure out the concrete social organizational function served by convention. Lessons for fifth-grade children can begin to make use of their understanding of convention to start to explore how conventions structure social life, and how they interact with morality. The lessons that follow will illustrate these goals. We begin with a use of *Charlie and the Chocolate Factory* to address conventions in grade 3. We will then shift to examples of lessons at grade 5 dealing with domain overlap between convention and morality.

Language Arts Charlie and the Chocolate Factory *(Grade 3)*

MODES OF DRESS (CLEANLINESS)

GOALS

Conventions seem arbitrary to children at this age. This lesson employs conventions of cleanliness and formal dress to engage students in moving toward the view that such conventions are established by authorities to establish some concrete order to things. In particular, how we dress is related to the formality of the context and the importance of a social event.

PROCEDURE

Once children complete their pairs reading, the teacher gives them a handout with the following passage and questions to discuss. The teacher reads the passage aloud to ensure that everyone has the content.

> "There's not a moment to lose. You must start making preparations at once! Wash your face, comb your hair, scrub your hands, brush your teeth, blow your nose, cut your nails, polish your shoes, iron your shirt, and for heaven's sake, get all the mud off your pants! You must be ready, my boy! You must be ready for the biggest day of your life!" (p. 57)

1. How come Grandpa Joe wanted Charlie to do all of those things?
2. Why does it matter how Charlie was dressed and how he looked?
3. What does it mean to dress up? When are we supposed to dress up? How come?

Once children have discussed these questions in pairs, the teacher leads the whole class in a discussion using the following questions as a guideline.

Questions to Guide Discussion

1. How come Grandpa Joe wanted Charlie to do all of those things?
2. Why does it matter how Charlie was dressed and how he looked?

3. What does it mean to dress up? When are we supposed to dress up? How come?

4. How should we dress when we go to school?

5. Should we be able to dress at school the same as when we play, or should we dress differently? How come?

6. How about if we go out to a restaurant with our parents? How should we dress then?

7. Shouldn't you be able to dress the way that you want to?

8. When are you free to dress any way that you want, and when should you dress up? How come? How can you tell?

The issue of dress in the above example is an interesting one because there are aspects of dress that are personal in nature. For example, even within the conventional constraints that children should be clean and wear nice clothes in formal social settings such as at a restaurant, school, or church, there is usually some latitude to allow for personal expression through such things as choice of color of the dress or shirt we wear. We will describe a lesson that builds on the personal domain component of dress in the section that follows. This boundary between what is personal and what is a legitimate matter of social convention adds to the complexity for children in negation phases (grades 3–4, 7–9) of thinking about social convention. Other social conventions, such as the use of titles to address adults of different status (e.g., teachers, judges), table manners, and tardiness are less subject to assimilation to the personal domain. As we will illustrate in the following chapters these issues are also present in language arts and social studies and can be used as content for lessons focusing on convention.

The Personal

The Primary Grades (Kindergarten–Grade 2)
Language Arts

As we saw above with the story "Bimbo the Big Bully" language arts can appeal to children's imaginations as they begin to generate reading skills. Young children are also exploring the boundaries between conventions that define what everyone does and personal expression that helps to create oneself as a unique person. Several children's books deal with such themes. One of the books that young children we have worked with find especially interesting is *Ella Sarah Gets Dressed* by Margaret Chodos-Irvine (2003). The book presents a story about a girl who wants to dress in a particular way despite the mild objections of her parents. The story, which can be read by second-grade children or read aloud to younger ones, pits personal choice and expression through dress against the wishes of authority. The story does not challenge the basic convention that children wear clothes. Nor does it deal with a social institutional setting where particular clothes are called for. Thus, the story is very similar in structure to the naturally occurring dispute that we observed between a young child and parents over personal expression though dress that was described in Chapter 2.

ELLA SARAH GETS DRESSED

One morning, Ella Sarah got up and said, "I want to wear my pink polka-dot pants, my dress with orange-and-green flowers, purple-and-blue striped socks, my yellow shoes, and my red hat."... Her mother said, "That outfit is too dressy. Why don't you wear your nice blue dress?" But Ella Sarah said, "No, I want to wear my pink polka-dot pants."

(Chodos-Irvine, 2003)

LESSON GOALS

1. Identify feelings and motives of characters in the story.
2. Consider how choice about personal issues may connect to establishing oneself as an individual.
3. Differentiate this situation from ones in which the child should conform to convention.

PROCEDURE

Have students read the story in pairs, or for nonreaders, the teacher would read the story out loud. Following the reading, work with students in small groups of up to 7 children for discussion.

Questions to Guide Discussion

1. Why did Ella Sarah want to wear the clothes that she chose?
2. How do you think Ella Sarah felt when her mom said that she should wear different clothes?
3. How do you think Ella Sarah's mom felt when Ella Sarah said, "No" and told her mom and her dad and her sister that she wanted to wear the clothes that she had picked out for herself?
4. Why do you think that Ella Sarah didn't wear the clothes that her family wanted her to wear, and instead wore the clothes that she wanted to wear?
5. Have you ever had a favorite thing to wear? Who should decide when you wear your favorite things? How come?
6. Suppose you could never decide for yourself what you wear. Would that be okay? How come?

7. Can you think of places where people have to wear special clothes? How about at church or a restaurant?

8. Suppose that Ella Sarah's mom had asked her to wear the blue dress because they were going out to a special place where kids are supposed to dress a certain way. Would Ella Sarah have been right to wear what she wanted to instead? How come?

This issues raised in this story are basic to normal children's development. As we saw in Chapter 2, personal choice is essential to individuation and autonomy. However, the child's defiance in this story can be viewed by some parents as sending the wrong message to children. Despite the book having received a Caldecott Medal and a large number of supportive reviews from parents, some parent reviewers have objected to its message. The following review, posted on Amazon.com, is illustrative.

> While I will say that the illastrations [sic] were lovely, and the text paints a very cute picture of a stubborn [sic] yet cute toddler, I have to say that this book was put up high on a shelf and will not be read again any time soon. WHY? Because throughout the book, Ella Sarah gets her way by being consistantly [sic] disobedient to her parents and older sibling, and throws (in my opinion) a temper tantrum to get her way! but in the end her BAD behavior is considered "CUTE" because after all, its [sic] more important to express your individuality. . . . It is very disappointing that a book like this received an acclaimed childrens[sic] literature award. The behavior that is portrayed and treated as acceptable (while it may be cute to Grandma) is not behavior I believe most parents would truly tolerate from their toddler.

Teachers engaging in education for children's moral and social development will always need to be mindful that asking children to consider and discuss actions that run counter to authority can be controversial and sometimes problematic. A basic premise of this book, based on developmental research and moral philosophy, is that genuine moral growth can only come about through consideration of such issues. A decision to take on topics of controversy has to be weighed carefully. In this case, our approach to the lesson did not end with Ella Sarah's defiance, but endeavored to engage children in sorting out legitimate areas and forms of protest and situations in which compliance with convention is the appropriate course of action.

Mixed Domain Issues: Conventional—Moral

Students at all ages confront issues that involve overlap between morality and social convention. For example, children in primary grades can experience a contradiction between school or classroom norms and what they perceive to be fair school practices (Thorkildsen, 1989, 2002). Children can be brought into meaningful discussion about such actual classroom rules and practices, as we learned in Chapters 4 and 5.

In terms of the academic curriculum, however, the most effective lessons engaging students in considering issues of moral-conventional conflict or overlap take place after children have constructed a concrete understanding of convention in relation to social structure and hierarchy. This generally does not emerge until about fifth or sixth grade. The following multi-day lesson is an example of how issues of overlap can be addressed in fifth- and sixth-grade social studies. The lesson deals with aspects of the institution of slavery. The teachers we have worked with have developed a number of lessons across grade levels dealing with the morality of slavery. The following lesson does not address slavery per se, but delves into the motivations that led plantation owners to constrain the conventions and customs of their slaves, and the impact of those actions. The lesson was developed for use with students in a predominantly White suburban school district. However, we have successfully used a similar simulation in predominantly African American and racially diverse classrooms. The key in all such contexts is to have role assignment be independent of the student's actual racial or ethnic background. Variations on this lesson can be used in later grades where one would expect more comprehensive arguments than can be advanced by fifth- and sixth-grade students.

SIMULATION ACTIVITY TO ACCOMPANY EXPLORATION OF SLAVERY (GRADE 5)

(Prepared by Sue Kleckner, Park Ridge, IL, District #64)

GOALS

The purpose of this activity is to help students gain insight into the reasons that slave owners attempted to control the customs and conventions of Africans as an aspect of the institution of slavery as it was practiced on plantations in the southern parts of Colonial America. Students will reflect on the functions of social convention and customs in establishing society and culture, and will consider the moral implications of the dominant culture eradicating the conventions and customs of the subordinate culture.

CONTENT AREA

Social Studies—Colonial America.

PROCEDURE

Phase I

Students are divided into five teams that are heterogeneous in terms of gender, ethnicity (where applicable), and academic ability. Four of the teams will play the role of African slaves. The fifth team, made up of four students, will represent plantation owners who want to run a successful, profitable plantation that raises a cash crop to be sold for a profit.

During one class period students who will play the role of slaves will meet with their team and decide on the important customs that will characterize their particular group. These customs can/will include clothing, men's work, women's work, ways of raising children, marriage customs, language, religious observances, daily rituals, and so on. Preferably, these customs would be based on research into actual tribes that made up groups of slaves. Alternatively, students can make up conventions and customs for their cultural group. This decision is based on time constraints and maturity of the group. The four students who will serve as plantation owners will spend the class period researching the history of southern plantations.

> **Teacher** We read in our chapter on the Southern colonies that plantation owners often outlawed or limited the practice of African customs and conventions among their slaves. You have been divided up into four groups, each group representing a group of slaves from an area of West Africa. Four of you will represent plantation owners trying to run a successful and profitable plantation. On any given plantation you would have slaves from each of these four groups.

Phase II

During the second class period the teacher asks each of the four groups to provide a brief resume of their customs. The teacher posts a butcher paper page on the wall listing the customs and conventions of each group. Once all of the customs and conventions are posted, the teacher leads the class in a discussion of the similarities and differences among the customs of each group.

Questions to Guide Discussion

1. Okay, what similarities do you see across each team?
2. What are the main differences?
3. Okay, now let's imagine that you want all of the people from these four tribes to work efficiently together. How well do you think that a plantation will operate if the groups retain all of their customs and conventions?
4. The teacher would focus the class on customs or practices that are in conflict. For example, the teacher would direct their attention to holidays or days of worship that fall on different days for different groups, different roles played by men and women from different groups, and so on, which would disrupt the social order of a plantation.

Homework

The four students acting as plantation owners gather together to decide what customs and practices they will not allow and what customs and conventions they will permit all groups to share. Finally, they will consider what customs and conventions they will impose from the dominant society in order to make their plantations more efficient.

Students in the four "tribal" groups write an essay indicating which customs and conventions of their group are most important to maintain and why.

Phase III

A third class period begins with the students in the role of plantation owners presenting the list of customs and conventions they will allow and which customs and conventions they will eliminate. The teacher posts the list of approved conventions and customs on the wall.

Students within the four "tribal" groups are given 15 minutes to convene and discuss their reactions to having their customs and conventions constrained. Each group is to address the following questions in their discussions.

1. How do you feel about having your customs eliminated or changed?
2. What effect does this have on your society?
3. How will it affect your children?

While the discussion among the tribal groups takes place, the students portraying plantation owners are to spend the time preparing answers to the following questions:

1. Why would you as plantation owners not want slaves to follow their customs?
2. What would be the problems if you had slaves from groups with different customs and conventions on your plantation?

Following the small group discussion, the teacher convenes the entire class. The teacher asks the class as a whole to address the questions they had discussed in small groups beginning with concerns of the plantation owners and then the slaves to address the issues of social convention. These questions about convention are then followed by questions on the morality of the actions taken by the plantation owners.

Convention

1. Why would plantation owners not want slaves to follow their customs?
2. What would be the problems for plantations if they had slaves from groups with different customs and conventions?
3. Why would slaves want to keep their conventions and customs?
4. How does adopting the conventions established by the plantation owners change the societies of the slaves?

Moral

Okay, let's take a minute to think and then we will have a vote. Okay, first we have the needs of the plantation owners to run their plantations efficiently. We also have the effect that eliminating conventions will have on the societies of the slaves.

Okay, close your eyes and raise your hands when we vote. Do you think that it was all right or do you think it was wrong for the plantation owners to decide what conventions and customs they will have on their plantations? Those who believe it was all right raise your hands; those who think it was wrong raise your hands. The teacher then engages the class in a discussion to flesh out the moral arguments surrounding the fairness of the plantation owners' actions. In most cases the plantation owner position ends up being the minority view. The teachers role in the beginning of the discussion is to make sure that all of the arguments are listened to, including those students who defend the decisions of the plantation owners. The ensuing discussion should follow the rules of communicative discourse described in Chapter 6 with the goal of moving toward a consensus on what is the moral position to take in this issue and the moral justification for that position.

Homework

At the end of the discussion the teacher addresses the class to set up the homework assignment.

Teacher Now let's think a minute. This actually happened in history. What impact do you think that it has had on the people who were slaves and their descendants? Suppose this were to happen to you now. Do you think that you would completely give up your customs? Would it matter to you?

How would you hang on to them if you wanted to? Do you think that any customs or conventions from the Africans survived?

The teacher then assigns students to work in pairs to use the library and Internet resources to find out what African customs and conventions continue within American society.

CHAPTER 8

Using the Academic Curriculum for Moral and Social Development in Middle School Grades (6–8)

I wonder if I've been changed in the night? Let me think. Was I the same when I got up this morning? I almost think I can remember feeling a little different. But if I'm not the same, the next question is "Who in the world am I?" Ah, that's the great puzzle!

—Lewis Carroll, *Alice in Wonderland*

The middle school years from ages 11 to 14 are an important transition period in children's social development. The increased cognitive abilities coupled with rapid physical changes associated with this age present challenges not only to schools and teachers, but also to the young people, who like Alice in the quote at the top of the chapter, are directly experiencing the impact of these dramatic physical, emotional, and cognitive shifts. Not surprisingly, early adolescence is associated with transitions in all three social cognitive domains.

Although some adults tend to view the middle school years in terms of problems and difficulties, most middle school teachers recognize this period as one filled with opportunities to help young people construct their personal identities and social and moral value systems. It is in this latter spirit that this chapter will discuss ways in which to engage social and moral development of early adolescents through the academic curriculum. These lessons were originally designed for use in grades 6–8. However, because children develop at different rates, the lessons may be adapted for use with students in ninth grade (freshman year) of high school. For reasons of chapter length the examples of lessons focusing on overlaps between morality and convention are not included here. Several examples are provided in Chapter 9 (high school) that can be adapted for use with students in grades 7 and 8.

Morality

As we learned in Chapter 3 the middle school years are associated with important gains and challenges in students' moral reasoning. On the plus side, most young people are moving away from the direct reciprocity, tit-for-tat conception of fairness that characterizes the justice reasoning of elementary grade students. Fairness for the young adolescent means more than coming out even. It also includes compassion and an increased willingness to consider the needs and abilities of people involved in moral situations. Thus, when it comes to issues involving the distribution of opportunities and goods, children at this age attempt to coordinate concerns for equality with attention to equity, opening them up to greater sensitivity to social injustice.

On the other hand, the increased cognitive capacities and social knowledge of middle schoolers can lead them to see "grey" areas in moral situations, which can result in decisions that younger and older children would find less than moral. When perceived moral ambiguity is coupled with the early adolescent expansion of the personal domain, middle school students tend to assert their "rights" and to appear more self-interested in ambiguous moral situations than do older high school students or students in middle elementary grades.

Thus, as most middle school teachers can testify, students at this age are morally complex and contradictory. The trick for us as moral educators is to engage the strands of moral idealism evident in the moral thinking of early adolescence to move them through this transitional period toward a more integrated conception of morality. The following lessons illustrate efforts to connect several strands in the moral thinking of middle school students. The first two lessons are from social studies; the third is from mathematics.

Social Studies

The first lesson was designed to be part of a sixth-grade world history unit on the ancient Egyptians. There are many moral issues that one could address within this topic area. The particular issue that was the focus of this lesson did not center upon Egyptian history or culture per se, but rather the way in which Western countries have obtained artifacts from ancient civilizations. This topic meshes rather nicely with early adolescent moral reasoning about situations that may result in indirect harm.

TREASURES IN THE PYRAMID

GOALS

This lesson addresses the moral ambiguity students at this age tend to perceive in situations of indirect harm. The "indirect stealing" scenario described in Chapter 3 in which the protagonist has to decide whether to tell a person he or she has dropped money while paying the bus driver, or not tell and keep the money is an example of an indirect harm situation. In contrast with direct harm, such as hitting someone, indirect harm results from the actor's failure to act in a way that would prevent harm to another person, or in which the actor takes advantage of a loss suffered by another person. The goal of this lesson is to sensitize students to the moral impact of the failure to be proactive in such indirect harm situations. In the following lesson, the morality of the indirect harm of keeping artifacts found in an ancient culture is weighed against the moral claims that could be made by the beneficiaries of the discovery and removal of the artifacts, such as the people who attend museums in Western countries.

PROCEDURE

The unit was drawn from a passage in the course textbook that is paraphrased below. Students were asked to read the passage and then to engage in small group discussion followed by a whole class teacher-led discussion.

> In the 1800s many people searched for treasure in ancient countries. They went to ancient sites, such as the pyramids in Egypt, searched for lost artifacts, and sold them for profit. One such treasure hunter was Giuseppe Ferlini. In 1834 he went to a site near the Nile River where he dug for two months under the pyramid of Amanishakheto. He discovered a chamber under the pyramid filled with beautiful items of gold, silver, and bronze. Ferlini returned to Germany with the treasure and sold it to a museum where it can still be seen today. Some people argue that these artifacts, like the findings of other treasure hunters, should be returned to the countries in which they were found.

Questions to Guide Discussion:

1. Do you think Giuseppe Ferlini did the right thing by selling the treasures to the museum? Or do you think he should have returned the artifacts to the Egyptian descendants of the people who created them? Explain your answer.
2. Many people learn about ancient Egypt and other cultures by visiting museums. Should these people's interests be taken into account or should we only be concerned with the interests of the descendants (Egyptians)?
3. Whose rights are more important here, the community's (Egypt) property rights, or the rights of treasure hunters like Ferlini to keep what they find? Explain.

The following questions are intended to link this abstract situation to students' everyday experiences and to help make a connection to themselves at a personal level. Some of the teachers we have worked with have started with the next set of questions, and then brought in the more abstract issue from Egyptian history. Our recommendation would be to alternate formats across lessons, moving between the academic and personal levels. In all cases we recommend that the lesson connect back to students' personal experience.

4. Have you ever found something valuable and wondered what to do with it? If yes, what did you choose to do?
5. Is it your responsibility to return an item to its rightful owner, or is it all right to keep or sell it? Explain.
6. Have you ever heard the expression "Finders keepers, losers weepers"? Do you agree with this phrase? Why/Why not?

Homework or In-Class Writing

Following the whole class discussion, students were asked to provide written responses to the following questions:

1. Do you think Giuseppe Ferlini did the right thing by selling the treasures to the museum? Or do you think he should have returned the artifacts to the Egyptian descendants of the people who created them? Explain your answer.
2. Whose rights are more important here, the community's (Egypt) property rights, or the rights of treasure hunters like Ferlini to keep what they find? Explain.

EXPANDING THE LESSON

This lesson can be expanded by directing students to use the Internet or library resources to investigate how museums are currently dealing with this type of situation. In our case, we were able to direct students to explore the Web site of the Field Museum of Natural History in Chicago, and to contact the curator of the permanent exhibit "Inside Ancient Egypt" to receive their policy on displaying the artifacts that include mummies of adults and children. The museum Mission Statement, which includes a clear ethical policy connecting the museum with the cultural groups represented in the museum collections, can be found at the following Web page: http://www.fieldmuseum.org/museum_info/mission_statement.htm. This expanded activity furthers the link between the class discussion and ethical issues dealt with in real life, and also contributes to students' academic research skills.

JOHN BROWN'S RAID

GOALS

This lesson engages students in weighing the ethical and moral implications of the use of violence to achieve a moral good. This lesson builds on the themes of justice versus vengeance raised in the lessons discussed in Chapter 7. However, the issues raised in this particular lesson open up questions as to whether violence is ever justified as a means to address a moral wrong. The central focus of the lesson comes from the antebellum period leading up to the Civil War. It is drawn from an issue discussed as part of American history taken by students in the eighth grade in the state of Illinois. The issue itself, however, and many aspects of the following lesson can be readily adapted for students in high school American history. The focus of the lesson is on a retaliatory raid led by John Brown and his sons against a settlement in Missouri.

PROCEDURE

Students are asked to read about John Brown in their textbook. Following their reading, the teacher presents the class with the following summary for small, group, and subsequent whole class discussion.

> In May, 1856, a border raid from Missouri, a pro-slavery state, devastated the anti-slavery town of Lawrence, Kansas. Within a few days, John Brown, who strongly opposed slavery, together with his sons and a few companions retaliated by attacking a settlement at Pottawatomie Creek, Missouri. The raid killed five settlers. John Brown hoped that his actions would spark a slave rebellion. However, that did not occur.

Questions for Discussion and Homework

1. Was John Brown justified in leading a retaliatory raid against the pro-slavery settlement? How come?
2. How far should a person go in retaliation? Is it right to hurt others as much as they have hurt you or the people that you care about? How come?
3. Is there a difference between vengeance and justice?
4. Brown had hoped that his actions would set off a slave rebellion. If that had taken place, would it have justified the raid? Why/Why not?

EXPANDING THE LESSON

The John Brown saga poses a series of rich moral questions. Indeed, while many of us would argue that what John Brown did was morally wrong, some adults would make the case that John Brown should be seen as a hero. My friend and colleague William Ayers and his wife Bernadine Dorn are among the people who pay homage to John Brown each year by visiting his gravesite on his birthday.

You may wish to take the discussion in several directions. One is to bring the issue closer to home and to build upon question 2 above to further discuss acts of retaliation adolescents take against people who have harmed them in some way.

Another route is to connect the John Brown raid with modern acts of political retaliation and violence such as abortion clinic bombers who believe their actions serve to protect the innocent unborn. With older high school students, you might bring in the argument advanced in defense of terrorism (which most people view as abhorrent and unjustified) as an act of self-defense used by less powerful political groups against an alleged more powerful oppressor.

One of the most effective extensions we have employed has been to follow up the discussion and homework about the John Brown incident with the writings of Martin Luther King Jr. and Malcolm X on the issue of violence as a means for social change and self-defense. This particular extension, which works effectively with middle school and high school students, has the added benefit of attending to racial and ethnic diversity in a natural and unforced way. Our approach has been to introduce two quotations that students can also find at the end of Spike Lee's movie *Do the Right Thing.*

> Violence as a way of achieving racial justice is both impractical and immoral. It is impractical because it is a descending spiral ending in destruction for all. The old law of an eye for an eye leaves everybody blind. It is immoral because it seeks to humiliate the opponent rather than win his understanding; it seeks to annihilate rather than to convert. Violence is immoral because it thrives on hatred rather than love. It destroys community and makes brotherhood impossible. It leaves society in monologue rather than dialogue. Violence ends by defeating itself. It creates bitterness in the survivors and brutality in the destroyers.   —Martin Luther King Jr.

> I think there are plenty of good people in America, but there are also plenty of bad people in America and the bad ones are the ones who seem to have all the power and be in these positions to block things that you and I need. Because this is the situation, you and I have to preserve the right to do what is necessary to bring an end to the situation, and it doesn't mean that I advocate violence, but at the same time I am not against using violence in self-defense. I don't even call it violence when it's self-defense, I call it intelligence.   —Malcolm X

The teacher presents each passage one at a time, preferable with an overhead or PowerPoint, and asks a student to read the passage aloud. Following the reading the students are instructed to discuss in small groups what the author meant, and then share their interpretations with the entire class. Once this has been done with each passage the teacher directs the students to discuss the following questions in small groups and then share their ideas during a whole class discussion. These questions then form the basis for a written homework assignment.

Questions for Discussion and Homework

1. Which of these positions do you favor? Why?
2. Can you integrate these two positions? How would you do it?

Mathematics

In both middle school and high school contexts instruction is generally no longer within a contained classroom. Instead students tend to shift classes and teachers with each subject area. This creates a concern among secondary teachers that the use of the curriculum for moral education can only be achieved in certain subject areas such as English or social studies in which the course content touches directly on aspects of social norms and behavior. Although it is undoubtedly easier to identify moral and social issues in those subject areas, it is not the case that issues of morality cannot be included within courses outside of literacy and social studies. In this chapter and in the following (Chapter 9) we will introduce lessons for moral development within the context of mathematics and the arts. In Chapter 9, I present an example from freshman algebra developed with one of our preservice teachers that illustrates the use of mathematics in the context of an everyday peer-based moral issue. The following math example, however, comes from a burgeoning movement to coordinate mathematics with what is referred to as "social justice" education. The specific example comes from a lesson developed by my colleague Rico Gutstein, intended for grades 7–8, on the topic of statistics and probability. The lesson is included with his permission. The social justice issue has to do with assumptions about racial profiling. Integrating contemporary social justice issues with moral education is consistent with the goal of engaging students in the process of critical moral reflection and moving beyond the formation of merely "nice" people. However, connecting social justice with academics is an issue of some controversy. Critics, such as Diane Ravitch (2005), express concerns that attention to contemporary moral issues such as social class or racial inequalities competes with the primary aims of education. Such criticisms might have merit if it were the case that attention to moral development came at the cost of academic success. In fact, there is mounting evidence that attention to moral and social development may enhance academic performance (Berkowitz, Battistich, & Beier, 2008; Durlak & Weissberg, 2007). Finally, encouraging students to employ their moral knowledge to improve society is a goal broadly shared by educators including proponents of mainstream character education (Lickona, 2004).

DRIVING WHILE BROWN

(Additional detail for this lesson may be found at: http://www.teachersforjustice. org/c-lessons/S-math)

GOALS

This lesson builds from the moral concerns of students at this age to coordinate issues of equity and equality. The lesson connects to students' intrinsic interest in social inequality. The mathematical topics include data analysis and probability (simulations, law of large numbers, theoretical/experimental possibilities). These aspects of mathematics and statistics are employed to determine whether racial profiling takes place with respect to tendencies of police to stop, search, or arrest individuals while driving on the basis of race or skin color. Students first simulate what should happen based on probabilities, and then compare their simulation with actual data. This comparison provides the basis for moral discussion and moral reflection. The following lesson focuses on driving data for Latinos. The lesson could readily be adjusted to focus on another group or social situation for which opportunities or problems are unequally distributed.

PROCEDURE

This lesson is designed to take place over a period of 3–5 days. The lesson is divided into three parts.

Part I

This aspect of the lesson is a review of basic ideas about statistical probability and the law of large numbers. Students working in pairs toss a coin 100 times. They then combine their results with the data from the entire class. The outcome demonstrates that the combined class data (large numbers) comes closest to 50-50.

Part II

This section of the lesson engages students in constructing a data table based on probabilities and asks them to interpret those data. This simulation makes use of population data for the city of Chicago.

Groups of 3–5 students are presented with a bag containing 9 black (African American), 9 tan (Euro-American/White), 6 red (Latino), and 1 green (Asians/Native American) cubes to approximate Chicago racial proportions. Students are not told how many cubes, or how many of each color are contained in the bag. Students reach into the bag without looking and select a cube, record its color, and replace the cube. Each time a student picks a cube the color is recorded on a chart. Students take turns recording results of 10 picks, and then another 10 picks, until they complete 100 picks in total. For each collection of 10 picks, students calculate the ratio of each color, and then calculate the ratio for the 100 picks in total. Students then individually provide *written* answers to the following questions:

1. Without opening the bag, how many cubes of each color do you think are in it? Why?
2. What happened as you picked more times, and what do you think would happen if you pick 1,000 times?

The class then discusses how this exercise allows them to see that events randomly distributed across a population will match the proportions of subgroups within that population.

Part III

This aspect of the lesson has two purposes. The first is to use what was learned in Part II to simulate the proportion of Latinos police would pull over for discretionary traffic stops based on the proportion of Latino drivers in the population.

This aspect of the activity engages students in deepening their understanding of the mathematical principles addressed in the lesson. The second aspect of this 2 for 1 activity is to stimulate moral development and social commitment.

Students are provided with the following data based on Illinois police reports for the Chicago metropolitan area for 1987–1997. In an area of about 1,000,000 motorists approximately 28,000 were Latinos. Over a determined period of time, police made 14,750 discretionary stops. A police officer in Illinois has the option to stop or not to stop a motorist (discretionary stop) if a driver changes lanes without signaling or drives 1–5 miles per hour over the speed limit. Of these stops, 3,100 were of Latino drivers. One can do a quick calculation and determine that Latinos made up 2.8% of the motorists, but also comprised about 20% of the motorists who were subject to discretionary stops by police. Students are asked to use the population data for motorists to set up a simulation for the rates at which Latinos would be expected to be stopped based on statistical expectations. In creating the simulation seventh- and eighth-grade students tend to either round off 2.8% and use 3 cubes within a set of 100, or attempt to be completely accurate and use 1 cube within 36. Students are then asked to make 100 picks from a bag containing the total number of cubes and present their data. The data from the entire class are then used to generate an overall probability. Groups are asked to respond to the following questions:

1. What percentage of motorists were Latinos?
2. What percentage of traffic stops were of Latinos?
3. How did you set up the simulation for this problem? How did you choose those numbers of cubes?
4. How many Latinos were picked out of 100, and what percentage is that?
5. What did you learn from this activity?
6. How did mathematics help you do this?

Questions for Moral Discussion and Homework

The following questions stem from this particular data set and are included here to illustrate how a moral discussion and follow-up would occur in response to findings such as the ones reported above.

1. What we discovered is that Latino motorists are more than 7 times as likely to be pulled over for a discretionary traffic stop by police than motorists in general. What do you think of that? Does this seem fair to you?
2. Why do you think this happens?
3. Suppose that a small percentage of people in a given ethnic group engage in illegal activities such as drug dealing. Do you think it would be right for the police to use their discretionary power to stop motorists from that ethnic group if the large majority of people are law-abiding citizens? How come?

4. Do you think this tendency for police to stop Latinos more often than people in general is a problem? How come?

5. If so, what do you think should be done about it? Can you think of anything that we might do as a class to raise awareness or help change things in our own community? [This last question could become the springboard for engagement in a class community service activity if the class indicates that they view the issue as a problem and offer concrete suggestions for how to respond.]

Social Convention

Middle school is the critical transition period during which young adolescents construct their understanding of the role conventions play in coordinating the interactions of people within a social system. In sixth and seventh grade the majority of students perceive conventions as simply the arbitrary dictates of authority. By late seventh and eighth grade students begin to construct an understanding of convention as a constituent component of social systems. The lessons provided here were designed to engage students in that conceptual shift. For about half of typical American students this transition is not completed until the freshman year of high school (ninth grade). Thus, the lessons presented in this section may be adapted for use with young high school students as well.

Social Studies

This section presents three lessons. The first two are drawn directly from topics covered in the curriculum. The first is a continuation of the unit on ancient Egypt employed in the "Treasures of the Pyramid" moral lesson provided above. The second example is a teacher-constructed scenario based on an aspect of American history. The third is a teacher-designed activity intended to stimulate students' understanding of convention and social systems.

ANCIENT EGYPT: DRESS AND SOCIAL CLASS

GOALS

This lesson focusing upon convention comes from the same unit on ancient Egypt as the "Treasures of the Pyramid" moral lesson above. The lesson focuses uon the use of titles to differentiate among people of differing social status or social class. This lesson has similarities to the lesson focusing on dress in Chapter 7. However, in this case, students are at a point in their social development where they are beginning to get a glimmer of how societies operate as complex hierarchical systems.

PROCEDURE

This lesson has two components, one focusing on the abstract issues from history, the other connecting to students' everyday use of titles at school. Some teachers prefer to introduce the lesson by starting first with the everyday issue. In this example, we begin with the topic addressed in the history lesson. Please note that even in the case of this abstract history lesson, the questions connect back to students' personal experience by linking the use of titles to refer to the pharaoh to contemporary use of titles to refer to the president.

The lesson begins by placing the students in groups. The teacher then asks a student to read the following passage aloud followed by small group and then whole class discussion.

> Throughout most of its history, Egypt was ruled by kings. These kings were thought to be representatives of the gods. Using the king's name directly was considered disrespectful, so people referred to him by his residence. They called him the "per aa," or pharaoh, which meant "great house" in Egyptian.

Questions for Discussion

1. Why do you think the people of ancient Egypt had a special title for their ruler? Explain.
2. Do you think that it would have been okay for a regular person to greet the pharaoh by saying "Hey Tut, how's it going?" Why not?
3. What is the proper way to greet the president? Why don't we just call him George? Why are people expected to call him President Bush, or Mr. President? Explain.
4. Suppose an individual, such as a news reporter, doesn't like or respect a particular president. Would it be okay to express this lack of regard by addressing the president without using a title such as Mr. President? Why?
5. Some people would argue that not using the president's title is disrespecting the country and not just the person. How does that work?
6. Could we have a society that doesn't use titles for people in different positions, such as Dr. or Your Honor for judges? How would that change society?

The following questions link the issue to students' everyday experiences.

1. How about at school? Why do we use titles here for teachers (Mr. and Ms.) but not for students?
2. What do these titles tell us about how school is structured?
3. Suppose we did away with titles at school. What do you think of that?

Homework or In-Class Writing

Following the discussion, students would be asked to provide individual written responses to the following questions.

1. Why do you think the people of ancient Egypt had a special title for their ruler? Explain.
2. What does that tell us about how Egyptian society was structured?
3. Some people would argue that it is disrespectful for a regular person to address someone like the president by first name. What makes that disrespectful when a president's first name is the person's name, after all?
4. Some people would argue that not using the president's title is disrespecting the country and not just the person. How does that work?

TIME AND PUNCTUALITY

GOALS

This lesson accompanies a unit on industrialization. It makes use of the shifts from rural agrarian society to engage students in reflecting on the conventions modern societies have adopted regarding time and punctuality. The issue of punctuality is one that vexes teachers of middle school students who seem to be forever late to class or planning to leave class early. Although this is generally viewed as a classroom management issue to be dealt with through rewards and punishments, it is also in many ways a matter of conceptualization of convention and of connection between school culture and home culture. Most middle school students view issues of punctuality as they do all other conventions: as simply the arbitrary dictates of authority. Thus, this curricular lesson may be seen as having a direct connection to an issue of classroom management.

This is also an issue that vexes future employers, especially of students from lower income urban settings whose home cultures do not share the punctuality conventions of the American mainstream workplace.

Finally, the lesson contributes to the more general developmental considerations about convention shared by each of the lessons in this section.

PROCEDURE

The teacher distributes the following passage and has it read aloud by one of the students. Following the reading, the teacher asks general questions to check for comprehension of the passage. The passages presents a plausible scenario constructed by one of our graduate students in collaboration with a classroom teacher. We have found that use of such scenarios helps to bring the issues to life. The shift from rural life to life centered around the factory resulted in many changes in people's lives. One of them had to do with how people dealt with time.

> The Johnson family was used to getting up at dawn and working until midday with a break for lunch, and other breaks during the day when someone needed a rest. Most days the Johnsons worked until late afternoon. Sometimes, if the weather was particularly hot, they would stop early. Other days

they might work until later. No one was keeping a close check on the time as long as the work got done.

When Mr. Johnson got a factory job, he found that things were different. He was expected to get to work at exactly the same time each morning. He had two 10-minute breaks each day; one in the morning, and one in the afternoon, plus a half-hour for lunch. Quitting time was exactly the same each day.

Mr. Johnson soon found that he was in trouble with his boss because he occasionally showed up late for work and sometimes took breaks that were longer than 10 minutes, or took breaks at unscheduled times. The boss explained to Mr. Johnson that the company had rules about time, and that he was expected to follow them. Mr. Johnson objected, saying that he didn't see why he had to follow a tight schedule as long as he got his work done.

Questions for Discussion

1. What do you think: Should Mr. Johnson continue to take unscheduled breaks and come to work late, or should he be punctual and follow the time schedule? How come?
2. Why do places of employment like factories have rules about punctuality?
   2a. What effect do you think it would have on the factory if people came to work at various times rather than on a schedule?
3. Do you think it matters whether a person is punctual as long as he or she gets the work done? How come?
4. How would it change society if people were not punctual?
5. In some societies such as in South America or the Caribbean punctuality is not considered as important. Is that all right? How come?
6. Suppose an American company was operating in South America. Would it be right for the U.S. company to expect its South American employees to be punctual and follow a schedule? Why?
7. What about at school? Are students expected to be on time? Why?
8. Does it matter whether people are on time or not? Why?
9. What about at parties? If a party starts at eight o'clock, should people show up exactly at eight? Why/why not? What's different about parties in terms of being punctual?
10. Why do rules about punctuality exist?

Homework

Write a 200-word essay on the following proposition:

> "People should be on time (punctual) in school and at work."

State whether you agree or disagree with the statement. Support your position with sound arguments. Also, say what you think are the best arguments that can be raised by someone who takes the opposite point of view. Finally, explain why your point of view has the strongest argument.

ANTHROPOLOGISTS AND MISSIONARIES: A SIMULATION

The following exercise was designed as part of my work with a teacher who wanted to make the concept of society concrete for her world history students. We have found this to be an especially effective tool for helping students to construct an understanding of the role of conventions in structuring social systems. This in turn has made discussions about culture and society that are common to courses in social studies, such as world history, take on deeper significance and relevance. The missionary aspect of the simulation also has the effect of increasing students' awareness of and respect for cultural diversity. This simulation has several parts and was originally set up to take one class period per week (Fridays) over a 4-week period. The short version presented here takes three class periods. It involves three primary components: (a) constructing a "society," (b) sending out anthropologists to learn about the conventions of neighboring societies, and (c) sending out missionaries to convert a neighboring society to adopt the conventions of the home society.

GOALS

Engage students in recognizing that arbitrary conventions establish the patterns of social interactions within societies. Societies differ in their conventions, and altering conventions alters society. Students also discover that moral rules governing interpersonal harm and welfare appear to be universal.

Phase 1

Constructing a society.

PROCEDURE

The teacher divides the class into teams of 5–6 students per team. Each team is directed to construct the rules and norms of a society in the following areas: interpersonal safety and well-being, clothing/dress, forms of address, rules for renting an apartment, age of consent, table manners, greetings, holidays. Groups are given a worksheet listing the categories, allowed one class period to begin the project, and instructed to work on it at home over the weekend. In the original version used with eighth-grade students, the teacher also directed groups to use materials such as papier-mâché to physically represent their society in order to maximize student identification with the project. Phase I in the original version took two class periods.

Phase 2

Anthropologists.

PROCEDURE

The teacher explains that there is a field of study called anthropology in which researchers visit other societies to learn about their rules and customs. Each group is instructed to select two members to serve as their anthropologist team to visit each of the other groups to learn the rules of the neighboring societies and report back their findings to the group. The teacher allows 5 minutes per team visit and rotates the anthropologist teams from one "society" to the next until all teams have visited each society. The remaining group members serve as the society members to explain their rules to the anthropologists. The anthropologist teams place their findings on a master sheet that lists each group and rule category. The anthropologists then return to their home societies and post their lists of findings. (Allow 30 minutes.)

Phase 3

Rules Discussion.

For each discussion segment the teacher alternates the discourse between small group and whole class discussion. (Allow 15–20 minutes.)

Moral Rules

Once the anthropologists return to share their findings and post their lists, the teacher directs the groups to begin a focused discussion around their findings. Groups are asked first to focus on the rules the anthropologists have obtained from each "society" for interpersonal safety and well-being. In our work with this exercise, the groups (societies) produce very similar lists of rules governing moral acts such as stealing, property damage, and assault. The groups (followed by the whole class) are asked to respond to the following questions:

1. What have you noticed about the rules in this category?
2. Why do you think the list of rules that you came up with are so similar?
3. Would it be okay for people in your society to do these things if you had not come up with these rules? How come?
4. Do you think it would be right for people in the societies to do these things if they did not have rules about them? How come?

Conventions

The teacher then asks the small groups to focus on the list of rules the anthropologists have generated for the remaining (conventional) norms established for each society. In our use of this exercise, the norms groups come up with vary widely for issues of convention. The groups (followed by the whole class) are asked to respond to the following questions:

5. What have you noticed about the rules in this category?
6. What do you think about the fact that the rules vary from one society to another?

7. Do you think it would be right for people in the other societies to do things that are not allowed in your society within this category of rules (such as how you greet people or what holidays you have) if they do not have rules about them? How come?
8. Would it be okay for people in your society to do the things that are now governed by the rules of your society if your society didn't have the rules about such things as how you greet people, or eliminate the rules that you now have? How come?

DOMAIN COMPARISON

The final phase of the exercise asks students to compare the types of norms (moral, conventional) and to consider what function they serve for society. The teacher engages the entire class in a discussion around the following questions:

9. What have you noticed that is different between the two types of rules and norms that your societies created?
   Right, we seem to have one set of rules that are common across societies. We also said before that these are basic rules that all societies have to have. We also have a second set of rules that vary from society to society. This kind of rule is called a "social convention."
10. Why do you think societies have social conventions? What purpose do they serve?
11. Suppose the society your group created did not have social conventions. How would that affect your society?

Phase 2

Homework
Students are asked to write a brief essay answering the following questions:

1. Why do you think societies have social conventions? What purpose do they serve?
2. Suppose the society your group created did not have social conventions. How would that affect your society?

Phase 3

Missionaries.

PROCEDURE

The purpose of this third component is to allow students to experience outside challenges to the conventions of their society and to consider what happens to a society when it adopts the conventions of another society. To prepare for this exercise, the teacher looks over the list of conventions created by each group in the class and identifies norms on similar issues (e.g., greetings, holidays) that differ between 2 or more of the student-constructed societies. The teacher then matches up a "missionary" assignment from a given group to a second group. This is done so that each group has a role for one missionary team, and each group is visited by one missionary team. The term "missionary" is one that we have used with teachers as a shorthand name for the exercise. The term "missionary" is never actually used in the class activities.

For example, one of the classes at a Catholic school where I worked included a group that had apartment rental policies requiring that prospective renters have a roommate and an apartment rental license from city hall. Another group in the same class adopted a holiday in which the members of the society were to be naked and throw water balloons at each other for recreation. For the simulated activity, the teacher asked the group to come up with an acceptable way in which to role play their holiday. The students quite creatively came up with paper signs to attach to themselves that read "naked," and shredded paper to throw at one another to simulate water balloons. The teacher then matched each of these groups with groups that had corresponding but different norms (e.g., different holidays, norms for apartment rental).

To initiate the exercise the teacher prepares the home society to expect to simulate the focal norm (e.g., their holiday or the process of apartment rental) for the exercise at the next class meeting. The teacher also asks each group to select two members who will serve as the visitor teams to another society. The teacher meets with the visiting teams and instructs them that they will be visiting another society and that their role is to try to convince the members of the other society to give up their convention/custom and adopt the convention/custom of their home society. For example, the society with the naked–water balloon holiday was assigned to a team from a culture that had a traditional picnic as the center of their holiday. The "missionary" team was instructed that their role was to convert the group with the naked–balloon-throwing holiday to celebrate the holiday clothed and without throwing water balloons and to have picnics instead.

At the beginning of class the teacher checks to see that all the groups are prepared to proceed. Once this is done, the visiting "missionary" teams are directed to visit the host societies (groups) and to engage in their "conversion" efforts. The teacher circulates among the groups to ensure that students remain on task. (Allow 20 minutes.)

Questions for Discussion

The visiting teams are directed to return to their home groups and participate in the following discussion. The small group discussion is followed by a teacher-led whole class discussion.

1. What happened when the visitors came to your group?
2. How did you feel when the visitors tried to have you change your convention to match the one from their society? How come?

3. What would happen if you changed all your conventions to match those of the other group? How would you feel about that?
4. How did the members of your group feel when they were trying to get the other group to change their conventions? How come you felt that way?
5. Are conventions important to societies? If so, how come?

Homework

Students are asked to write a brief essay responding to the following questions:

1. How did your group react to having the visitors try to change the conventions of your group to match their convention? How come?
2. Are conventions important to societies? Why/why not?

Personal

One of the major shifts in social cognition during middle school is the tendency to expand what young people view as within their personal domain rather than matters of convention or prudence. This shift is central to the young adolescent's emerging sense of self and identity. The following two lessons were designed to capitalize on this aspect of social development. The first is from literature. The second makes use of role play and visual arts to help students situate what is personal in relation to other social norms.

Literature/English

CRASH (NOVEL BY JERRY SPINELLI)

GOALS

This lesson was one of several used in conjunction with students' reading of the novel *Crash* as part of the middle school reading list in Park Ridge Elementary District #64. The goal was to connect with middle school students' efforts to establish the connection between personal choices about dress, appearance, and mannerisms, and what it means to be authentic or "phony." A similar discourse with freshman high school students can be achieved with J. D. Salinger's *Catcher in the Rye*.

PROCEDURE

The following lesson builds from a passage in which the character Crash narrates about the first day of school:

"The bell wasn't going to ring for another fifteen minutes, but everybody was already there. Partly it's first-day excitement. But mostly it's checking everybody out. Seeing what they look like after the summer. . . . I'd say one-quarter is checking out other kids' clothes, and three-quarters is showing off your own. Your new sneaks, your labels. Talking prices."

The teacher has a student read the above passage aloud. This is followed with small group discussion, and then a teacher-led whole class discussion around the following questions. Afterwards, students write an essay that they begin in class and complete as homework.

Discussion Questions

1. How does the passage fit your own experience on the first day of school? Is it an accurate or inaccurate account of what happens here at school?
2. How do clothes serve to illustrate who you are? How does that work?
3. Some people argue that if everyone in a clique dresses the same, then you can't be different or unique from everyone else. What do you think about this?
4. Do you think that people who wear the same designer clothes are fakes? Does the type of clothing you wear make a difference in how phony or real you are?
5. Who do you think is more of a fake: Webb or Crash? Explain why you think so.

In-Class Writing and Homework

Write a 200-word essay on the following topic. Be sure to address each question in your essay.

There is a saying that "Clothes make the person."

1. Use the passage from *Crash* to interpret this statement.
2. In what sense would you say that this statement is accurate? In what sense is it not accurate?
3. How do clothes contribute to whether a person is phony or real?

THE MESSY ROOM (ROLE PLAY)

GOALS

This role play is based on research findings by Judith Smetana (2005) indicating that the primary source of adolescent–parent conflict in early and middle adolescence is over issues that adolescents view as personal matters, but that the parents respond to as part of the conventions of the home or community, or issues of the child's safety. In one of her papers, titled "Clean Your Room," Smetana (Smetana, Daddis, & Chuang, 2003) identifies the adolescent–parent battle to get the child to clean his or her bedroom as a prototypical issue for

American families. The role play simulates that dispute and asks the participants to problem solve how the young person might best handle the conflict with the parents. This exercise helps students to interpret their own feelings about such disputes and contributes to healthy classroom management, but also gives students greater insights into the motivations of characters and themes in literature.

Generally teachers employ this role play either as a purely social development activity for home room or in conjunction with a reading in literacy (English) class. As will be made clear below, the role play can be extended to initiate an activity in math class on the use of Venn diagrams.

PROCEDURE

The teacher assigns roles to 1 boy as the child, 1 girl as the mom, and 1 boy as the narrator. Each student in the class, acting as observers, is provided a copy of the following script. The role play alternates between acting out scenes and discussion of a given scene.

Role Play Script

NARRATOR: In this scene we have a boy named Daniel, who is 11, and his mom. It is Saturday morning and the mom wants Daniel to clean up his messy room.

MOM: Daniel, it's Saturday, and it's time for you to clean up your room.

DANIEL: Oh mom, why do I have to do this? It doesn't look bad to me.

MOM: Well, it looks like a mess, and today's the day that we are supposed to get the house cleaned up.

Discussion

TEACHER: (Says to entire class) Okay, turn to the person next to you and share what you think Daniel should do here. How come? Who do you think is right in this case, Daniel or his mom? How come?

(Teacher then opens up the discussion to the entire class.)

Role Play (Continued)

TEACHER: (To the boy who plays Daniel) Really get into your role as Daniel and tell us how you see the situation. (The child playing Daniel then lays out his case. Invariably the case includes the argument that it is *his* room and that he should not have to clean it if he doesn't want to.)

Discussion (Continued)

TEACHER: To the other students, (first for pairs discussion and then whole class) Do you think he has a point here in arguing that it is his room after all? (Teacher should also highlight other points that the child playing Daniel might offer on his behalf.)

Role Play (Continued)

TEACHER: (To the girl who plays the mom in the skit), in your role as the mom, explain to us how you see this situation. Tell us why you want the room cleaned up, and why you think it's right to expect your son to go along.

Discussion (Continued)

TEACHER: Okay, what do the rest of you think about what the mom has to say?

Problem Solving

TEACHER: Okay, let's brainstorm here. Work with your partner and come up with advice we could give Daniel that would help him out in this situation.

(Then to whole class) Okay, let's hear what ideas we have come up with.

Note to teacher: Let the children generate their own solutions, but gently guide them toward solutions that allow the child to arrive at a fair compromise that recognizes the child's claim to his room, and yet allows him to meet the mother's request in a broad sense.

Homework or In-Class Writing

Write a 200-word essay responding to the following questions:

1. Provide what you think is Daniel's best case for whether he should or should not clean up his room if he doesn't want to.
2. Explain what you think would be the best way for Daniel to resolve the situation with his mother.

EXPANDING THE LESSON: HOME ROOM ACTIVITY (OR MATH ACTIVITY USE OF GRAPHS, VENN DIAGRAMS, AND DATA)

GOALS

The previous role play can be used to illustrate the notion that some issues that come up between parents and children can be subject to negotiation. However, one could argue that some issues should be left entirely within the child's discretion, while other things really should be controlled by parents. Cross-cultural research on this issue discussed in Chapter 2 has found that adolescents and parents distinguish among personal, moral, prudential, and conventional issues when it comes to parental authority (Smetana, 2005). Adolescents are ceded authority when it comes to personal issues. The teacher can expand this role play lesson by asking students to work in pairs to generate a list of behaviors and choices that should be up to the child, up to the parent, or shared decisions. The basic exercise is one that I have used in work with parents of adolescents. However, it works just as well with young people.

The social development goal is to provide students an opportunity to share with one another their views about legitimate areas of personal and parental authority. This provides students with some social context within which to interpret their interactions with their own parents. The home room teacher can note students who are outliers on either dimension of personal and parental control, and seek help from school counselors for students (and their families) whose views seem widely divergent from those of the rest of the class.

PROCEDURE

The teacher generates a worksheet that lists activities or behavioral choices that a young person might make that comprise personal, conventional, prudential (safety), or overlapping issues. Instructions at the top of the worksheet direct the student to indicate whether the action should be up to the child, the parent, or shared. A sample worksheet follows. The list is sorted by category for illustrative purposes. The list given to students would be randomized. Following the pairs work, the teacher collects the lists to generate a tally score for items that fall within each category. Following the generation of the list representing the collective thoughts of the class, the teacher leads the following discussion. (Note: In math classes, teachers have used the data from the student-generated lists to engage the class in constructing data tables or visual graphic representations of item categorizations.)

Questions for Discussion (a subset could be used as homework or in-class writing)

1. What do you see as being in common with the behaviors and activities that you think should be entirely up to the child? Why should the parent not try to control these things?
2. What do you see as being in common with items that you think parents should control? Do these things fall into one category or into several categories?
3. What do you see as being in common with the items that fall in between?
   3a. How should we deal with these kinds of things when parents and kids disagree?

Sample Worksheet

Rate each item as something that should be "up to the child to decide" (C), "up to the parent/parent should control" (P), or "overlap between parental and child control" [(P/c) = primarily the parent, (C/p) primarily the child].

Personal

Friends

Keep secret diary (should parent be able to read?)

Hairstyle

TV shows

Music

Moral

Throwing fireworks at neighbor's dog

Stealing from others

Hitting and hurting others

Conventional

Whether or not to dress up for church

Whether or not to eat with family at Thanksgiving meal

Prudential (self-harm)

Alcohol use

Drug use

Overlapping

What foods to eat for snacks

Tattoos

Watching R-rated movies

Sleep over at friend's house

Not wearing a coat on a very cold day

What courses to take at school

Whether or not to go to church

What clothes to wear to school

Bedtime

Whether or not to clean up bedroom

Body piercing

CHAPTER 9

Using the Academic Curriculum for Moral and Social Development in High School

The teenager seems to have replaced the Communist as the appropriate target for public controversy and foreboding.

—Edgar Friedenberg, *The Vanishing Adolescent*

Development occurs at different rates, and many students who enter high school as freshmen are developmentally similar to early adolescents in eighth grade. For that reason, I advise teachers of freshmen students to make use of the suggestions from both Chapters 8 and 9 in thinking about integrating moral and social development into curricular lessons. The focus of most of the lessons in this chapter will be on middle adolescence (ages 15–18) or the sophomore through senior years of high school. Students at this point in development have generally constructed an understanding of the role of conventions in structuring social systems. They have also resolved some of the moral quandaries associated with indirect harm that were opened up in early adolescent moral thinking. These new social cognitive capacities mean that moral and social curricula can begin to focus greater attention than in earlier years on the relations between morality and society, and the connections between morality and social institutions. Indeed, some developmental researchers have suggested that what characterizes moral development in adolescence is the increased capacity to coordinate morality with nonmoral considerations (Smetana & Turiel, 2003). Nonetheless, this period of development is also marked by transitions within domains, especially in the personal domain of selfhood and identity (Nucci, 1996). The lessons that follow are designed to map onto these developmental trends both within domains and coordination across domains.

Morality

Mathematics

THE PAPER ROUTE

(Adapted from a lesson by Lisa Jason)

We will begin with a lesson designed for use in freshman algebra. This lesson may also be used with advanced eighth graders. It asks students to apply their basic knowledge of equations and word problems to solve a distributive justice situation in an everyday setting. The situation itself is adapted from a developmental interview constructed by William Damon (1977) designed to be engaging to young people.

GOALS

The developmental goal of the lesson is to consolidate students' conceptions of the relations between equity and equality in interpersonal distributive justice. The academic goal is to develop students' ability to employ algebra to resolve word problems.

PROCEDURE

Students are presented the following scenario and questions to discuss in pairs:

Four kids who are neighbors (John, Mark, Sally, and Mary) decide to work together on a paper route to make some money. John and Mary are both 15 and in high school, while Mark and Sally are both 12 years old and seventh graders. At the end of their first week they earn $48. But now they have a problem. They didn't decide ahead of time how to divide up the money that they had earned.

   a. Sally argues that the fairest way is to divide up the money equally.
   b. Mary argues that Sally was lazy and only delivered half as many papers as Mary. So Sally should get half as much as Mary and the other kids.
   c. Mark argues that he and John were stronger than Mary and Sally, who are girls, and together carried 25% more than the girls did altogether. So the boys should each get 25% more than each of the girls.
   d. John agrees that the reason Sally carried fewer papers than Mary is that she is lazy. He also argues that even though Mary isn't as strong as the boys, she worked just as hard. However, he also argues that the older kids (he and Mary) should get 25% more than the younger kids because older kids have more expenses than younger ones do. So, in

his mind, he and Mary should get the same amount and 25% more than Mark, but Sally should get half as much as Mark because she was lazy.

1. Please create algebraic equations that would express each solution for the best way to divide the $48.
2. Provide a written answer for the solution you and your partner think is the fairest.
3. Explain why you think that is the fairest solution, and provide your argument as to why the other solutions are not as fair.

SOLUTIONS

(provided by Lisa Jason)

a. $a + b + c + d = 48$
$X + X + X + X = 48$
$4X = 48$
$X = \$12.00$

b. $a + b + c + d = 48$
$X + X + 0.5X + X = 48$
$3.5X = 48$
$X = \$13.72$ (Mary, John, Mark)
$c = \$6.86$ (Sally)

c. $a + b + c + d = 48$
$1.25X + 1.25X + X + X = 48$
$4.5X = 48$
$X = 10.67$
$a = 1.25 (10.67) = \$13.33$ (John)
$b = 1.25 (10.67) = \$13.33$ (Mark)
$c = \$10.67$ (Sally)
$d = \$10.67$ (Mary)

d. $a + b + c + d = 48$
$a = d = X + 0.25$
$b = X$
$c = 0.5X$
$1.25X + X + 0.5X + 1.25X = 48$
$4X = 48$
$X = 12$
$a = \$15$ (John)
$b = \$12$ (Mark)
$c = \$6$ (Sally)
$d = \$15$ (Mary)

Following the pairs work, the teacher leads the students in a whole class discussion, focusing first on the problem solutions, and then the positions pairs took with respect to which solution they considered to be most fair.

Homework

Students are given the opportunity to revise their solutions and their written positions regarding the solution they consider to be most fair.

Sciences

The following lesson was included in a high school psychology class. It concerns the ethical constraints guiding research with human subjects. Other lessons in the natural sciences can focus on the ethical uses of scientific knowledge (e.g., cloning; genetic selection or genetic engineering of children). Science teachers we have worked with have found it profitable to cast such controversies within the structure of dilemma discussions. The following lesson employs a mixture of discussion and group project work.

THE TUSKEGEE SYPHILIS STUDY: CREATING AN IRB

GOALS

This lesson draws from the historical incident that served as the catalyst for the development of Institutional Review Boards to govern the ethics of the use of human subjects for scientific research sponsored by the federal government. The purpose of the lesson is to engage students in the use of their moral reasoning to construct a moral institution. The "hands on" nature of the exercise allows students the experience of engaging critical moral judgment to create a moral institution, which in turn provides a basis from which to judge existing moral institutions. In particular, this exercise provides them the opportunity to critically evaluate past actions of scientists, and the existing institutions designed to govern the ethics of research with human subjects. Thus, the lesson deals with a fundamental aspect of scientific literacy, important for an informed general public, as well as contributing to moral growth.

PROCEDURE

Students are provided a description of the events that comprised the Tuskegee syphilis study. This can be done through a teacher-prepared worksheet or by directing students to a suitable Web site. The basic elements of the issue are as follows. In 1933, the U.S. Public Health Service in Macon County, Alabama, began an investigation to chart the phases of syphilis when the disease is left untreated. Macon County was selected for the study because it had an exceptionally high prevalence of the disease. A total of 399 African American men with latent syphilis and 201 men without the disease were enrolled in the study. The people enrolled in the study were poor and had high rates of illiteracy. The participants in the study were led by the study researchers to believe that they were being treated for syphilis. The study lasted for 40 years. During that time participants received sporadic examinations, but no antisyphilitic treatment. In 1942 some of the participants in the study were being drafted into the armed forces to fight in World War II. To prevent these draftees from receiving antisyphilitic treatment, the investigators provided the Macon County Selective Service Board with a list of 256 names of men under the age of 45 years who were to be excluded from the list of draftees needing treatment. The Board agreed to exclude these men. Finally, when an effective therapy was available with the introduction of penicillin in 1943, the Public Health Service did not use the drug on the Tuskegee participants unless they asked for it. By the time the study was exposed in 1972, 28 men had died of syphilis, 100 others were dead due to syphilis-related complications, at least 40 wives had been infected, and 19 children had contracted the disease at birth (source: Centers for Disease Control).

Students are asked to read the above information and then are placed in groups of 4–6 and asked to discuss the following questions:

1. What do you think about the way in which this research was carried out? Would you say that the way that it was carried out was ethical? How come?
2. What would you say was the primary value of the study (what knowledge would be gained)?
3. What would you consider to be the primary ethical limitations of the way that the study was carried out? Please list each limitation and explain why.
4. Does the knowledge to be gained from the study justify the procedures that were used in the research? Why/Why not?

Following this group work, the teacher leads a whole-class discussion in which the ethical limitations of the study are enumerated and discussed. Following this discussion the teacher introduces the IRB project.

IRB Project

The teacher introduces the class to the concept of the Institutional Review Board and explains that all current scientists who wish to conduct research with human subjects must submit a protocol that describes their research procedure for review of the ethics of the proposed research design. Students are then assigned to work in pairs to consider what they would include within every IRB protocol, with the following guidelines:

1. What is informed consent? Should informed consent always be required? How come?
   1a. How about if a study doesn't involve an experiment, such as simply observing how people act, or giving them a survey. Should the researchers have to get informed consent in that case? Why/why not?
2. What should be included in the information that is given to obtain informed consent? What should the participants be told? How come?
3. What qualifications should someone have in order to give informed consent (e.g., age, mental capacity)?
4. Should researchers be allowed to study people (e.g., children) who cannot give informed consent on their own? Why? How would you handle that?
5. Who if anyone should be allowed to give informed consent for research to be done with someone else, such as young children or students in school?
6. What other things do you think should be included in an IRB to ensure that the study is ethical? How come?

Paper

Using the above guidelines and the information the students gained through in-class pairs work, each student is asked to write a 2-page paper responding to the above questions.

Follow-Up

Following this exercise, students are given the IRB guidelines for research with human subjects from a local research university Web site. Half of the class receives guidelines for medical research, and half guidelines for the social sciences. Students work in pairs to answer the following questions:

1. What is your evaluation of these IRB guidelines?
2. Is there anything included that you would eliminate? How come?
3. Is there anything missing that you think should be included? Why?

During whole class discussion, the teacher would point out that the guidelines for the social sciences and medical research are different, and would ask the following questions:

1. Why do you think the IRB guidelines for medical research are different from the ones for social sciences such as psychology?
2. Do we need IRB guidelines for the social sciences at all? How come?
3. Do we need IRB guidelines if the research does not involve an experiment? Why/why not?

Social Convention

At this point in development, high school students have constructed an understanding of societies as normative systems. This allows them to engage for the first time in an informed comparison of societies both across cultures and across time. Thus, the lesson that will be included here as well as the subsequent lessons that explore the overlap between morality and convention build on this ability of adolescents to engage in reflection upon societies as systems.

Visual Arts

DEPICTIONS OF WOMEN ACROSS TIME IN THE ARTS

(Adapted from a lesson by Emily Moravec)

GOALS

This lesson is designed to take place in a studio art class with high school seniors. The initial discussion about the conventions that frame the representation of women in different periods could be limited to art history. The full lesson as presented here moves beyond that discussion to include construction of a drawing. The academic goal is to foster competence in freehand drawing as well as to engage students in an understanding of artistic expression.

The social development goal of the lesson is to engage students in understanding how the arbitrary conventions of a given time structure society. This is accomplished in this lesson by following the depiction of women through the visual arts in different historical periods. The lesson should also stimulate students to recognize how the conventions of society interact with artistic expression. Thus art is both a mirror of the times, and a catalyst for reflection and social change.

PROCEDURE

Phase 1

Reflecting on the depiction of women through time.

The lesson begins with a visual exploration of images of women in paintings and sculpture from different historical periods. This can be done either through a slide show presented by the teacher or by directing students to view images on the Internet. For purposes of this lesson, only images from the students' dominant culture would be shown (in this case, Western art). The presentation would include a sampling of at least 10 time periods. This phase could also include reading about the gender and family conventions of each period, especially if the lesson were part of an art history class. Students would be placed in mixed gender groups of 2–3 students for an initial discussion followed by a whole class discussion of the following questions.

Questions for Phase 1

1. What changes did you notice in the ways in which women were portrayed with respect to conventions of posture, dress, and facial expression? What do these changes tell you about the role of women in these different time periods?
2. What changes did you notice in terms of the activities women were depicted as being involved in? What did that tell you about the role of women in the society of the time?
3. What changes did you notice in the ways in which women were depicted in the company of children and men? What does this tell you about the conventions of gender and family of the time?
4. How does art capture the conventions of society? How might an artist influence the conventions of his or her time? What effect do you think that has on society? Explain.

Homework

Students are directed to find an image in the media or in art that is consistent with their view of a contemporary conventional woman. The student then finds a visual depiction of the opposite, a woman who doesn't seem to fit the typical or conventional vision as maintained by the student. Each image is to be accompanied by a 1–2-page essay describing how the image fits the student's concept of a conventional or unconventional woman.

Phase 2

Performance.

In the performance component of the lesson, students work in pairs (mixed gender when possible). Pairs are instructed to collaborate on an artistic representation (drawing) of a contemporary conventional woman.

GOALS

There are two sets of goals for this activity. The social development goal is to engage students in a dialogue over the conventions that define a conventional woman of today. A reflective component of the post performance part of the lesson builds on this reflection to engage in a comparison of today's conventional woman with the women of prior historical periods. This contributes further to students' understanding of the role that conventions play in structuring and defining the society of a given time.

The second goal is to help students experience the concept of artistic integrity by allowing them to experience how it feels to create an artistic work that involves compromise with another person.

PROCEDURE

The teacher begins the activity with the following instructions:

"I would like you to work together with your partner to construct a drawing that represents a contemporary conventional woman. First, you need to discuss the elements that would define a conventional woman of today. Then you would need to discuss and collaborate on the actual composition and drawing of the conventional woman you and your partner wish to represent. You may continue to engage in dialogue as you complete your drawing."

Follow-Up Discussion

The following questions would be discussed in pairs and then shared with the entire class.

1. Do you think that the drawing you have created accurately represents a conventional woman of today? What elements did you include that define the woman in your drawing as conventional?
2. Do any of the representations we have come up with as a class remind you of a time period from the past? What are the similarities and differences that you see?
3. Did you and your partner disagree about the best way to represent a conventional woman of today? Why?
4. How did you end up handling your disagreement?

Homework

Students will be asked to write a 2-page essay on the following questions:

1. How do the conventions of a time period define what it means to be a woman?
2. How do artists capture this in their work?
3. How might an artist engage in a critique of society through the representation of the women of the time period?
4. In our class project you worked with another person to create your drawing. How would your representation look if you were the only person who had worked on this project? How come?

Personal Domain

Middle adolescence continues the process of establishing the balance between what is personal and what should legitimately be regulated by social or moral considerations. During the high school years, young people are connecting their notions of the personal with a sense of self as having psychological "depth" (Nucci, 1996). Unlike middle school students who define individuality reactively as being "different from others," high school students begin to think about individuality in terms of the coordination between an inner core, "the real me," and the outer display of that real self through one's dress, mannerisms, and life choices. Concerns about individuality, authenticity, and self-consistency form part of the overall constellation of tasks that psychologists since Erik Erikson (1968) have recognized as the fundamental search for identity associated with this developmental period in modern societies (Moshman, 2004). The concern for authenticity is epitomized by J. D. Salinger's character Holden Caulfield in *Catcher in the Rye*. In Chapter 8 we discussed a lesson that included concerns for authenticity (what it means to be a phony).

A second way in which the personal domain is expressed in the high school years is through resistance to authority and claims to "rights" on the part of high school students. The following lessons illustrate ways in which to use the curriculum to positively channel those developmental impulses.

American Literature

WHAT IT MEANS TO BE AN INDIVIDUAL

GOALS

The social development goal of this lesson is to engage students in reflection upon the connection between control over aspects of the personal with the construction of a deep sense of self and individuality. One of the difficult challenges for contemporary adolescents is to balance personal choices with the requirements for group membership and respect for the rights of others. The following two lessons were designed for sophomore-level American literature to be used in conjunction with a unit on Henry David Thoreau and Ralph Waldo Emerson. The academic goals include familiarity with part of the "canon" of American literature and improving expository writing skills.

PROCEDURE

The teacher directs students to work in small groups to discuss the following quotations. Two are from the transcendentalist authors Thoreau and Emerson, and one is from the twentieth-century poet E. E. Cummings.

"Whoso would be a man must be a non-conformist." From *Self Reliance* by Ralph Waldo Emerson.   • Muhammad Ali
    - Lebron James

"If a man does not keep pace with his companions, perhaps it is because he *LeBron* hears a different drummer. Let him step to the music which he hears, however *Common* measured or far away." From *Civil Disobedience* by Henry David Thoreau.

"To be nobody but yourself—in a world which is doing its best, night and day, to make you like everybody else—means to fight the hardest battle which any human being can fight, and never stop fighting." E. E. Cummings *— A.C Green — Michelle Obama*

Questions for Discussion

1. Interpret each of the quotations in terms of their basic message. What are these authors telling us?
2. Do you agree with Emerson that one has to be a nonconformist in order to be a person? How come? In what sense do you think he means that?
   2a. Does this mean that we have to be completely different from other people in order to be a person? Why/why not?
3. What is Thoreau's basic point when he says, "Let him step to the music which he hears"? What is he saying to us in terms of how we should treat our peers?
4. What are the struggles that you face "to be nobody but yourself" as E. E. Cummings puts it? How do you handle those issues in your daily life?

ESSAY ASSIGNMENT

Write a 2-page essay in which you respond to the following theme, "What it means to be an individual." In your essay explain how one establishes and maintains oneself as an individual while also being a member of a community. Address the challenges that you face to remain "nobody but yourself." Explain how you can be yourself, while also doing things that are just like other people. Finally, address what you need to do in order to allow others to be themselves.

Combining Morality with Convention and the Personal (Fostering Domain Coordination)

The remaining lessons in this chapter are illustrative examples asking students to coordinate their moral understandings with concepts of social convention and/or the personal to arrive at balanced social judgments. Weighing moral and nonmoral elements of social situations is an aspect of everyday adult life. From the traditional developmental perspective advanced by Kohlberg (1984) and his colleagues, these multidimensional forms of moral reasoning were believed to fall within a single global developmental stage. What we have learned through research is that contextualized moral decision making is more complex and variable than that. This is never more evident than in the social and moral judgments of high school-aged students. The following lessons were designed to stimulate reasoning *across* domains rather than subordinate students' moral discourse to a single developmental dimension.

A tendency in adolescence, however, is to subordinate mixed domain issues entirely to matters of morality. This tendency is an aspect of adolescent idealism. The art of moral education is to support that idealism while also helping students to coordinate moral imperatives with the societal requirements of structure and organization. Of course, the counter tendency of many adults is to suppress the moral insights of youth in the name of social stability and our supposed greater grasp of social "reality." However, the position being advanced in this book is that being open to the moral challenges that emerge from our students is part of our own commitment as moral professionals. In the lessons that follow, we attempted to structure each lesson such that students are guided to integrate their conceptions of what is morally right or ideal with the needs of society for structure and organization.

American Literature/English

A TIME I DEFIED AUTHORITY (MORALITY AND THE PERSONAL)

GOALS

This lesson was designed to be used in conjunction with the reading of Henry David Thoreau's *Civil Disobedience*. The goal of the lesson is to encourage students to construct an understanding of morally legitimate opposition to authority. This particular lesson entails coordination between concepts of the personal and moral concepts of rights. In this first activity the lesson focuses on students' proximal experiences with adult authority. The follow-up activity serves to deepen their conceptual understanding of "civil" disobedience. It also expands the domain coordination to include social convention.

PROCEDURE

Students are asked to read Henry David Thoreau's *Civil Disobedience*. They are then placed in small groups and then the whole class discusses the following questions:

1. How does Thoreau justify civil disobedience? Do you agree with his arguments?
2. What would not constitute a legitimate basis from which to defy authority? Explain. In your group come up with 3 examples of legitimate and 3 examples of illegitimate defiance of authority. Explain your selections.

ESSAY ASSIGNMENT

Write a 2–3-page essay on the following theme: "A Time I Defied Authority." In your essay describe a situation in which you legitimately defied an authority such as a parent or teacher. Present the circumstances that led to your defiance, and explain why your defiance was justifiable as well as how the form your defiance took was justifiable. In your arguments feel free to make use of the points made by Thoreau in *Civil Disobedience*.

Expanding the Lesson (Morality and Convention)

This lesson can be expanded by asking students to read Martin Luther King's "Letter from a Birmingham Jail." The goals for this expansion are twofold. First, from the perspective of academic goals, it moves the discourse about civil disobedience into contemporary American political history. Thus students can make connections between issues raised in literature with social events. It also shifts the voice from white America to the civil rights of people of color. This addresses cultural diversity within the curriculum in an unforced manner.

Second, in terms of moral development goals, it shifts the moral context of defiance of authority from an individual to a societal perspective. This entails coordination between morality and convention, and not just attention to the personal. This lesson focusing on Martin Luther King could, of course, also take place in a class on American history.

PROCEDURE

Part I

Introducing the issue.

The teacher introduces the lesson by asking students to work in pairs to address the following question: "Is it ever morally justifiable to act outside the law?" Prior to the pairs discussion the teacher asks for a show of hands to see which students agree and disagree with the above statement. To the extent possible pairs are comprised of students who hold opposite positions on the issue. In guiding the discussion the teacher gives the following parameters.

1. Work together to try to reach an agreed-upon position.
2. Base your arguments on moral justifications. A personal desire to do something that is against the law is not a moral argument. Simply reciting a religious law or rule also is not an argument. An argument means that you have to give reasons that support your position.

Following the pairs discussion, the teacher brings the class together, elicits the arguments raised in the pairs discussion, and lists them on an overhead or on an easel. The teacher maintains the list for later discussion of the "Letter from a Birmingham Jail" and for essay assignment 1, which follows.

PART II

"Letter from a Birmingham Jail."

The teacher asks students to read Martin Luther King's "Letter from a Birmingham Jail." This can be done as a homework assignment in preparation for class discussion. From the theoretical position of Lawrence Kohlberg, this document by Dr. King exemplifies principled moral thinking that would be beyond the moral development of typical high school students. From a domain theory perspective, however, high school students can be scaffolded through a discussion of the letter by Dr. King that would allow them to coordinate their moral understandings with an evaluation of the morality of societal systems. The writing assignments for this lesson call for a considerable amount of conceptual organization and integration. Some students will require teacher support to complete these writing assignments. In those cases the teacher can supplement writing by allowing the student to make a taped oral argument from which the student can write a less elaborate essay.

To introduce the reading the teacher summarizes the circumstances of the letter, which Dr. King wrote in response to a published statement by eight African American church leaders objecting to the demonstrations that King was leading in the city of Birmingham, Alabama. Among the objections they raised was concern that King, who was also a minister, was supporting the violation of the law. King wrote the letter while in jail for leading protest demonstrations. Once students have had an opportunity to read Dr. King's letter, the teacher places students in small groups for discussion of the following questions. The small group discussion is followed by a whole class discussion of the same questions.

1. Why does Martin Luther King feel justified as an outsider to engage in civil disobedience in Birmingham, Alabama? Do you agree with his argument?
2. What does King mean when he says, "Injustice anywhere is a threat to justice everywhere"?
   2a. Does this mean that we should be concerned about injustice that occurs in other countries? What gives us the right to do that?
   2b. Suppose that someone in Canada believes strongly that a practice that we do in the United States is unjust. Should a Canadian be allowed to engage in civil disobedience in the United States in order to address what the Canadian sees as an unjust practice in our country?
3. Why did Dr. King move to demonstrations instead of negotiation? Was he opposed to negotiation? Do you think Dr. King was wrong or right to engage in demonstrations rather than continuing to negotiate?
4. What does Dr. King mean by the statement, "We know from painful experience that freedom is never voluntarily given by the oppressor; it must be demanded by the oppressed"? What does that statement mean in terms of what the oppressed are morally justified in doing in response? How come? What are they *not* morally justified in doing? How come?

5. How does Dr. King distinguish between "just" and "unjust" laws?
   5a. What makes segregation statutes unjust laws?
6. Interpret the following statement from the letter: "Any law that uplifts human personality is just. Any law that degrades human personality is unjust."
7. Did Dr. King advocate defying the law? Why/why not? Why did he think his approach showed respect for the law?
8. What were King's main criticisms of white moderates? What do you think of those criticisms?
9. Why did Dr. King feel that he was morally obligated to participate in civil disobedience in Birmingham, Alabama? What do you think: Was he morally justified in breaking the law through his civil disobedience? Why/why not?

ESSAY ASSIGNMENT 1

(The goal of assignment 1 is to engage students in an analysis of the issues of convention at stake in this situation.)

Imagine that you are a judge in Birmingham, Alabama, with the responsibility of handling the case of Martin Luther King Jr. Provide a 1–2-page response to Dr. King's letter. In your response you may use the arguments included in the handout from our class discussion that provide objections to the notion that one can morally go above the law. *In your essay make sure to address the importance of the law for maintaining social order.*

When the assignment has been graded, the teacher places students in groups of 4–6 to share the arguments that they made in their essays. The teacher then calls on students to share the arguments they made with the entire class.

ESSAY ASSIGNMENT 2

(The goal of this assignment is to foster students' understanding of the moral basis for King's arguments regarding civil disobedience. The assignment asks students to coordinate the moral aspects of King's argument with the requirements for convention in order to sustain a social system.)

Following the above discussion of essay assignment 1, the teacher provides the following instructions for assignment 2:

Write a 2-page essay in which you address the following issues:

1. Interpret the following statement: "Any law that uplifts human personality is just. Any law that degrades human personality is unjust."
2. Imagine yourself as Dr. King. Respond to the arguments you made as the judge in essay 1 to morally justify your actions of civil disobedience. For full credit make sure to take into account the arguments that **you** made in essay 1 regarding the importance of the law for maintaining social order. As Dr. King

argue how your actions were necessary in order to improve society. Finally, show how your actions (as Dr. King) served both the moral concerns for justice and the needs of society for laws and conventions that maintain social order.

When the assignment has been graded, the teacher places students in groups of 4–6 to share the arguments that they made in their essays. The teacher then calls on students to share the arguments they made with the entire class. In this discussion the teacher highlights the moral and societal aspects of Dr. King's approach to civil disobedience.

THE MORAL LIVES OF ULYSSES JEFFRIES AND HUCKLEBERRY FINN

Snoop Dogg Meets Mark Twain

(Adapted from a lesson by Roy Bounds)

Teachers of English and American literature are often confronted with public controversies over the selection of literature for their students. The following lesson takes two controversial pieces to address issues of morality, convention, and the moral growth of individuals within the constraints of their social worlds. The lesson was originally intended for use with inner-city students. The selected works address issues of race and social class from radically different perspectives and time periods. The lesson discussed here is from a larger unit involving both books in which many other issues raised in these books are discussed.

GOALS

This lesson engages students in a comparative analysis of the evolution of the morality of two major characters from different time periods. This engages students in constructing an understanding of how personal morality is affected by the conventions of the times, and how an individual can transcend those norms through moral self-reflection. The lesson also permits students to compare their own morality with that of the characters from the novels and to the current society's conventional moral expectations. The characters in both novels are imperfect from a moral point of view. Their imperfections allow students space within which to engage in moral evaluation and comparison with themselves as evolving moral beings. The term *moral self* has been used to describe the moral component of self (Lapsley, 2008). Finally, the lesson addresses social issues of race and class both in terms of the content of each book, and through the race of the authors.

PROCEDURE

Students are assigned in pairs to read *Huckleberry Finn* by Mark Twain and *Love Don't Live Here No More* by Snoop Dogg. Students who have lower reading abilities or learning disabilities read condensed versions of each book. The following questions are used to structure discussion of the values elements of the two books. The questions are followed by letters indicating the domain addressed by the question (M = moral, C = conventional).

Questions for Discussion

Huckleberry Finn.

1. Huckleberry Finn and the fugitive slave, Jim, are both escaping society, Huck because he feels he doesn't fit in, and Jim because of slavery. However, throughout the novel Huck appears to be in charge of Jim, even though Jim is a grown man and Huck a teenage boy. Why was that the case? What does this tell us about how American society was structured during the time period when this story took place? (C)
2. In various places in the book, Huck is depicted as playing tricks on Jim. Can you provide some examples of where that occurs? What do you think about Huck's behaviors toward Jim in those situations? Would you say that it was OK for Huck to do those things? How come? (M, C)
3. In what ways does Huck's behavior toward Jim reflect the conventions of his time period? Explain. (C)
4. Huck does not always appear to agree with the conventions of the times when it comes to his interactions with Jim. Can you identify some situations where Huck goes against the conventions of his era in his interactions with Jim? Explain how what Huck did in your examples went contrary to the conventions of the time. (C)
   4a. Using the examples from your answer to the previous question, would you say that Huck was wrong or right to act the way he did? How come? (C)
   4b. How would the society of that time have been different if everyone acted toward Jim the way that Huck did in your examples? (C, M)
5. How would you evaluate Huck's moral position in terms of how he interacts with Jim? Are there things about Huck's actions that you agree with? What would they be and why? Are there things you would disagree with and why? (M)
6. Overall, how would you rate Huck Finn as a person? Explain. (Connection to "moral self.")

Ulysses (*Love Don't Live Here No More*):

1. Ulysses is an up-and-coming drug dealer in his community. What do you think about that? (This open question may invoke a range of moral and conventional as well as pragmatic responses.)
2. He uses a lot of the money he gains through drug dealing to help his mother and his brother. How does this affect your view of Ulysses? Does it justify his actions as a drug dealer? Why/why not? (M)
3. In what sense do the actions of Ulysses reflect the conventions of his community? Do they also reflect some of the values of the larger society? Explain. (C)
4. In what ways does Ulysses make moral choices that go counter to the conventions of his "street" culture? Can you give examples where that occurs? What do you think about those choices? (C, M)
5. Overall, how would you rate Ulysses as a person? Explain. (Connection to the "moral self.")

General issues.

1. Huck Finn and Ulysses are teenagers growing up in different surroundings and in different historical periods. In each case, their behavior is influenced by the conventions of their society. What is also true about both characters is that they make choices to act in ways that go against the expected norms of behavior in order to do what they believe is the right thing in terms of how they treat others. Can you list at least one example for each character that illustrates this point? Explain how your examples illustrate this point. (C, M)
2. Both Huck and Ulysses are on their way to becoming adults. Given the choices they have made and the actions they have taken, what sort of person do you think each character will become when they grow up? For each character do you think he will become a "good" person as an adult? Why/why not? (Coordination of morality and convention. Connection to the "moral self.")
3. Can you think of any conventions from our community or the larger society that direct young people your age to act in ways that are unfair or not in the best interest of other people? How should a person your age handle those things? What advice would you give to someone your age about how to handle those conventional expectations? (C, M; Connection to "moral self.")

ESSAY PLAYWRITING ASSIGNMENT

This assignment can be written in class or as a homework assignment. It is done in pairs with the students who have read the books together. The teacher can decide whether or not to select some of the resulting plays to be enacted in class with follow-up discussion. The teacher introduces the assignment as follows:

> For this assignment you are to work together as playwrights. In a stage play we can make the impossible happen. The premise of this play is that Huck

Finn and Ulysses find themselves brought together in a time warp. They are alone and in a room in a timeless setting. A voice speaks to them, saying, "Young men, you have been brought here from different times to learn about each other. You will be returned to your place and time in a few hours. In the meanwhile, make yourselves comfortable and get to know each other."

The teacher then directs the students to write the dialogue that occurs between Huck and Ulysses with the following instructions:.

1. In your dialogue have your characters tell about their lives and what they believe in with regard to what they are doing.
2. Have the Huck character explain about running away with Jim and the things that have gone on. Have Huck explain about the rules and norms about race during his time period. Have Huck also tell about how he thinks about those norms and what he thinks about Jim.
3. Have Ulysses explain to Huck that he is a drug dealer, and also what he is trying to do with respect to his family and the norms of the world he lives in. Have each character challenge (in a friendly way) the values and lifestyle of the other person.
4. You will need to decide whether or not your characters will like each other. You will also need to decide whether or not they listen to each other's ideas.

Social Studies: American History

JOURNALISM

GOALS

An important event in American history was the construction of the Bill of Rights. Making those elements of American government come to life is a central responsibility of American education. In Illinois and many other states, it is part of state education law that high schools teach students about the U.S. Constitution. All students must pass a test on the Constitution in order to graduate. The following lesson addresses aspects of this requirement by bringing an issue of First Amendment freedoms into the lives of high school students.

This lesson was drawn from a newspaper article describing an actual incident that had taken place regarding a student newspaper. The issue addressed in the lesson asks students to consider moral issues of rights and free speech, moral concerns for harm and fairness, and conventions that maintain the organization and structure of the high school as a societal institution. Understanding the moral consequences of violations of individual privacy also touches on students' conceptions from the personal domain. Concepts from the personal domain are also engaged in constructing arguments for rights to free speech. Thus, this lesson invokes coordination across multiple domains.

PROCEDURE

The teacher provides students the following description of an event from an actual high school community.

A high school newspaper staff and editor decided that it would be a good idea to do a story on families of divorce. They interviewed many students, some of whom expressed negative feelings about themselves and toward their parents. The views were summarized in an article and presented for publishing. When the principal saw the article, he did not permit it to be published.

In the article no students' names were used, but families could be identified from some of the details mentioned. The principal argued that because it was possible to identify individuals and families, the rights of those people to privacy were denied. He felt that the school as publisher of the newspaper had a right to censor articles such as this. He felt that the issue was too sensitive to deal with in a school newspaper.

The students objected on the grounds that the principal's action abridged their First Amendment rights to free speech and free press about an issue that is important to young people.

Following the reading of the description and clarification of the issues, the teacher places students in small groups to discuss the following questions:

1. Who do you think was right in this case, the students or the principal? How come?
2. The issues covered by the story were very important ones to students. To what extent do you think a student newspaper is obligated to publish sensitive issues like the one covered in this story? How come?
3. Even though no names were mentioned, the details of the story were such that people could identify the families of the students involved. What do you think about that? Do the families have a right to privacy about such things? How come? Why does it matter?
4. What should take precedence here, the rights of a newspaper to publish information important to its readers, or the families' right to privacy? Why?
5. In any publication someone oversees the content of articles. Who should assume this responsibility in the high school, the principal or the student editor? Why?
6. In terms of the previous question, how would the school as a social system (or society) be different depending on whether it is the school principal or the student editor who oversees the contents of the school newspaper? Explain.

Homework Essay

Write a 2–3-page essay focusing on the events described in the school newspaper incident. For this essay, imagine that you are a member of the Supreme Court. For this exercise you are not constrained by prior court decisions. Decide whom you will support—the school and its principal as publisher of the newspaper, or the student editors and staff. Write an essay that presents an argument in support of your position.

Focus on the following conflicts:

1. Free speech and freedom of the press as opposed to the right of privacy for the people being written about.
2. The right of students to public discussion of issues important to them, as opposed to adult authorities who can override the actions of minors.

As you write, answer the following questions:

1. Although no names were mentioned, the details of the story were such that people could identify the families of the students involved. In this situation the right to air issues for public discussion conflicts with the right of families to maintain privacy. Whose rights should take precedence? How come?
2. In any publication someone oversees the content of articles. Who should assume this responsibility in the high school, the principal or the student editor? Why?
3. In this situation, the principal is acting within his role as publisher and as the primary adult authority in the school. The students feel that his action conflicts with their First Amendment rights and freedoms. Thinking in terms of the school as a society, how can these conflicting positions best be reconciled? Explain.

Social Studies: American History

THE GLASSBOROUGH BOTTLE FACTORY

GOALS

This lesson makes use of a fictional scenario to engage students in their learning about industrial labor practices in late-nineteenth-century America. This is one of the first lessons we constructed as part of the research testing the efficacy of attention to domains for social development (Nucci, 2001; Nucci & Weber, 1991). The lesson has since been modified as we have worked with teachers over the years. This is a two-part lesson that touches on all three social cognitive domains, and illustrates how what appears to be abstract academic content can be connected to the moral implications of how students live their daily lives.

The lesson content is a classic case of domain overlap in which prevailing social conventions support the exploitation of one group of people (children) to the benefit of another social group (factory owners and consumers). With respect to social convention, the lesson serves to consolidate students' understanding of how social norms structure social organization. With regard to morality, the lesson extends students' basic notions of fairness and harm by asking students to consider whether one has a moral right to engage in harm in order to remain economically viable. The moral dilemma contained in this lesson is one that challenges students' idealistic assumptions about morality and social justice. There is no simple answer in which no one is harmed. With regard to the personal, the lesson engages students in reflection on the rights of individuals to engage in actions that others consider harmful to the self. Finally, the lesson is designed to engage students in an effort to coordinate all of these factors in arriving at a moral social judgment.

The goals of this lesson extend beyond the impact of the particular academic content of late-nineteenth-century America. The issues raised in the lesson have contemporary counterparts that permit students to evaluate current social practices and their own moral responsibilities. The discussion questions and activities developed by the teachers we have worked with draw students head on into issues of moral and cultural relativism, tolerance, and moral chauvinism. These are questions that are important in helping students to begin to take moral stands, and to recognize the relationships those moral positions have to social structure and culture. The structure of the lesson, by having students parse the moral, conventional, and personal aspects of the problem, provides them with the scaffold to develop a set of analytic tools for engaging in principled reflection on a thorny social issue. It also has the potential to give them a window into the process of moral self-reflection. Part II of the lesson employs a *service learning* activity to foster that personal connection.

PROCEDURE

Part I

Following the assigned reading of the textbook, the teacher provides students with the following quotations and scenario to stimulate small group discussion. In the example below the questions used with students are followed by letters indicating the domain addressed by the question (M = moral, C = conventional, P = personal).

1. "The most beautiful sight we see is the child at labor; as early as he may get to labor, the more beautiful, the more useful does his life become."

Asa Chandler (founder of Coca-Cola)

2. "In Lawrence, Massachusetts, half the textile workers in the mills were girls between the ages of 14 and 18."

3. "A considerable number of boys and girls die within the first two or three years of beginning work. Thirty-six of every one hundred of all the men and women who work in the mill die by the time they are 25 years old. The life span of the average mill worker in Lawrence is 22 years shorter than that of the owner."

The late 1800s was a period of rapid industrial growth in the United States. Competition among businesses was fierce as companies competed against one another for customers. In order to cut costs some businesses hired children under the age of 15 because they would work for lower wages than adults. This placed companies that did not hire children at a disadvantage. One business caught in this situation was the Glassborough bottle factory.

The owner of the Glassborough bottle factory, Mr. Galle, did not wish to hire children because his factory was dangerous and the children would have to work long hours after school. On the other hand, if he didn't hire children he would not be able to sell his bottles for a competitive price, and he would risk going out of business. In the end, Mr. Galle decided to hire children to work in his factory.

Discussion Questions

1. Was Mr. Galle right or wrong to have hired children to work in his factory? Why/Why not?
2. In Glassborough it was customary for children to work alongside adults on the farms and in the factories. How should that affect what Mr. Galle should do? (C)
3. What impact do child labor laws have on the way society is structured? (C)
4. Why might a society want to have children work alongside adults in factories? (C)
5. Did Mr. Galle have a right to hire children in order to remain competitive? Was it fair for him to have done that? (M)
6. In hiring children to work in his factory, Mr. Galle is placing them in a situation of considerable personal danger. What are Mr. Galle's obligations, given those conditions? (M)
7. Should children under the age of 15 have a right to work in a dangerous factory such as Mr. Galle's if they wish to? (P)
8. Taking everything into account, what would have been the right thing for Mr. Galle to have done in this situation? (M, C)

Homework Essay

Imagine yourself as an editorial writer for a newspaper in the 1890s. Write a 2-page editorial on the practice of hiring children to work in factories. Your editorial must take a stand either in support or in opposition to the practice. Use the ideas that came up during your class discussion of the questions in the handout to help support the arguments you make in your editorial.

PROCEDURE: Part II

GOALS

The second part of the lesson was designed to connect the events of the 1890s to the economies of emerging nations in which child labor is used for the manufacture of goods exported to the United States. The social development goals were to engage students in relating the conditions of the 1890s to their current role as potential consumers of products produced with child labor. The abstract moral issue of child labor is thus shifted to the concrete morality of their own behavior as consumers. The optional service-learning component provides students with an opportunity to put their moral ideals into action.

PROCEDURE

The teacher places students into small groups for a follow-up discussion of the issues raised by the child labor unit from U.S. history.

Questions

1. Today, many products manufactured by American companies are produced in countries that allow young children to work in factories. Can you name any of those products?
2. Is it okay for individual Americans to knowingly buy those products? (M, P)
3. Some people would argue that they have a right to buy products at the lowest price, and that it is not their responsibility if the manufacturer in a foreign country hires children as workers. What do you think about that argument? Do you agree or disagree? Why? (P, M)
4. Should Americans take any actions to change the policies of the governments that allow child labor? (M, P)
5. Do members of one society have a right to intervene in the social practices of another society? (M, C)
6. On what moral basis, if any, can one society judge the customs and conventions of another society to be morally wrong? (M, C)
7. Do Americans have the right as consumers to boycott the purchase of products produced with child labor as a way to force companies in other countries to change their practices? How come? (M, P)

ESSAY

Write a 300-word essay responding to the following questions. Use the ideas that came up in your in-class discussion.

1. Do you think it is wrong or all right for individual Americans to knowingly purchase products produced with child labor? Why?
2. Would it be wrong or right for American consumers to boycott the purchase of products produced by child labor as a way to force companies in other countries to change their hiring practices? How come?

Expanding the Lesson: Service Learning, "Fair Trade"

The original version of the lesson was limited to discussion and writing. However, the lesson has been expanded to include an optional service-learning component. Many schools and districts have added service learning as part of high school graduation requirements. There is emerging evidence indicating that well-run service-learning programs lead to an increased level of civic engagement (Andersen, 1998; Youniss, McLellan, & Mazer, 2001; Youniss & Yates, 1997) and are associated with an increase in positive moral action and a decrease in rates of delinquent conduct (Hart, Atkins, & Ford, 1998).

At least two factors appear to be important for service learning to have a positive impact on students' social growth. The first is that some degree of choice as to the nature of the particular activity a student will take part in seems to be important for the activity to have positive benefit (Andersen, 1998; Barker & Eccles, 1997; Leming, 1999). The importance of choice is linked to student motivation as well as identity formation. In this regard, Leming (1999) reported that when programs force students into so-called "voluntary" service activities, they result in alienation among adolescents who see through what they perceive to be blatant attempts by schools to make them into particular sorts of people. The second critical factor is that the service-learning activity be linked to a period of reflection (Andersen, 1998; Youniss, McLellan, & Mazer, 2001; Youniss & Yates, 1997).

The following example illustrates how service learning can be incorporated in the curriculum. The Chicago-area school district that we worked with in constructing this lesson did not have a formal service-learning requirement. However, many students within the district opted to engage in service-learning activities to enhance their graduation dossiers. These activities included such things as peer tutoring, peer mediation, participation in service clubs that sponsored activities such as work at a neighborhood or church-sponsored food pantry, volunteer work at a school for students with special needs, and participation in Amnesty International. Thus, students had a number of ways to contribute to society from different political perspectives. However, not all of these activities included the reflective component research has found to be essential for moral growth. Nor did many of the activities tie directly back into the academic curriculum.

The particular activity described here follows naturally from the course content and is consistent with the moral education goal of connecting students' capacity to engage in critical moral reflection about social practices with their actual social behavior. In this case, the notion of community service entails civic activism.

PROCEDURE

The teacher would employ the above discussion on child labor as an introduction to the service-learning activity.

The question of whether or not to buy products made with child labor or other practices considered unfair to workers has been taken up by advocates of what is called "fair trade." What I would like you to do is go on the Internet and find out about fair trade. I would also like you to find out how much money is spent by teenagers each year in the American economy. Tomorrow, we will discuss actions that we might take as a service-learning activity based on what we learn about fair trade and the economics of teen spending.

The teacher would provide a set of Web sites for students to explore. In the following class, the teacher would gather information students have obtained about fair trade and teen spending. The teacher would then introduce the service-learning project.

We discovered through our online research that the aggregate spending of American teens in 2006 was $79.7 billion. That is a lot of money. What do you think would happen if that spending by teens were directed away from companies that employ child labor or that engage in other unfair labor practices, and directed toward companies that abide by international standards for the hiring and treatment of their workers? Well, we can take steps in that direction if you choose to do so. The teacher would provide the following list of activities:

1. Work together to generate a list of companies that engage in fair trade practices, observing international standards for hiring, in the production of chocolate, clothing, shoes, and other goods commonly purchased by teenagers.
2. Generate informational leaflets to distribute to students at school describing fair trade and listing companies that follow fair trade practices.

The teacher would then ask students if they have other ideas about activities that they believe would help affect the purchase of goods that meet fair trade guidelines. Some of the suggestions students have come up with have included:

1. Distribute the same leaflets at the local mall to inform shoppers.
2. Meet with local merchants to urge them to carry and highlight fair trade products at their stores.

3. Lead a boycott of a local chain store selling clothing manufactured with child labor.

Reflective Discussion. The purpose of the discussion is to consolidate students' moral values and to help them incorporate those moral understandings as an aspect of the persons they are becoming. Finally, these discussions emphasize students' sense of empowerment and citizenship. The following are some key questions that can be used to lead such a discussion:

1. What impact do you feel your activities have had on other people?
2. What impact do you think your activities have had on our local community and your goal of affecting child labor and other unfair labor practices?
3. How does that make you feel about yourself?
4. What changes do you see in yourself as a result of your participation in this activity?

CHAPTER 10

Closing Thoughts

I like a teacher who gives you something to take home to think about besides homework.

—Lily Tomlin as "Edith Ann"

E very teacher knows that it is easier to train than to educate, and easier to control students than it is to help them to develop self-control and concern for others. In my more than 30 years of working with teachers and would-be teachers, I have met few who would aspire to be trainers and controllers of students. We began this book by looking at the results of research on children's moral and social development. From that research we have learned that morality is distinct from the conventions of society, and from what people consider to be matters of personal choice and privacy. That research provides ample evidence that the natural tendency of students is to actively interpret and evaluate the social and moral aspects of their lives in an effort to understand and function within their everyday social interactions.

As teachers we have a choice of whether to make use of those natural developmental patterns or to impose a ready-made cultural belief system upon them. A teacher who is an educator will see the moral necessity of working to facilitate development. This means taking the time to analyze the elements of classroom structure, rules, and procedures in relation to domains of moral and social values. It means looking at how classroom behavior and misbehavior are managed, and how teacher authority is implemented and maintained. It also means taking the time to identify moral and social issues embedded within the regular academic curriculum and constructing lessons that contribute 2 for 1 academic and moral development student gains.

In this book I have shared what we have learned to help teachers achieve those rather formidable moral and academic goals. The approach described in this book is challenging. I have mentioned at various points in the book that a teacher wishing to implement a domain-concordant approach to teaching will need to have patience and perseverance. The approach to classroom management described in Section II asks teachers to assume the more challenging role of educator rather than controller of student behavior. The approach to curriculum asks the teacher to be a creator rather than consumer of lesson plans and materials. Altogether, the approach asks the teacher to become a constructivist educator who challenges students to examine their assumptions and to generate more encompassing conceptions of morality. Such an educator recognizes that turning out students who are "nice people" is not enough.

Teachers who wish to continue the conversation begun in this book can explore resources on the Office for Studies in Moral Education Web site, http://MoralEd.org.

References

Ainsworth, M. (1973). The development of infant-mother attachment. In B. M. Caldwell and H. N. Ricciuti (Eds.), *Review of Child Development Research.* Vol. 3. Chicago: University of Chicago Press.

Andersen, S. M. (1998). *Service learning: A national strategy for youth development.* A Position Paper issued by the Task Force on Education Policy. Washington, DC: Institute for Communitarian Policy Studies, George Washington University.

Aronson, E., & Patnoe, S. (1997). *The jigsaw classroom: Building cooperation in the classroom.* New York: Longman.

Arsenio W. F., Gold, J., & Adams, E. (2004). Adolescents' emotion expectancies regarding aggressive and nonaggressive events: Connections with behavior problems. *Journal of Experimental Child Psychology, 89,* 338–355.

Arsenio, W., & Lover, A. (1995). Children's conceptions of sociomoral affect: Happy victimizers, mixed emotions, and other expectancies. In M. Killen & D. Hart (Eds.), *Morality in everyday life* (pp. 87–130). New York: Cambridge University Press.

Arthur, J. (2008). Traditional approaches to character education in Britain and America. In L. Nucci & D. Narvaez (Eds.), H*andbook of moral and character education* (pp. 80–98). New York: Routledge.

Astington, J. W. (1993). *The child's discovery of the mind.* Cambridge, MA: Harvard University Press.

Barker, B., & Eccles, J. (April, 1997). *Student council volunteering, basketball, or marching band: What kind of extracurricular involvement matters?* Symposium: Adolescent involvement in community. Biennial meeting of the Society for Research in Child Development. Washington, D.C.

Battistich, V., Solomon, D., Watson, M., & Schaps, E. (1997). Caring school communities. *Educational Psychologist, 32,* 137–151.

Baumrind, D. (2005). Taking a stand in a morally pluralistic society: Constructive obedience and responsible dissent in moral/character education. In L. Nucci (Ed.), *Conflict, contradiction and contrarian elements in moral development and moral education.* Mahwah, NJ: Erlbaum.

Berkowitz, M. W. (1997). The complete moral person: Anatomy and formation. In J. M. Dubois (Ed.), *Moral issues in psychology: Personalist contributions to selected problems* (pp. 11–41). Lanham, MD: University Press of America.

Berkowitz, M., Battistich, V., & Beier, M. (2008). What works in character education: What is known and what needs to be known. In L. Nucci & D. Narvaez (Eds.), *Handbook of moral and character education* (pp. 414–430). New York: Routledge.

Berkowitz, M., & Gibbs, J. (1983). Measuring the developmental features of moral discourse. *Merrill-Palmer Quarterly, 24,* 399–410.

Berkowitz, M., Gibbs, J., & Broughton, J. (1980). The relation of moral judgment stage to developmental effects of peer dialogues. *Merrill-Palmer Quarterly, 26,* 341–357.

Bigler, R. S., & Liben, L. (2006). A developmental intergroup theory of social stereotypes and prejudice. *Advances in Child Development and Behavior, 34,* 39–89.

Blatt, M., & Kohlberg, L. (1975). The effects of classroom moral discussion upon children's level of moral judgment. *Journal of Moral Education, 4,* 129–161.

Blumenfeld, P. C., Pintrich, P. R., & Hamilton, V. L. (1987). Teacher talk and students' reasoning about morals, conventions, and achievement. *Child Development, 58,* 1389–1401.

Bochenek, M., & Brown, A. (2001). *Hatred in the hallways: Violence and discrimination against lesbian, gay, bisexual, and transgender students in U.S. schools.* New York: Human Rights Watch.

Bowlby, J. (1958). The nature of the child's tie to his mother. *International Journal of Psychoanalysis, 39,* 350–373.

Brown, C. S., & Bigler, R. S. (2004). Children's perceptions of gender discrimination. *Developmental Psychology, 40,* 714–726.

Brummett, J. (2003, April 13). United Christian states of America (Column). *Las Vegas Review-Journal,* p. A15.

Character Counts Coalition. (1993). *Ethics in action.* Marina del Rey, CA: Joseph and Edna Josephson Institute of Ethics, May/June.

Chodos-Irvine, M. (2003). *Ella Sarah gets dressed.* Orlando, FL: Harcourt.

Corsaro, W. (1985). *Peer culture in the early years.* Norwood, NJ: Ablex.

Cumberland-Li, A., Eisenberg, N., Champion, C., Gershoff, E., & Fabes, R. A. (2003). The relation of parental emotionality and related dispositional traits to parental expression of emotion and children's social functioning. *Motivation and Emotion, 27,* 27–56.

Dahl, R. (1973/2005). *Charlie and the chocolate factory.* London, UK: Puffin Books.

Damon, W. (1975). Early conceptions of positive justice as related to the development of concrete operations. *Child Development, 46,* 301–312.

Dale, E., & O'Rourke, J. (1976). *The living word vocabulary, the words we know: A national vocabulary inventory.* Elgin, IL: Dome.

Damon, W. (1977). *The social world of the child.* San Francisco: Jossey-Bass.

Damon, W. (1988). *The moral child.* New York: Free Press.

Damon, W., & Hart, W. (1988). *Self-understanding in childhood and adolescence.* Cambridge, MA: Cambridge University Press.

D'Augelli, A. (1998). Developmental implications of victimization of lesbian, gay and bisexual youths. In G. Herek (Ed.), *Stigma and sexual orientation: Understanding prejudice against lesbians, gay men, and bisexuals* (pp. 187–210). Thousand Oaks: Sage Publications.

Davidson, M. (1974). *Nine true dolphin stories.* New York: Scholastic.

Davidson, P., Turiel, E., & Black, A. (1983). The effect of stimulus familiarity on the use of criteria and justifications in children's social reasoning. *British Journal of Developmental Psychology, 1,* 46–65.

Deci, E. (1995). *Why we do what we do: The dynamics of personal autonomy.* New York: G. P. Putnam.

Deutsch, M. (1993). Educating for a peaceful world. *American Psychologist, 48,* 510–517.

DeVries, R., & Zan, B. (1994*). Moral classrooms, moral children: Creating a constructivist atmosphere for early education.* New York: Teachers College Press.

Dodsworth-Rugani, K. (1982). *The development of concepts of social structure and their relationship to school rules and authority.* Unpublished doctoral dissertation, University of California, Berkeley.

Durkheim, E. (1925/1961). *Moral education.* Glencoe, IL: The Free Press.

Durlak, D., & Weissberg, R. (2007). *The impact of after-school programs that promote social and emotional skills.* Chicago, IL: The Collaborative for Social and Emotional Learning.

Eccles, J. S., Midgley, C., Wigfield, A., Buchanan, C. M., Reuman, D., Flanagan, C., et al. (1993). Development during adolescence: The impact of stage-environment fit on adolescents' experiences in schools and families. *American Psychologist, 48,* 90–101.

Eccles, J. S., Wigfield, A., & Schiefele, U. (1998). Motivation to succeed. In W. Damon (Ed.), *Handbook of child psychology: Vol. 3. Social, emotional, and personality development,* N. Eisenberg (Ed.), (5th ed., pp. 1017–1095). New York: Wiley.

Eisenberg, N. (1986). *Altruistic emotion, cognition and behavior.* Hillsdale, NJ: Erlbaum.

Elias, M., Parker, S., Kash, V. M., Weissberg, R., & O'Brien, M. (2008). Social and emotional learning, moral education, and character education. In L. Nucci & D. Narvaez (Eds.), *Handbook of moral and character education* (pp. 248–266). New York: Routledge.

Emde, R., Birigen, Z., Clyman, R., & Openheim, D. (1991). The moral self of infancy: Affective core and procedural knowledge. *Developmental Review, 11,* 251–270.

Erikson, E. (1968). *Identity, youth, and crisis.* New York: W. W. Norton.

Evertson, C., & Weinstein, C. (Eds.). (2006). *Handbook of classroom management: Research, practice, and contemporary issues.* Mahwah, NJ: Lawrence Erlbaum.

Geiger, K., & Turiel, E. (1983). Disruptive school behavior and concepts of social convention in early adolescence. *Journal of Educational Psychology, 75,* 677–685.

Gelman, S. (2003). *The essential child: Origins of essentialism in everyday thought.* Oxford, UK: Oxford University Press.

Gerskoff, L., & Thelen, E. (2004). U-shaped changes in behavior: A dynamic systems perspective. *Journal of Cognition and Development, 5,* 11–36.

Gralinski, H., & Kopp, C. (1993). Everyday rules for behavior: Mothers' requests to young children. *Developmental Psychology, 29,* 573–584.

Greenberg, M. T., Weissberg, R. P., O'Brien, M. U., Zins, J. E., Fredericks, L., Resnik, H., et al. (2003). *American Psychologist, 58*(6/7), 466–474.

Habermas, J. (1991). *Moral consciousness and communicative action.* Cambridge: MIT Press.

Hansen, D. T. (1996). Teaching and the moral life of classrooms. *Journal for a Just and Caring Education, 2,* 59–74.

Hart, D., Atkins, R., & Ford, D. (1998). Urban America as a context for the development of moral identity in adolescence. *Journal of Social Issues, 54,* 513–530.

Hasebe, Y., Nucci, L., & Nucci, M. (2004). Parental control of the personal domain and adolescent symptoms of psychopathology: A cross-national study in the U.S. and Japan. *Child Development, 75,* 1–14.

Horn, S. S. (2003). Adolescents' reasoning about exclusion from social groups. *Developmental Psychology, 39,* 71–84.

Horn, S. S. (2006). Heterosexual adolescents' and young adults' beliefs and attitudes about homosexuality and gay and lesbian peers. *Cognitive Development, 21,* 420–440.

Horn, S. S., & Nucci, L. (2006). Harassment of gay and lesbian youth and school violence in America: An analysis and directions for intervention. In C. Daiute, Z. Beykont, C. Higson-Smith, & L. Nucci (Eds.), *International perspectives on youth conflict and development.* Oxford, UK: Oxford University Press.

Jackson, P. W., Boostrom, R., & Hansen, D. T. (1993). *The moral life of schools.* San Francisco: Jossey-Bass.

James, R., & Blair, R. (2005). Morality in the autistic child. *Journal of autism and developmental disorders, 26,* 571–579.

Johnson, D. W., Johnson, R., Dudley, B., Ward, M., & Magnuson, D. (1995). The impact of peer mediation training on the management of school and home conflicts. *American Educational Research Journal, 32*, 829–844.

Joosse, B. (2002). *Stars in the darkness*. San Francisco: Chronicle Books.

Katz, L. F., & Gottman, J. M. (1991). Marital discord and child outcomes: A social psychophysiological approach. In J. Garber & K. Dodge (Eds.), *The development of emotion regulation and dysregulation* (pp. 129–153). New York: Cambridge University Press.

Killen, M. (1991). Social and moral development in early childhood. In W. Kurtines & J. Gewirtz (Eds.), *Handbook of moral behavior and development: Vol. 2, Research* (pp. 115–138). Hillsdale, NJ: Erlbaum.

Killen, M., Breton, S., Ferguson, H., & Handler, K. (1994). Preschooler's evaluations of teacher methods of intervention in social transgressions. *Merrill-Palmer Quarterly, 40,* 399–416.

Killen, M., & Smetana, J. (1999). Social interactions in preschool classrooms and the development of young children's conceptions of the personal. *Child Development, 70*, 486–501.

Klonsky, M. (2007). Small schools workshop. www.smallschools.com/index.html.

Kochanska, K. (1993). Toward a synthesis of parental socialization and child temperament in early development of conscience. *Child Development, 64,* 325–347.

Kohlberg, L. (1984). *Essays on moral development*: *Vol. 2, The psychology of moral development*. San Francisco: Harper and Row.

Kohlberg, L., & Turiel, E. (1971). Moral development and moral education. In G. Lesser (Ed.), *Psychology and educational practice*. Chicago: Scott Foresman.

Kohn, A. (1997, February). How not to teach values. *Phi Delta Kappan,* 429–439.

Lapsley, D. (1996). *Moral psychology*. Boulder, CO: Westview.

Lapsley, D. (2008). Moral-self identity as the aim of moral education. In L. Nucci & D. Narvaez (Eds.), *Handbook of moral and character education* (pp. 30–52). New York: Routledge.

Laupa, M., & Turiel, E. (1986). Children's conceptions of adult and peer authority. *Child Development, 57,* 405–412.

Laupa, M., & Turiel, T. (1993). Children's conceptions of authority and social context. *Journal of Educational Psychology, 85,* 191–197.

Leming, J. (1999). The impact of integrating a structured ethical reflection program into high school service-learning experiences of students' sociomoral development.

Leslie, A., Mallon, R., & Dicorcia, J. (2006). Transgressors, victims, and cry babies: Is basic moral judgment spared in autism? *Social Neurosciences, 1,* 270–283.

Lickona, T. (2004). *Character matters: How to help our children develop good judgment, integrity, and other essential virtues.* Carmichael, CA: Touchstone Books.

Lind, G. (1996, April). *Which educational environment promotes self-sustaining democratic development?* Paper presented at the annual meeting of the American Educational Research Association, New York.

Lind, G. (2006). The Konstanz method for dilemma discussion. www.unikonstanz.de/ag-moral/moral/dildisk.htm

Metz, M. H. (March, 1978). *Clashes in the classroom: The importance of norms for authority.* Paper presented at the annual meeting of the American Educational Research Association, Toronto.

Moshman, D. (2004). *Adolescent psychological development: Rationality, morality, and identity.* Mahwah, NJ: Lawrence Erlbaum.

Nicholls, J. (1984). Achievement motivation: Conceptions of ability, subjective experience, task choice, and performance. *Psychological Review, 9,* 328–346.

Nicholls, J. (1989). *The competitive ethos and democratic education.* Cambridge, MA: Harvard University Press.

Nicholls, J., & Miller, A. (1984). Development and its discontents: The differentiation of the concept of ability. In J. Nicholls (Ed.), *Advances in motivation and achievement: The development of achievement motivation* (pp. 185–218). Greenwich, CT: JAI Press.

Nicholls, J., & Thorkildsen, T. (1988). Children's distinctions among matters of intellectual convention, logic, and fact. *Child Development, 59,* 939–949.

Noam, G. (1993). "Normative vulnerabilities" of self and their transformations in moral action. In G. Noam (Ed.), *The moral self* (pp. 209–238). Cambridge, MA: MIT Press.

Noddings, N. (2002). *Educating moral people: A caring alternative to character.* New York: Teachers College Press.

Nucci, L. (1977). *Social development: Personal, conventional, and moral concepts.* Doctoral dissertation, University of California, Santa Cruz.

Nucci, L. (1984). Evaluating teachers as social agents: Students' ratings of domain-appropriate and domain-inappropriate teacher responses to transgressions. *American Educational Research Journal, 21,* 367–378.

Nucci, L. (1985). Children's conceptions of morality, societal convention, and religious prescription. In C. Harding (Ed.), *Moral dilemmas: Philosophical and psychological issues in the development of moral reasoning* (pp. 115–136). Chicago, IL: Precedent Press.

Nucci, L. (1996). Morality and the personal sphere of actions. In E. Reed, E. Turiel, & T. Brown (Eds.), *Values and knowledge* (pp. 41–60). Hillsdale, NJ.: Lawrence Erlbaum.

Nucci, L. (2001). *Education in the moral domain.* Cambridge, UK: Cambridge University Press.

Nucci, L. (2004). Morality and convention. Video.

Nucci, L. (2006). Classroom management for moral development. In C. Evertson & C. Weinstein (Eds.), *Handbook of classroom management: Research, practice, & contemporary issues.* Mahwah, NJ: Lawrence Erlbaum.

Nucci, L., Becker, K., & Horn, S. (2004). *Assessing the development of adolescent concepts of social convention.* Paper presented at the annual meeting of the Jean Piaget Society, Toronto, Canada.

Nucci, L., & Charlier, P. (April, 1983). *Cognitive development in the societal domain and comprehension of social studies content.* Paper presented at the annual meeting of the American Educational Research Association, Montreal.

Nucci, L., Drill, K., Larson, C., & Browne, C. (2006). Preparing pre-service teachers for character education in urban elementary schools: The UIC initiative. *Journal for Research in Character Education, 3,* 81–96.

Nucci, L., & Katsarou, E. (2004). Student support: Building relationships, discipline and social emotional learning. Workshop presented to the faculty of the National Teachers Academy, Chicago, IL.

Nucci, L., & Nucci, M. S. (1982a). Children's responses to moral and social-conventional transgressions in free-play settings. *Child Development, 53,* 1337–1342.

Nucci, L., & Nucci, M. S. (1982b). Children's social interactions in the context of moral and conventional transgressions. *Child Development, 53,* 403–412.

Nucci, L., & Turiel, E. (1978). Social interactions and the development of social concepts in pre-school children. *Child Development, 49,* 400–407.

Nucci, L., & Turiel, E. (2007). Development in the moral domain: The role of conflict and relationships in children's and adolescents' welfare and harm judgments. Paper presented as part of the symposium "Moral development within domain and within context" at the biennial meeting of the Society for Research in Child Development, Boston, MA.

Nucci, L., Turiel, E., & Encarnacion-Gawrych, G. (1983). Children's social interactions and social concepts in the Virgin Islands. *Journal of Cross-Cultural Psychology, 14,* 469–487.

Nucci, L., & Weber, E. (1991). Research on classroom applications of the domain approach to values education. In W. Kurtines & J. Gewirtz (Eds.), *Handbook of moral behavior and development: Vol. 3, Applications* (pp. 251–266). Hillsdale, NJ: Erlbaum.

Nucci, L., & Weber, E. K. (1995). Social interactions in the home and the development of young children's conceptions within the personal domain. *Child Development, 66,* 1438–1452.

Oser, F. K., & Veugelers, W. (2003). *Teaching in moral and democratic education.* Bern: Peter Lang Verlag.

Piaget, J. (1932). *The moral judgment of the child.* New York: Free Press.

Piaget, J. (1962). Will and action. *Bulletin of the Menninger Clinic, 26,* 138–145.

Power, C., Higgins, A., & Kohlberg, L. (1989). *Lawrence Kohlberg's approach to moral education*. New York: Columbia University Press.

Ravitch, D. (June 20, 2005). Ethnomathematics: Even math education is being politicized. *Wall Street Journal*.

Rivers, I., & D'Augelli, A. (2001). The victimization of lesbian, gay and bisexual youths. In A. D'Augelli & C. Patterson (Eds.), *Lesbian, gay, and bisexual identities and youth* (pp. 199–223). New York: Oxford University Press.

Russell, S., Franz, B., & Driscoll, A. (2001). Same-sex romantic attraction and experiences of violence in adolescence. *American Journal of Public Health, 91,* 903–906.

Ryan, K. (1989). In defense of character education. In L. Nucci (Ed.), *Moral development and character education: A dialogue* (pp. 3–17). Berkeley: McCutchan.

Schwartz, M. (2007). *Effective character education.* New York: McGraw Hill.

Shields, D. L., & Bredemeier, B. J. (2008). Sports and the development of character. In L. Nucci & D. Narvaez (Eds.), *Handbook of moral and character education* (pp. 500–519). New York: Routledge.

Shweder, R., Mahapatra, M., & Miller, J. (1987). Culture and moral development. In J. Kagan & S. Lamb (Eds.), *The emergence of morality in young children*. Chicago: University of Chicago Press.

Smetana, J. (1989). Toddlers' social interactions in the context of moral and conventional transgressions in the home. *Developmental Psychology, 25,* 499–508.

Smetana, J. G. (1995). Context, conflict, and constraint in adolescent-parent authority relationships. In M. Killen & D. Hart (Eds.), *Morality in everyday life: Developmental perspectives* (pp. 225–255). Cambridge, UK: Cambridge University Press.

Smetana, J. G. (2002). Culture, autonomy, and personal jurisdiction in adolescent-parent relationships. In H. W. Reese & R. Kail (Eds.), *Advances in child development and behavior, Vol. 29* (pp. 51–87). New York: Academic Press.

Smetana, J. G. (2005). Adolescent-parent conflict: Resistance and subversion as developmental process. In L. Nucci (Ed.), *Conflict, contradiction and contrarian elements in moral development and education* (pp. 69–91). Mahwah, NJ: Lawrence Erlbaum.

Smetana, J. G. (2006). Social cognitive domain theory: Consistencies and variations in children's moral and social judgments. In M. Killen & J. Smetana (Eds.), *Handbook of moral development* (pp. 119–154). Mahwah, NJ: Erlbaum.

Smetana, J., & Bitz, B. (1996). Adolescents' conceptions of teachers' authority and their relations to rule violations in school. *Child Development, 67,* 1153–1172.

Smetana, J., & Braeges, J. 1990. The development of toddlers' moral and conventional judgments. *Merrill-Palmer Quarterly, 36,* 329–346.

Smetana, J. G., Campione-Barr, N., & Daddis, C. (2004). Developmental and longitudinal antecedents of family decision-making: Defining health behavioral autonomy for African American adolescents. *Child Development, 75,* 1418–1434.

Smetana, J., & Daddis, C. (2002). Domain specific antecedents of psychological control, parental monitoring and adolescent autonomy: The role of parenting beliefs and practices. *Child Development, 73,* 563–580.

Smetana, J., Daddis, C., & Chuang, S. (2003). "Clean your room!": A longitudinal investigation of adolescent-parent conflict and conflict resolution in middle-class African-American families. *Journal of Adolescent Research, 18,* 631–650.

Smetana, J. G., & Turiel, E. (2003). Morality during adolesence. In G. R. Adams & M. Berzonski (Eds.), *The Blackwell handbook of adolescence* (pp. 247–268). Oxford, UK: Blackwell.

Sroufe, L. A. (1983). Infant-caregiver attachment and patterns of adaptation in preschool: The roots of maladjustment and competence. In M. Perlmutter (Ed.), *Minnesota Symposium on Child Psychology* (Vol. 16, pp. 41–81). Minneapolis: University of Minnesota Press.

Staub, E. (1971). Helping a person in distress: The influence of implicit and explicit "rules" of conduct on children and adults. *Journal of Personality and Social Psychology, 17,* 137–144.

Subbotsky, E. V. (1995). The development of pragmatic and nonpragmatic motivation. *Human Development, 38,* 217–234.

Thorkildsen, T. A. (1989). Justice in the classroom: The student's view. *Child Development, 60,* 323–334.

Thorkildsen, T. A. (2002). The way tests teach: Children's theories of how much testing is fair in school. In M. Leicester, C. Modgil, & S. Modgil (Eds.), *Values, education, and cultural diversity.* London: Cassell.

Turiel, E. (1983). *The development of social knowledge: Morality and convention.* Cambridge, England: Cambridge University Press.

Turiel, E. (2002). *The culture of morality: Social development, context, and conflict.* Cambridge, UK: Cambridge University Press.

Turiel, E., & Davidson, P. (1986). Heterogeneity, inconsistency, and asynchrony in the development of cognitive structures. In I. Levin (Ed.), *Stage and structure: Reopening the debate* (pp. 106–143). Norwood, NJ: Ablex.

Wainryb, C. (1991). Understanding differences in moral judgments: The role of informational assumptions. *Child Development, 62,* 840–851.

Watson, M. (2003). *Learning to trust: Transforming difficult elementary classrooms through developmental discipline.* San Francisco, CA: Jossey-Bass.

Watson, M. (2008). Developmental discipline and moral education. In L. Nucci & D. Narvaez (Eds.), *Handbook of moral and character education* (pp. 175–203). New York: Routledge.

Weissberg, R. P. (2005, August). *Social and emotional learning for school and life success.* Invited Address for the Society for Community Research and Action (APA Division 27) Distinguished Contribution to Theory and Research Award at the Annual Meeting of the American Psychological Association, Washington, DC.

Weissberg, R. P., & O'Brien, M. U. (2004). What works in school-based social and emotional learning programs for positive youth development. *The Annals of the American Academy of Political and Social Science, 591,* 86–97.

Weston, D., & Turiel, E. (1980). Act-rule relations: Children's concepts of social rules. *Developmental Psychology, 16,* 417–424.

Wilson, J. Q. (1993). *The moral sense.* New York: The Free Press.

Wolf, A. (2002). *Get out of my life, but first could you drive me and Cheryl to the mall: A parent's guide to the new teenager.* New York: Farrar, Straus, and Giroux.

Wynne, E. (1987). Students and schools. In K. Ryan & G. F. McLean (Eds.), *Character development in schools and beyond* (pp. 97–118). New York: Praeger.

Wynne, E. (1989). Transmitting traditional values in contemporary schools. In L. Nucci. (Ed.), *Moral development and character education: A dialogue* (pp. 19–36). Berkeley: McCutchan.

Wynne, E., & Ryan, K. (1993). *Reclaiming our schools: A handbook on teaching character, academics, and discipline.* New York: Macmillan.

Youniss, J. (1980). *Parents and peers in social development.* Chicago: University of Chicago Press.

Youniss, J., McLellan, J. A., & Mazer, B. (2001). Voluntary service, peer group orientation, and civic engagement. *Journal of Adolescence Research, 16,* 456–468.

Youniss, J., & Yates, M. (1997). *Community service and social responsibility in youth.* Chicago: University of Chicago Press.

Name Index

Subject Index

Academic curriculum
  See also Discussions
  basic principles, 94–98
  discussions, 103–109
  for elementary grades, 111–129
  goals, 92–94
  for high school grades, 155–181
  identifying and categorizing issues by domain,
    100–101
  lesson formats, 98–100
  for middle school grades, 131–153
  practical applications, 98–102
Adolescence
  See also Lesson plans, for high school grades
  age-related changes in personal domain, 29, 32–33
  developmental changes and school rules, 61–63
  development changes in social convention, 36, 39–42
  distributive justice/fairness, development of, 43–46
  harm and welfare, development of, 44, 46–50
  identity crisis, 33–34
  moral development and social-emotional climate, 71–73
  rules and, 56–63
  social problem solving, 79–81
Adults
  bias and influence on children, 57
  responses to moral and social convention
    transgressions, 20
Age-related changes in personal domain, 28–33
Ambiguously personal issues, 33–34
Amish, moral issues and, 13
"Ancient Egypt: Dress and Social Class," 140–142
"Anthropologists and Missionaries: A Simulation," 144–146
Assumptions, factual, 93
Autonomy, 69

Behavior
  misbehavior, responding to, 83–85
  supporting positive, 82–83
Belonging, 69–70

Bias, influence on children of adult, 57
Bibliotherapy, 114
"Bimbo the Big Bully" (Davidson), 112–113

Catcher in the Rye (Salinger), 164
Catholics, moral issues and, 12–13
Character education, 1
Charlie and the Chocolate Factory (Dahl), 115–118,
    122–123
Chicago Public School system, 81
Children
  age-related changes in personal domain, 28–32
  developmental changes and school rules, 58–61
  development changes in social convention, 34–42
  distributive justice/fairness, development of, 43–46
  harm and welfare, development of, 44, 46–50
  moral development and social-emotional climate, 70–73
  personal domain and social interactions, 20–22
  responses to moral and social convention transgressions,
    18–19
  rules and, 56–63
  social experiential origins of children's morality, 18–19
  social problem solving, 75–79
Civil Disobedience (Thoreau), 166–167
Classroom climate
  moral development and emotion, 67–70
  moral development and social-emotional climate, 70–73
Classroom climate, elements of
  autonomy, 69
  belonging, 69–70
  competence, 70
  fairness, 70
Classroom social conventions, 57–63
Communicative discussions, 104–105
Competence, 70
Conceptual discussion, 102
Conflict discussion, 102
Conventional domain, 93
Crash (Spinelli), 148–149

199